Moby-Dick and Calvinism

Moby-Dick
and Calvinism

A World Dismantled

T. Walter Herbert, Jr.

RUTGERS UNIVERSITY PRESS
New Brunswick, New Jersey

Library of Congress Cataloging in Publication Data

Herbert, Thomas Walter, Jr. 1938-
  Moby-Dick and Calvinism.

  Includes bibliographical references and index.
    1. Melville, Herman, 1819-1891. Moby Dick.
  2. Melville, Herman, 1819-1891 — Religion and ethics.
  3. Calvinism in literature. I. Title.
  PS2384.M62H37   813'.3   76-56252
  ISBN 0-8135-0829-0

Copyright©1977 by Rutgers, the State University of New Jersey.
Manufactured in the United States of America.

Second Printing

Publication of this book was supported by a grant from the American
Council of Learned Societies

To my parents,
Jean Linton Herbert
and Thomas Walter Herbert

Contents

Preface   ix
Editions and Abbreviations   xii

Introduction   1

Part One   21

I. A Proud Coherence   23

II. A Unitarian Tragedy   45

III. Child of the Devil   57

IV. Sane Madness   69

Part Two   93

V. Ishmael as Spiritual Voyager   95

VI. The Dignity of Man: Mapple and Bulkington   109

VII. Ahab Reprobate   117

VIII. The Infidel's Cosmic Resentment   127

IX. Ahab Transfigured   141

X. Ishmael Adrift   159

Conclusion   171
Index   179

Preface

It has been true for some time that by writing one reasonably intelligible book on Melville a man could secure a better living in America than Melville managed to win by writing the whole body of his work. It is possible that this period is now drawing to a close; but while it has lasted his writings have received such an immense volume of commentary that yet another article on Melville, to say nothing of a scholarly book, should be obliged to present reasons for its existence.

Dramatic historical changes frequently have their harbingers in the secret pains and aspirations of individuals. The secularization of Western consciousness during the nineteenth century is a well-recognized development, and Melville is similarly well recognized as one of its prophets. *Moby-Dick* has been hailed, ever since the rediscovery of Melville in the 1920's, as having adopted viewpoints more characteristic of our era than of his own. Yet an important part of this story remains unknown, and with it a major aspect of Melville's creative achievement.

Part One of this book gives a biographical account of Melville's inner struggle with the theological ideas that were losing authority during his time, and Part Two explains his way of handling those ideas in *Moby-Dick*.

This is not a study of literary sources, primarily, but of cultural transformation in its most intimate laboratory. The religious conceptions Melville uses in *Moby-Dick* were part of the essential fabric of his mind; they structured a world that he had accepted as a direct account of reality. Yet he came to withdraw his psychic investment in this tradition and to place its governing ideas in a framework that radically altered their meanings.

Melville's reshaping of theological tradition pervades *Moby-Dick*. It appears in the basic plan of the narrative, in the charac-

terization of the leading figures, and in scores of individual meditations. When these reshapings are understood, it becomes
evident that *Moby-Dick* dramatizes the spiritual situation in
which an established ordering of things gives way. The state
of being caught "between two worlds, one dead, the other power-
less to be born," was not a theme of complaint for Melville.
He achieved instead such revelations of the human condition
as become possible between the worlds, when no existing system
of thought makes a credible claim to represent the final truth.

So understood, as a book that reworks the traditions of its
own time, *Moby-Dick* emerges as something larger than a precursor of the modern secular consciousness. It claims its place among
the major literary achievements of our civilization, one which
triumphs over the vast changing of the ages by incorporating
a reflection upon such changes into its vision of things.

* * *

It is a pleasure to thank those who have given me help. I
owe a personal debt of gratitude to Mrs. Edward Elliott, Mr.
John B. Elliott, and Miss Marjorie White.

At various stages of its development the manuscript of this
book received attention from scholars whose criticisms led me
to improve it. I want to thank Leland M. Burr, Leopold
Damrosch, Jr., Michael J. Colacurcio, Lee Andrew Elioseff,
Walter Herbert, Howard C. Horsford, and Merton M. Sealts,
Jr. The late Professor Lawrance Thompson led the seminar in
which this project was begun and assisted it generously thereafter, offering vigorous challenges and encouragements.

The following institutions have offered invaluable assistance:
the Gardner Sage Library at New Brunswick Theological Seminary, the Houghton Library at Harvard University, the Manu-
scripts and Archives Division of the New York Public Library,
the Speer Library at Princeton Theological Seminary, and the
Firestone Library at Princeton University. I wish to express my
appreciation for grants that I received from the University of
Kentucky Research Foundation.

Manuscript sources are quoted by permission of the Houghton
Library, Harvard University, and the New York Public Library.

My wife, Marjorie, aided in the work with great constancy and resourcefulness.

T. Walter Herbert, Jr.

Georgetown, Texas
August, 1976

Editions and Abbreviations

The following editions of works of Herman Melville are cited in the text:

"Hawthorne and His Mosses," in Herman Melville, *Moby-Dick*, ed. Harrison Hayford and Hershel Parker (New York, 1967), pp. 535-551. Cited in the text as "Mosses."

The Letters of Herman Melville, ed. Merrell R. Davis and William H. Gilman (New Haven, 1960). Cited in the text as *Letters*.

Mardi and a Voyage Thither, ed. Harrison Hayford, Hershel Parker, and G. Thomas Tanselle (Evanston, Ill., 1970).

Moby-Dick, ed. Harrison Hayford and Hershel Parker (New York, 1967). Citations give chapter titles as well as page numbers.

Pierre or, The Ambiguities, ed. with an introduction by Henry A. Murray (1949; reptd. New York, 1962). I cite the introduction to this edition.

Redburn, His First Voyage, ed. Harrison Hayford, Hershel Parker, and G. Thomas Tanselle (Evanston, Ill., 1969).

White-Jacket or The World in a Man-of-War, ed. Harrison Hayford, Hershel Parker, and G. Thomas Tanselle (Evanston, Ill., 1970).

The following abbreviations are used throughout the notes:

ARC — Archives of the Reformed Dutch Church, Gardner Sage Library, New Brunswick Theological Seminary.

Gilman — William H. Gilman, *Melville's Early Life and Redburn* (New York. 1951).

GLC — Gansevoort-Lansing Collection, New York Public Library.

Leyda — Jay Leyda, *The Melville Log*, 2 vols. (New York, 1951).

Sealts — Merton M. Sealts, Jr., *Melville's Reading, a Checklist of Books Owned and Borrowed* (Madison, 1966).

Introduction

Among the papers Melville left when he died is a brief story that can be taken as a reflection upon the strange course of his own life; it concerns the last days of an aged man-of-war's man named Daniel Orme.[1] Orme is aloof and moody, an imposing man whose immense physical size and bearing suggest a spiritual stature at odds with his humble surroundings. His associates regard him with superstitious distaste verging on dread. His personal history is unknown, but it is rumored that the warfare of his earlier years was not always in legitimate naval service. Something disconcerting in his personal presence contributes to the suspicion that he had at one time been a buccaneer. The figure of Orme recalls the spiritual questers who dominate the works Melville had written four decades earlier in the mighty flourishing of his art. Ishmael and Captain Ahab, like Pierre, Taji, and Tommo, are men of ambiguous meaning; they cross the legal and moral boundaries that prevent decent souls from entering a realm of terrible, inscrutable, and wondrous experience.

Orme is preoccupied by a reminder of the tumults of a former time. He has the habit of opening his shirt, when he thinks himself alone, to contemplate a curious figure on his chest, a tattooed crucifix across which there runs a thin white scar. No one can say whether the scar was received honorably in regular warfare, or whether it reminds Orme of adventures outside the law, yet it bespeaks a deadly confrontation at some final horizon of life. The Christian tradition offers no more comprehensive and powerful symbol than the one tattooed over Orme's heart.

This book proposes *Moby-Dick* as the battle that marred the crucifix, the battle whose memento is this image of a piety split

---

1. "Daniel Orme," in Herman Melville, *Billy Budd, Sailor and Other Stories,* ed. Harold Beaver (1967; reptd. Harmondsworth, England, 1970), pp. 411-417.

by elemental conflict. *Moby-Dick* is more than a major episode in Melville's life-long struggle with religious issues; it records the decisive combat in which the sacred image was defaced. Melville himself could not be certain whether the spiritual struggle chronicled by the great whaling story was legitimate or piratical because that struggle had discredited the religious standards in which he considered that moral judgments had to be grounded. It remained for him an ambiguous theme of meditation in later years because of this fact, and also because it was in part a battle within himself. The conflict that still preoccupied him forty years after the composition of *Moby-Dick* was inherent in his character, and had its source at the very origin of his mental life.

In writing *Moby-Dick*, Melville confronted a spiritual conflict that had been generated during his childhood and youth. His writings reveal, to be sure, that he read widely in philosophy and religion as an adult, and that his reading provoked energetic responses. But those responses were shaped by deeply ingrained preoccupations and uncertainties that became part of his character early in life. He was not merely unable to choose among the various schemes of truth that his reading and experience made available; his doubts ran so deep as to divide the personal center in which religious ideas were deliberated. He experienced the contradictions between incompatible theories as an acute personal conflict, but instead of retreating before this painful circumstance, he was inspired to undertake a zealous meditative quest. He came to believe that he might reach fundamental new religious insights by challenging his deepest consternations, and in *Moby-Dick* he boldly risked the coherence of his mental life in order to investigate what he called "the sane madness of vital truth" ("Mosses," p. 542).

Moby-Dick exemplifies a special kind of creativeness, in which the issues of a personal disturbance receive articulation in a work of major cultural significance. Melville was not the only American in the early nineteenth century who was so severely plagued by religious doubts as to fear for his sanity, and every student knows that Melville's writing was "influenced" by traditions of religious thought. What sets Melville apart is not the psychological and cultural conditions that acted upon him, but the creative mastery with which he reacted upon them. His masterwork does not merely echo religious concerns of his time, in variations determined by his private interests; it achieves the integrity and special timbre of an original utterance.

Since Melville's religious milieu is here viewed retrospectively, it is possible to make assumptions about psychological development that would not have been intelligible to Melville or to any of his contemporaries. No reader of Melville can remain indifferent to the fact that point of view can shape the perceptions of the viewer, since that process is one of Melville's most prominent thematic concerns. Virtually no other writer so persistently reminds the critic that a useful perspective can harden into an "approach" claiming final authority for its angle of salience, and that relevant procedures of analysis can become a "methodology" that administers processes of inference according to a dogmatic set of rules. Melville's religious conflict, in particular, drove him to make the coherence of truth itself a subject matter for thought, so that one who makes the effort to investigate that conflict is under a special obligation to explain his premises.

My major premise is that models of reality have a major role in the formation of human character. Lines of research in sociology, anthropology, and psychology have converged upon the recognition that individual persons, as well as communities, render experience intelligible by employing conceptions of the world.[2] The world views accepted by different communities at different times are exceedingly diverse, as our rapidly expanding knowledge of human cultures has made overwhelmingly clear. And yet, it seems likewise evident that the essence of man himself is not to be found by superimposing the mental topographies of all times and nations upon each other, in the hope of finding a recurrent configuration. The distinctively human trait, rather, is the necessity of some such system of meaning for the conduct of life. Personality within a culture coalesces about the scheme

2. See Peter L. Berger and Thomas Luckman, *The Social Construction of Reality* (Garden City, 1966), and Erik H. Erikson, *Identity, Youth and Crisis* (New York, 1968), esp. pp. 188-191. The fullest and most compelling statement of this view is found in Clifford Geertz, *The Interpretation of Cultures* (New York, 1973), in particular the lead essay, "Thick Description: Toward an Interpretive Theory of Culture."

of basic attitudes which the culture mediates to every newborn in making him a member of his society. The metaphor of "membership" asserts the intimacy of this relation, the extent to which accepted conventions of thought and action reach into the individual and establish the terms on which he must achieve whatever individuality is to be distinctively his own.

Religious conceptions describe the ultimate context of experience. They set forth a cognitive perimeter within which more immediate structures of meaning have their place, and lay down fundamental coordinates from which they take their bearings. This notion of the religious is inherent in the root meaning of the term; as *religio* refers to the binding together of things, so religious belief conveys the assurance that the various systems of meanings by which men organize their lives have indeed a secure purchase on a coherent final actuality, a purchase strong enough to quell the fear that an ultimate arbitrariness, the reign of sheer accident, determines human striving. Melville's religious conflict includes his perplexities regarding the specific traditions of religious belief that his culture made available to him; but it also involves his confrontation with the possibility of final unmeaning, the confrontation that is native to religious thought.

The theory that man is a creature who lives and moves and has his being amid a texture of socially transmitted meanings is further pertinent to Melville's religious meditations because of its implications for the definition of sanity and madness. Implicit in any diagnosis of insanity is a conception of the real world, and of what ideas and feelings constitute a suitable response to it. The terrors that haunt a severely neurotic man are simply not realistic to his relatively untroubled fellows, and may seem to him like substanceless figments when he returns to a normal state of mind. He becomes sane, indeed, when he is able once again to participate without undue stress in the communally attested view of reality by which sanity is defined.

Since all definitions of madness are grounded in a doctrine of the real, it is possible for a man in the midst of severe psychic distress to direct his energies against the terms on which he fears himself to be crazy, to explore his personal turmoil for its ontological meanings. Instead of seeking to regulate his inner life in accordance with conventional estimates of reality, he may defiantly seek to turn the tables on his inner and outer accusers, so as to challenge the conceptual framework on which their judgment rests. Such, in schematic terms, is the thesis of this book: that Melville achieved in *Moby-Dick* a sophisticated, acute, and prophetic attack on the scheme of theological ideas that was taken as an accurate description of ultimate reality in his time.

Melville deals with historic theological issues that may seem quite remote to us, scarcely worth the energies of a great genius. Yet the enigmas that he sought to penetrate were generic to the structure of ideas that molded his consciousness, so that the need to review the historical context of his work is anything but antiquarian. It is directed rather toward an understanding of the fact that although Melville lived in a world very different from our own, and thought in the idiom that his world provided, he nonetheless addresses us directly. Like other masters of literary art, Melville succeeded in taking command of certain basic conventions of thought that were so potent as to dominate the meditations of his contemporaries.

***

During the early nineteenth century (before Melville's birth in 1819 and for several decades thereafter) the Christian community in America was the scene of a proliferating debate. The Unitarians, in their stronghold at Harvard College, stood at one extreme of a thickly populated spectrum of views; opposing them at the other extreme were the most conservative Calvinists. Essential to the controversy were differing interpretations of the moral relation between God and man: liberals argued that God had endowed his human creatures with inherent rights that divine Providence would not violate, whereas orthodox believers stressed the suffering and evils of life as evidence for their view that the Almighty was rightly angered by the innate depravity of the race. These topics of debate were not new, but can be traced back through the Arminian controversies of the seventeenth century to the quarrel between Augustine and Pelagius in the fifth century. In the early nineteenth century, however, these debates came to seem intractable and were denounced increasingly as a waste of motion.

Melville's religious perplexities were shaped by the fact that he absorbed in childhood the opposing theories of Unitarianism

and the most conservative orthodoxy. His saturation in these
hostile traditions occurred under conditions that made it impossible for him to accept either, and gave him instead a deeply
rooted preoccupation with the problems posed by their incompatible interpretations of experience.

Beyond such specific traditions of religious teaching there lay,
however, a shared conception of reality, a fundamental conceptual framework that supposed the ultimate structure of reality
to be conveyed by some idea of "God." In absorbing this basic
outlook, Melville accepted its corollaries, that the nature of
"God" was at least partly knowable, and that such knowledge
established a rule for the conduct of life. The theocentric system
of understanding provided something far more basic than a set
of answers to man's questions about the world. It provided a
set of terms in which questions and answers could be framed,
a conceptual structure within which debates could be carried
on intelligibly.[3]

3. For a good discussion of the character and historical influence of such
basic conceptual frameworks see Susanne K. Langer, *Philosophy in a New Key,
a Study of the Symbolism of Reason, Rite and Art* (Cambridge, Mass., 1942). There
is a considerable literature on such schemes and their importance for the
interpretation of literature and the study of intellectual history at large. The
term "basic conceptual framework" is derived from Langer and seems best
for the purposes of this book. "Myth," a term in general use, and applied
to Melville by James Baird's *Ishmael* (Baltimore, 1956), properly indicates
a fusion of thought and emotion, but suggests that they are joined in images
and narrative, evident constructions of fancy. To call nineteenth-century theology a "myth" would not do justice to the literalness with which the scheme
was taken. Thomas Kuhn, applying this analytical concept to the history
of science, has proposed the term "paradigm." See *The Structure of Scientific
Revolutions,* 2d ed. (rev.) (Chicago, 1970). For my thesis, however, "paradigm"
fails to suggest the emotional investment that these frameworks absorb, the
way they channel feelings along special pathways, as well as order rational
processes.
    When applied to culture, the use of such conceptions invites debate about
what system was really dominant in a given period and when, precisely, it
collapsed. Langer argues that the "Christian system" faded in the late Middle
Ages, and that a new philosophical epoch was born with the emergence of
Cartesian dualism. This is evidently incompatible with the view taken here,
that the system encountered a major crisis in the nineteenth century. Yet
another student might find grounds for arguing that contemporary theological
writers like Barth, Tillich, and the Niebuhrs have given Christian thought
a historical flowering in our own time.
    As Thomas Kuhn observes, however, an area of investigation may enter
a crisis state and seem to meet a dead end, only to be revitalized by the

The theocentric system had its metaphysical and epistemological components, abstract theoretical issues that provided a rich field for the elaboration of opposing views. But the system also performed an immediate ethical function, that of defining the terms on which the practical policies of men could receive the sanction of an ultimate authority. The spiritual power to be derived from a proper relationship to the Godhead had its mundane counterpart, since it was presumed that human enterprises could only gain effectiveness by their conformity with the theocentric contours of reality itself. Edward Beecher emphasized the comprehensive moral illumination to be expected from a correct interpretation of the divine order when he proposed his solution to the problems that divided religious leaders. "We need a system that shall give us the power intelligently to meet and logically to solve all of the great religious and social problems which we are called on to encounter in the great work of converting the world, and thoroughly reorganizing human society."[4]

In *The Conflict of Ages; or, The Great Debate on the Moral Relations of God and Man* (1853), Beecher reviewed the liberal-orthodox controversies in abundant detail, and sought to explain why they had not been resolved. He identified a fundamental dislocation in Christian theology itself that had introduced "perpetual internal conflict into the very vitals of the system." The whole tradition of Christian theology seemed to him like a malfunctioning machine whose "main moving powers" worked against each other (p. 10). "The principles of honor and right," which acknowledge inherent human dignity, had never been reconciled

---

accession of new formulative notions (see pp. 83-84). The intellectual struggles that look like the death agony of a tradition may appear to be growing pains in the judgment of a later time. Just as every constructive advance must have its destructive aspect, so an apparently irreversible decay may foster the seeds of an unexpected renewal.

It becomes clear, then, that nothing so ambitious as a final judgment on the vitality of the Christian tradition is necessary in order to particularize the specific issues around which intractable debates proliferated in the early nineteenth century, and to recognize that they are symptomatic of a basic crisis.

4. Edward Beecher, *The Conflict of Ages; or, The Great Debate on the Moral Relations of God and Man* (Boston, 1854), p. iii. Subsequent references to this edition appear in the text.

with "the facts of the ruin of man," which make up the manifold
afflictions of the race. Invoking a personal turmoil that more
than once had shaken his mental balance, Beecher declared that
when these contrary "moving powers" operate directly on a
single mind, they force it to an insane conclusion: the divine
scheme of things itself appears malevolent (pp. 184-191).

Beecher argued that because of this central enigma the "internal struggles and convulsions" of the Christian community had
"wasted an amount of energy great almost beyond imagination."
"In the eyes of intelligent spectators, not familiar with theological debates, religion itself has been dishonored" (*The Conflict
of Ages*, p. 13). Beecher may well have sensed that more was
at stake in these wasteful controversies than the loss of intellectual prestige that religious leaders had suffered. If theological
knowledge itself had so drastic a moral quandary at its heart,
then its claim to confer moral authority could not be sustained.
Beecher had the evidence on which he might have become aware
that his tradition of thought was in a fundamental crisis; both
the proliferating debates and the persistent central contradiction
suggested a need for basic renovation. Beecher once confided
to his brother that he hoped to act as a "moral Copernicus,"[5]
as though planning to reframe the whole field of moral thought,
to clear away the stifling complexities of current theory and
open a path for energetic advance. But in the published work,
Beecher retreated from such a bold claim, arguing for a way
to correct the "misadjustment" of theological discourse; and although his account of the dilemma inspired widespread public
debate, scarcely anyone accepted his solution.[6]

---

5. Robert Meredith, *The Politics of the Universe* (Nashville, 1968), p. 132.

6. Meredith, p. 145, notes that *The Conflict* went through five printings in
three months and seven "editions" (which were also reprintings) in two years;
he also discusses the extensive controversy prompted by the book (see pp.
145-178). Henry James, Sr., the Swedenborgian, replied to Beecher in terms
that suggest how widespread a spiritual *malaise* he had identified. "Your atti-
tude is very broadly representative. Your theologic experience reflects that
of numberless thousands, though it is at the same time true that only one
here and there is seen lifting his hands to heaven, and loudly imploring deliverance, while the vast majority lock the sullen pain in their own bosoms,
and dying, make no sign." See *The Nature of Evil, Considered in a Letter to the
Rev. Edward Beecher, D.D. Author of "The Conflict of Ages"* (New York, 1855),
pp. 9-10.

A historic shift in perspective was afoot even as the theologians continued their self-defeating quarrels. The nineteenth century witnessed a major transition of thought, both in Europe and America, as the world view promulgated by Christian theocentrism yielded to various secular frames of reference which encompassed competing theories on the ultimate context of man's life and his moral duties.[7] Melville is generally recognized, with Kierkegaard and Nietzsche, as a prophet of this spiritual revolution.

The history of Melville criticism richly illustrates the analogies between his intellectual investigations and the philosophical schemes that displaced the theocentric system. His work is alive with intellectual impulses that anticipate modern movements of thought, and has prompted so many interpretations within modern conceptual frameworks that one scholar has protested that a complete canvass would list "most of the bugbears haunting the minds of modern intellectuals."[8] Very good studies of this kind share a common weakness with the less successful: they do not sufficiently take into account the distinctive intellectual idiom in which Melville worked. Melville did not challenge the theocentric presuppositions of his time from a standpoint in symbolist theory, or psychoanalytic theory, or naturalism, or phenomenology, or existentialism. The aesthetic structures of *Moby-Dick* evoke the religious crisis that gave birth to such contemporary doctrines because Melville challenged the theocentric scheme by working within its own terms.[9]

7. Merle Curti, *The Growth of American Thought*, 3d ed. (New York, 1964), pp. 517-539, or Floyd Stovall, "The Decline of Romantic Idealism, 1855-1871," in *Transitions in American Literary History*, ed. Harry Hayden Clark (Durham, 1953), pp. 315-378, may be consulted for good summaries of the well-recognized features of this process as it developed in America. A divided and demoralized theological community faced, after the Civil War, an increased intellectual challenge from Darwinism, the new astronomy and physics, and the higher criticism of the Bible. Melville's interest in these external challenges, and his way of responding to them, is ably discussed by Walter Bezanson in his introduction to *Clarel* (New York, 1960). The argument of this study concerns the endemic problems of Christian thought, the internal crisis that weakened its reply to these challenges.

8. Leon Howard, *Herman Melville, a Biography* (1951; reptd. Berkeley, 1967), p. 341.

9. James Baird, *Ishmael*, (Baltimore, 1956), discusses Melville as a figure of cultural transition, who achieved the "modulation of idiom" required when

Melville's spiritual exploration in *Moby-Dick* employs specific themes and motifs of Calvinist and liberal theology, and of the controversy between them.[10] He uses these materials in forms

---

inherited symbols are exhausted. "Melville, the artist, is a supreme example of the artistic creator engaged in the act of making new symbols to replace the 'lost' symbols of Protestant Christianity" (p. xv). Baird's very provocative study disavows interest in the specific historical context of Melville's thought, and thus misses the importance of his way of turning Christian symbols against their received meanings. Milton R. Stern, *The Fine Hammered Steel of Herman Melville* (1957; reptd. Urbana, 1968), better discerns the special character of Melville's inverted usages when he describes him as employing a romantic symbology to express consistently antiromantic themes. "Romantic symbology generally, and transcendental symbology especially, is aimed by cosmic idealism." But Melville's essential vision, Stern recognizes, is anti-idealistic, so that he uses "cosmic symbols, whose antiromantic meanings will be tested by experience" ("Foreword"). Thus Melville becomes "the first major American author to turn the symbology already created by the transcendentalists to the relativistic purposes of naturalism" (p. 10). I have sought to illuminate the intellectual conflicts that this transitional position imposed upon Melville himself, and to show that the most forceful idealist system that Melville had at his disposal was not transcendentalism but Protestant theology.

10. Critical studies that have examined Melville's religious ideas have led to disputes in which there seems to be truth on both sides. Certain of these disputes can be resolved when Melville's radically subversive way of using Christian conceptions is recognized. A major issue, for example, is the "justice" of Captain Ahab's fate. Nathalia Wright implies that Melville accepted the authority of the Christian scheme and used it to condemn Ahab's wickedness. Explaining the parallel between Captain Ahab's death and that of his Old Testament counterpart, King Ahab, Wright notes that "the destruction of the *Pequod* is appalling indeed. But it is a fitting end for the monomania of Ahab. . . . So in the case of King Ahab the account of his death is elaborated by more details of violence than are to be found in that of any of the Israelite kings before him. The reason is not far to seek. He vexed Jehovah more than all the rest." See Nathalia Wright, *Melville's Use of the Bible* (Durham, 1949), p. 67. Several other writers have agreed that Ahab goes to a divinely warranted doom.

Howard P. Vincent, in *The Trying Out of Moby-Dick* (1949; reptd. Carbondale, 1965), finds the controlling rationale in Father Mapple's sermon: "whereas Jonah at last heeded the will of God in time to save the ship and to still the storm, Ahab, unrepentant, imposes his will upon his men so that both he and the *Pequod* crew are destroyed" (p. 72). Captain Ahab, Vincent concludes, "should have been one of the silent worshipers at the Seaman's Bethel" (p. 75). Newton Arvin, *Herman Melville, a Critical Biography* (1950; reptd. New York, 1964), also relies on Mapple's sermon for his definition of Melville's essential view: it "is intended to make us understand that Ahab, like Jonah, has in a certain sense sinned through his proud refusal to obey God's will, or its equivalent; pride and disobedience, in at any rate some dimly Christian senses, are at the root of Ahab's wickedness" (pp. 179-180).

that imply that the champions of opposing versions of Christian
doctrine were quarreling over the trusteeship of a dead tradition.
He commandeers polemical conventions for his own purposes,
using them so as to violate their conventional meanings. At the
core of his radical doubt lies the same question that had vexed
Beecher: how can the God of traditional theocentrism possibly
be worthy of the devotion of moral men? But Melville is not
simply meditating once again the "problem of evil"; he disrupts
the entire conceptual framework in which "evil" was perceived
as a "problem." Whereas Beecher sought desperately to make
an "adjustment" in the defective machinery of theological discourse, Melville asserted its disintegration.

* * *

Melville arrived at his evocation of cultural crisis as he explored a severe personal conflict. His preoccupation with outdat-
ed religious questions was a source of dismay to his most intimate
literary associates. Evert Duyckinck, the learned editor and critic
who befriended Melville, was amused to find that Melville was

---

Although Arvin recognizes the contempt for "Christian" submissiveness that
Melville implies in his chapter on "The Tail" (p. 180), he concludes his analysis by returning to the theme of "cosmic submissiveness." He says that Father
Mapple uses the "familiar language of faith" in a way that blurs his essential
message, namely, that man may arrive at a kind of peace by obeying the
" 'will' of nature," which has "something godlike in it" (pp. 192-193).
   These studies diminish the cogency of Ahab's indictment of the divine order,
and the seriousness with which Melville developed and presented that indictment. Lawrance Thompson follows up this central Melvillian preoccupation;
he claims that Ahab embodies a heroic rebellion against cosmic malignity
and goes to his death as the victim of an evil God. But Thompson, like those
with whom he differs, holds that Melville accepted the conceptual framework
provided by Christian theology as an account of reality. Noting that Melville
was thoroughly schooled in the "dogma of John Calvin," Thompson argues
that instead of rejecting it, Melville came to believe in its more repulsive
features: "believing more firmly than ever in the God of John Calvin, he
began to resent and hate the attributes of God, particularly the seemingly
tyrannous harshness and cruelty and malice of God. Thus, instead of losing
faith in his Calvinistic God, Melville made a scapegoat of him." Lawrance
Thompson, *Melville's Quarrel With God* (Princeton, 1952), pp. 4-5. In Thompson's view, "God" remains a stable target for Melville's resentment; he insists
that theocentric assumptions continued to make sense of experience for Melville even when the resultant order became intolerable. Correspondingly,
Thompson does not observe that Melville attacks the presuppositions of
Ahab's cosmic rebellion in ways that severely qualify the moral validity of
his heroism. Ahab is not the spokesman for a "quarrel with God"; Melville

"another representative of the old Arminius."[11] But his amusement gave way to a monitory disapproval after the publication
of *Moby-Dick*. "It is a curious fact that there are no more bilious
people in the world, more completely filled with megrims and
head shakings, than some of these very people who are constantly
inveighing against the religious melancholy of priestcraft."[12]
Duyckinck's objection was not based on religious scruple, but
on his taste. Like many another reader of Melville, he was
repelled by what seemed to him "bilious"; he hated to see a
rare talent wasted on so paltry a topic as "religious melancholy."

Hawthorne had more sympathy for Melville's darker meditations, but he too grew weary of their apparent obsessiveness.
Five years after the publication of *Moby-Dick*, Hawthorne noted
his continued wrestling with religious enigmas. "Melville, as he
always does, began to reason of Providence and futurity, and
of everything else that lies beyond human ken, and informed
me that he had 'pretty much made up his mind to be annihilat-
ed'; but still he does not seem to rest in that anticipation; and,
I think, will never rest until he gets hold of a definite belief.
It is strange how he persists — and has persisted ever since I
knew him, and probably long before — in wandering to-and-fro
over these deserts, as dismal and monotonous as the sand hills
amid which we were sitting."[13]

Dr. Henry Murray, whose psychoanalyic discussion of *Pierre*
is a landmark of Melville criticism, argues that Melville's obsessive interest in such issues was a symptom of neurotic distress.
Murray holds that the loftiness of the questions that plagued
Melville served to conceal the true character of his difficulty:
"A man in his position, who is incapable of willing his way
out of inner discord, is likely to find the unsolvable problems
of traditional philosophy irresistibly alluring . . . . By wrestling

---

absorbs him into a larger spiritual investigation that does justice to Ahab's
indictment of the divine while recognizing its limitations. The destruction
of the Pequod is not presented as an act of God, evil or otherwise; it culminates
Melville's exploration of the enigmas that undermined the notion of "God"
as an adequate means of interpreting experience.

11. Leyda, I, 273.

12. *Ibid.*, p. 437.

13. Nathaniel Hawthorne, *The English Notebooks*, ed. Randall Stewart (New
York, 1941), pp. 432-433.

with these ... enigmas of thought and persuading himself and others that his happiness depends on his finding the talismanic secret (which he knows is impossible), he dresses his mental preoccupations in robes of historic dignity, covers the naked facts of his personal distress, and indefinitely postpones the dreaded curative decision" (*Pierre*, p. xvii).

This contention is to a degree quite persuasive, but it presupposes an excessively sharp dichotomy between the "naked facts" of psychic distress and the enigmas of philosophy, as though psychoanalysis could discern a meaningful pattern in those "facts," without employing philosophical suppositions. Murray himself uses Freudian and Jungian theory together, without concerning himself with the intellectual conflicts between them, and as a result his discussion is at points confused.[14] His interpreta-

14. Henry Murray celebrates Melville's surrender to the forces of the unconscious (see his introduction to *Pierre*, p. xcvii), which he defines in Jungian terms as a chaos seeking resolution in mythic images (pp. xxvii, xxxi) but also describes as informed by the classic Freudian strife. "Thus, many years before Freud, Melville, opening his mind to undercurrents of feeling and imagery, discovered the Oedipus Complex" (p. xxxvii). Both of these schemes are applied by Murray to the relationship between Pierre and Isabel. In the Jungian framework, Melville's depiction of this relationship adumbrates the psychic and cultural potencies of the "anima experience." (See pp. li-lv.) But Murray also sees it as a ramification of the Oedipal dilemma, Pierre's participation in the emotional and moral consternations of the "incest motive."

The fact that Murray does not clarify the relation between these two characterizations of Isabel's meaning leads to a basic confusion in his discussion of Melville's spiritual failure in *Pierre*. Melville's failure, he argues, is reflected in Pierre's failure to consummate the relationship with Isabel: "He orders Isabel to call him brother no more, insisting that there is no certain proof of their kinship. Thus, by decree, he abolishes the incest barrier. Next he asserts that it is 'the gods' who are to blame if the combustibles they put in him are discharged: man is not morally responsible. This fundamental conclusion is succeeded by a far-reaching thought — that the ideal of purity is wide of the mark, that 'demi-gods trample on trash, and Virtue and Vice are trash!' For an instant, Pierre sees some saving way out of the devastating conflict and — reaching the highest pitch of positive religious conviction that can be found in the whole length of Melville's writings — cries: 'I will gospelize the world anew, and show them deeper secrets than the Apocalypse: — I will write it, I will write it!'

"This second glimpse of Melville's 'scared white doe' marks the turning point of the novel. After this one tumultuous uprising and definitive suppression of instinct, Pierre's love for Isabel begins to fade. Note that Pierre does not say, 'I will do it, I will do it!; he exclaims, 'I will write it, I will write it!' But he does not write it. His work takes another course. We hear no more of Pierre's new gospel" (p. lxxxii).

tion is further limited because it accepts an assumption that both of these pioneering theorists may be said to have shared.

It is not necessary to enter into the now highly complex exegetical controversies about the "real" meaning of Freud's or Jung's work in order to recognize that both writers have been taken as holding that the character of neurosis is determined by trans-historical factors. Freud's emphasis on a set of quasi-biological drives has led interpreters to suppose that the forces that generate neurotic illness have a specific pattern as timeless and universal as the features of Jung's collective unconscious. Both Freud and Jung have seemed to imply that making contact with the essence of psychic life requires the apprehension of permanent mental structures and processes. Despite opposing contentions regarding the nature of these fundamental dynamic patterns, theorists in both traditions have argued that they are *reflected in* specific cultural phenomena rather than *arise from* them. Murray does not feel compelled to choose between Freudian and Jungian presuppositions in order to praise Melville for having discovered in his own psychic depths a realm of absolute experience that transcends the particularities of his immediate cultural setting. Melville drove "a shaft into the primitive strata of his mind. *There* he was outside the boundaries of his culture, dissociated from his space-time, and almost in possession of a universality of understanding that reached round the world and back into Pagan centuries" (*Pierre,* p. xxx).[15]

It seems clear that Murray locates the turning point in Pierre's failure to "do it," to carry through on his abolition of the incest barrier. What remains unclear is how sexual relations with Isabel would have yielded a new gospel. Murray himself is vague on the critical point; he asserts that Pierre glimpses *some* saving way out of the conflict. Murray's reason for associating Isabel with a new gospel lies, not in her meaning within the Freudian sexual dilemma, but in her function as a Jungian anima. The anima is potentially an agent of cultural advance, harboring the secret of a new gospel, because she embodies "scores of nameless intuitions and impulses, the open expression of which has been barred by culture" (p. lii). This wealth of prophetic meanings is correlated with the activities proscribed by the "incest barrier" in that both are "barred by culture," but this negative correlation itself means only that they represent opposing theories of the repressed aspects of the mind.

15. Correspondingly, although Murray summarizes numerous details from Melville's life that are used in *Pierre,* he derives little significant insight from them. Instead of suggesting important features of Melville's creative achievement, they only show that the novel is "autobiographical." Murray in fact

More recent psychoanalytic investigation has revealed that neurotic problems receive their character as they develop in the interplay between an individual and his specific human environment; this interplay engages the traditions of thought that the culture supplies an individual for the comprehension of his experience. Erik Erikson argues that healthy maturing requires the acquisition of a stable sense of "self," which is wedded to a coherent image of the world. He observes that traditional systems of thought provide the context within which this psychic task is carried out, giving the individual culturally attested forms of ordering experience that permit him to take his bearings and formulate his own special identity.[16] If the formulative notions provided by the culture are themselves confused, or cannot be applied to experience without severe discrepancy, neurotic problems will result whose features reflect the underlying cultural dislocation. Erikson follows Erich Fromm, Karen Horney, and Harry Stack Sullivan in stressing the importance of cultural factors in neurosis; but Erikson pushes this argument a critical further step.[17] If culture can determine the specific forms of personal neurosis, rare individuals can explore their inner conflicts in ways that illuminate and influence culture.[18]

The argument of this book holds that the intellectual conflict between liberal and Calvinistic points of view was a potent ingredient in Melville's psychic difficulties, not as a mask for "deeper" problems merely, but as an authentic locus of psychic distress. The theocentric system gave him a fundamental idiom in which to comprehend himself and his world; problems of doctrine were for him continuous with problems of experience.

---

warns against seeking aesthetic significance in Melville's use of such particulars. "It would be a fatal mistake to regard his autobiographical writings mainly as egotistical exhibitions of purely personal experiences, because, by opening his mind to the spontaneities of the impersonal unconscious and identifying with a procession of archetypal figures, he succeeded in memorably portraying dispositions that are universal" (p. xxxi). The "universality" of Melville's art lies in his approximation of the psychic universals revealed by (here Jungian) psychoanalytic theory.

16. Erik H. Erikson, *Identity, Youth and Crisis* (New York, 1968), pp. 188-191.

17. For a good summary see Clara Thompson and Patrick Mullahy, *Psychoanalysis: Evolution and Development, a Review of Theory and Therapy* (New York, 1950), pp. 193-224.

18. See Erik H. Erikson, *Young Man Luther* (New York, 1958).

In order to illustrate how traditional patterns of thought may give structure to chronic psychological distress, it may be useful to reconsider Hawthorne's famous complaint about Melville's "dismal and monotonous" topics of conversation, shifting the emphasis from Melville's obsessiveness to Hawthorne's *ennui*.

Hawthorne had himself contemplated the possibility of "annihilation," and it led him to a conclusion so dreadful that he could only give it utterance in the act of denial. He had been profoundly shaken by his mother's deathbed sufferings, and transcribed in his journal the meditations it aroused. "God would not have made the close so dark and wretched, if there were nothing beyond; for then it would have been a fiend that created us, and measured out our existence, and not God. It would be something beyond wrong — it would be insult — to be thrust out of life into annihilation in this miserable way. So, out of the very bitterness of death, I gather the sweet assurance of a better state of being."[19]

Hawthorne's effort to find the meaning of his private grief brought him face to face with the same moral enigma that Edward Beecher had expounded in his grand survey of the "conflict of ages." Hawthorne refused to believe in "annihilation" for reasons that were shaped by the hectored questions concerning divine Providence. He convinced himself that "a better state of being" had to be supposed because the misery of life itself appeared so excessive as to demand reparation in the hereafter. If human beings simply disappear into nothing, Hawthorne implied, there is no realm in which a just God can compensate for the undeserved earthly sufferings of his creatures. Hawthorne's agonized meditation reveals his basic kinship with those who took the liberal side of the controversy. The orthodox belief that God ordains the bitterness of death as a punishment for sin simply does not occur to him.

But Hawthorne's is scarcely a positive faith; his assertion of religious hope is animated essentially by his horrified recoil from the prospect of conceiving existence as an insult measured out by a transcendent fiend. Instead of providing tangible solace, the theocentric framework in which Hawthorne interpreted his

---

19. Randall Stewart, *Nathaniel Hawthorne, a Biography* (New Haven, 1948), p. 90.

mother's death yielded an insane nightmare. The logic is as inexorable as it is perverse: 1. His mother did not deserve to suffer this way; 2. If there is no "better state of being," God is a fiend. For Hawthorne a strenuous denial seemed the only way out. His "sweet assurance" does not rest on a foundation of unshakable divine truth, nor is it received as a gift of grace; it is something that Hawthorne is compelled to "gather." As Melville explored the disconcerting prospect that Hawthorne wished to obviate, he came to see quite clearly how such a failure of religious belief could inspire passionate assertions of its success. He disposed of the resultant emotional and intellectual dishonesty in a single sentence: "Faith, like a jackal, feeds among the tombs, and even from these dead doubts she gathers her most vital hope" (*Moby-Dick*, "The Chapel," p. 41).

Melville's questions fatigued Hawthorne, not because he found it easy to answer them, but because it was difficult for him to face their implications.[20] They troubled him on levels of his mind that he did not care to explore, where real grief received expression in a frame of reference that skewed it into metaphysical horror, and a perfectly consistent logic brought in conclusions that were manifestly crazy. Alfred North Whitehead once observed that boredom can be symptomatic of a fundamental intellectual dislocation: a basic "life-tedium" sets in when the concepts used to analyze experience no longer make sense of the realities to which they are applied, since psychic energy is absorbed by the effort to keep up a coherent mental life in the midst of incoherent feelings and ideas.[21]

Melville would seem to have experienced the very reverse of

---

20. This book was in the last stages of preparation when Edwin Haviland Miller's *Melville* (New York, 1975) appeared, so that it was not possible to give it the consideration that its scope and psychoanalytic approach invite. Miller's evocations of Melville's psychic difficulties are often compelling, but he follows Murray in adopting premises that confer derivative status upon Melville's struggle with cultural traditions. Melville spoke to Hawthorne about religious matters, Miller affirms, because he "knew that his confessions had to be phrased in metaphysical or religious language in order to disguise and to distance the personal hurts hidden beneath the grandiose phrases" (p. 287). Looking for "personal hurts" in the conversation at Liverpool, Miller construes Melville's comment about "annihilation" as a threat to commit suicide.

21. Alfred North Whitehead, *Process and Reality* (New York, 1929), pp. 22-24.

Hawthornian boredom,[22] to have suffered attacks of feverish excitement when he permitted the spiritual dislocations within himself to surface. He knew quite well that these states of mind carried him out of the range of "normal" mental experience. But he became convinced that his truest creativeness lay in braving this tumult, winning the articulation of a "vital truth," in contention with apparent madness. At the culmination of his religious conflict, he enlisted the example of Shakespeare as an earnest of the transcendent achievement for which he ran his psychic risk. "But it is those deep far-away things in him; those occasional flashings-forth of the intuitive Truth in him; those short, quick probings at the very axis of reality: — these are the things that make Shakespeare, Shakespeare. Through the mouths of the dark characters of Hamlet, Timon, Lear, and Iago, he craftily says, or sometimes insinuates the things, which we feel to be so terrifically true, that it were all but madness for any good man, in his own proper character, to utter, or even hint of them. Tormented into desperation, Lear the frantic King tears off the mask, and speaks the sane madness of vital truth" ("Mosses," pp. 541-542).

Melville's madness became sane as he explored the meanings of his personal crisis in a form that illuminates the crisis of his age, anticipating the imminent collapse of the theocentric world view. But the true stature of *Moby-Dick* remains obscure so long as we view it as conveying only the death agony of a superseded interpretation of moral experience. We cannot pretend to a mo-

---

22. Weariness and *ennui* plagued Hawthorne increasingly as the years passed, sometimes leading to periods of virtual despair. The association of this recurrent distress with his profound misgivings about the meaning of death is suggested by the fact that he suffered an especially acute attack during the illness of Una in Rome (Stewart, pp. 204-205). His efforts to maintain a belief in the "hereafter," so as to fortify himself against such despair did not end with the meditation by his mother's bedside. A notebook entry of 1855 indicates his continuing search for assurance: "God himself cannot compensate us for being born, in any period short of eternity. All the misery we endure here constitutes a claim for another life; and, still more, all the happiness, because all true happiness involves something more than the earth owns, and [needs] something more than a mortal capacity for the enjoyment of it" (*English Notebooks*, p. 101). The continuity of thought between this comment and the earlier one, as he reinforces the assurance gathered from the miseries of life with a further assurance based on its joys, only emphasizes the need he felt to shore up a faith that continuously threatened to disintegrate.

nopoly of truth by which to make an absolute assessment of
the shortcomings of earlier systems. Melville's struggle should
not be viewed as the harassment of a noble spirit who would
have functioned smoothly in contemporary categories, a gifted
primitive who brilliantly foresaw ourselves.

What Melville centrally conveys is the confrontation with that
depth of experience which is always beyond all systems. He
evokes what appears to be the most enduring feature of those
basic conceptual frameworks in which men articulate their nego-
tiations with experience, namely their historical finitude. The
impermanence of these intellectual institutions is their most permanent characteristic; none stands forth in radical newness,
transcending the history that gave it birth. As Melville broke
out of the intellectual framework in which he was trained, he
came to a revitalized awareness of the mysteries that have stirred
religious meditation from the earliest ages of Western thought.
"I read Solomon more and more," he confided to Hawthorne,
"and every time see deeper and deeper unspeakable meanings
in him" (*Letters,* p. 130). When he uttered the core of his religious
discoveries in *Moby-Dick,* Melville revealed their essential kinship
with that ancient charter of religious doubt. " 'All is vanity,' "
ALL. This wilful world hath not got hold of unchristian Solomon's wisdom yet" ("The Try-Works," p. 355).

If the theocentric interpretation of moral experience has been
superseded, this does not mean that religion itself may be con-
fined to a place in the procession of basic conceptual frameworks
by which man has sought to make his experience intelligible,
as though history were a Comptean progress that makes the
wisdom of earlier ages obsolete. The truest religious awareness
has had exponents in every age, who have perceived the limitations and impermanence of current systems, noting the vanity
of all that claim to have taken possession of an eternal truth.
Works of art that convey this tragic aspect of experience deserve
to survive the attrition of the ages, and the creative struggle
that produces such art deserves as intimate an examination as
the surviving records allow.

Part One

I

A Proud Coherence

B asic conceptions of reality are instilled during childhood. In America when Melville was reared, these conceptions included theological ideas; in other cultural settings the focus may be avowedly secular. But in each case the initial training establishes a notion of the ultimate coordinates of reality that is extraordinarily tenacious.

To indicate how Melville's childhood will be viewed in this book, it may be useful to consider two influential writers who have used secular and theological perspectives in discussing the impact of early experiences. Both Sigmund Freud and Horace Bushnell observed the striking congruity between adult religious attitudes and the patterns of thought and feeling established in childhood, but they assessed this congruity in very different ways.

Freud used the term "religion" in its restrictive sense, as referring to the belief in supernatural beings; and he argued that it is the cultural product of a universal psychological inclination, the desire of adults to return to the more comfortable world of infancy. Religion is thus an "illusion," which draws its strength, not from any correspondence with reality, but from man's insistent desire for protection from the terrors of nature, the cruelties of fate, and the privations of his communal life. Helpless before these menacing features of his experience, man turns to an illusory Father whose divine lordship recapitulates the parental oversight of childhood, even as man's adult impotence recapitulates the helplessness of infancy. Thus the power and love and threat of the earthly father are projected into the Godhead.

This interpretation depends, in turn, on a conception of reality that Freud summarized concisely: "to many questions science can as yet give no answer; but scientific work is our only way to the knowledge of external reality." Freud wrote *The Future of an Illusion* expressly to proclaim the necessity of an *"education to reality,"*[1] by which man would be enabled to cast off his protracted childishness and accept the world as science describes it.

Yet even in advancing this argument, Freud finds it necessary to come to terms with the fact that religious conviction seems to be inherent in the character of certain mature believers and to inform thought and feeling with such tenacity as to raise doubts regarding the derivative and compensatory function that he assigns to it. He concedes momentarily that the essential nature of man might indeed not permit the wholesale abolition of religion that he recommends. His way of disposing of this problem focuses on the impact of early training.

Can an anthropologist give the cranial index of a people whose custom it is to deform their children's heads by bandaging them from their earliest years? Think of the distressing contrast between the radiant intelligence of a healthy child and the feeble mentality of the average adult. Is it so utterly impossible that it is just religious upbringing which is largely to blame for this relative degeneration? ... We introduce ... [the child] to the doctrines of religion at a time when he is neither interested in them nor capable of grasping their import .... So when the child's mind awakens, the doctrines of religion are already unassailable .... So long as a man's early years are influenced by the religious thought-inhibition ... we cannot really say what he is actually like.[2]

In Freud's view, thus, a man whose character has been formed by theological conceptions must be considered a kind of medical oddity, a distorted being in whom the lineaments of reality itself have been altogether obscured. The measurements employed by a scientific approach to mental life will yield misleading results, Freud implies, so long as they are applied to specimens of hu-

---

1. Sigmund Freud, *The Future of an Illusion,* trans. W. D. Robson-Scott (Garden City, 1957), pp. 55, 89.

2. *Ibid.,* pp. 84-86.

manity that have been warped so drastically. Thus Freud seeks
to maintain his grip on the conception of reality that he termed
"scientific" by conceding that he cannot "really say" what a
religiously indoctrinated man "is actually like." Only when the
education to reality that he proposes has had its proper effect
will the true nature of man be visible: he wishes to replace a
religious indoctrination with a scientific one.

Horace Bushnell was as ambitious as Freud in advocating
an improvement in child-rearing practices, but he did not share
Freud's conception of reality. *Christian Nurture* (1861) was a major
achievement of theological reflection in nineteenth-century
America and is still hailed as a classic of religious education;
in it Bushnell insists that believers should "take possession of
the organic laws of the family, and wield them as instruments
. . . of a regenerative purpose."[3] Consistently theocentric in his
estimate of the reality to which children should be educated,
Bushnell criticizes his fellow Christians for their failure to make
use of the lawfully patterned dynamic systems by which human
mentality is formed. He describes the impact of a sophisticated
parental example, a candid and pervasive Christian faithfulness
"all glowing about the young soul, as a warm and genial nurture,
and forming in it, by methods that are silent and imperceptible,
a spirit of duty and religious obedience to God" (pp. 12-13).

Freud argues that the idea of God is a fiction that absorbs
into itself the feelings that children develop toward their parents;
he holds that this fiction is sustained in culture by the unwill-
ingness of grown men and women to face the world without
the comfort of believing that a divine Parent finally controls
all earthly happenings. Bushnell likewise stressed the transmuta-
tion of filial attitudes into religious attitudes, but on the assumption that this process is ordained by God: "The parents are to
fill . . . an office strictly religious; personating God in the child's
feeling and conscience, and bending it, thus, to what . . . we
call a filial piety. So that when the unseen Father and Lord
is Himself discovered, there is to be a piety made ready for
him; a kind of house-religion, that may widen out into the measures of God's ideal majesty and empire . . . . [Children] could

3. Horace Bushnell, *Christian Nurture*, introd. Luther A. Weigle (New Haven,
1967), p. 91. Subsequent references to this edition appear in the text.

not make a beginning with ideas of God, or with God as an unseen Spirit; therefore they had parents given to them in the Lord — the Lord to be in them, there to personate and finite himself, and gather to such human motherhood and fatherhood, a piety transferable to Himself, as the knowledge of his nobler, unseen Fatherhood arrives" (*Christian Nurture,* p. 271).

Freud and Bushnell are quite in agreement on the thesis that family life instills in children "a piety transferable" into adult pieties, capable of supporting explicit adult convictions about the nature of reality; and each is anxious lest the mentality of children coalesce about erroneous formulations of the real.

My own interpretation of Melville's youth takes its basic premise from the implicit recognition that Bushnell and Freud share. In looking for the origins of Melville's religious conflict, I do not propose to interpret his rearing in Christian terms as theologically erroneous, or in Freudian terms as emotionally distorted. I conceive the early period, rather, as having transmitted a consolidation of meanings that was theocentric, the kind of training that Bushnell recommended and that Freud likened to the practice of head-bandaging.

This analysis centers, not upon the "reality" about which they disagreed so sharply, but upon the processes of transmission. The "house-religion" of Herman Melville's family did not make for the ideological continuity that Freud and Bushnell contemplated. Instead of preserving the theocentric heritage intact, the circumstances of Melville's rearing transmitted it as a matrix of psychic conflict.

***

Herman Melville's father, Allan, was eager to claim the satisfactions and shoulder the responsibilities of standing in a family tradition that had been marked by historic achievements. On a business trip to Europe the year before Herman was born he made a special pilgrimage to Scoonie Parish in the Town of Leven in Scotland, in order to reaffirm this familial piety at one of its major shrines. "The Revd Andrew Melvill a Reformer & contemporary of John Knox was the minister of this parish," he wrote his wife. Allan's connection to Scoonie, and to the famous Scotch reformer, was all the stronger because his

great-grandfather, Thomas Melvill, had served the parish for
nearly fifty years. Allan discovered that "the very pulpit . . .
from which my Great Grandfather . . . dispensed the sacred
truths of the Gospel is still in use. I entered it with awe & reverence & most devoutly wished that I might leave behind as good
a name as embalms the memory of this truly pious [man]."[4]
The heritage Allan wished to perpetuate gave a prominent place
to Christian belief, although it is evident that the awe and reverence Allan felt were as much inspired by the Melvills' record
of distinction as by their commitment to the sacred truths of
the Gospel.

The "house-religion" that conditioned Herman's rearing was
thus pervaded by an insistence upon the necessity of religious
belief to the formation of a virtuous manly character. In recom-
mending with emphasis that *"the child is to grow up a Christian,
and never know himself as being otherwise"* (*Christian Nurture*, p. 4),
Horace Bushnell described a feature of the rearing that Herman
received. But instead of forming a halo of divine sanction about
the perpetuation of a proud family tradition, Christian belief
became problematical for Herman because of the confusion and
bitterness attendant upon the breakdown of that tradition.

He was not baptized "Herman Melville." In those days the
family still spelled its name "Melvill," and changed the spelling
as it sought to disentangle itself from the moral and economic
disgrace into which Allan plunged. Allan did not leave behind
a good name; he bequeathed a complex liability.

The fall of Allan Melvill did not occur until Herman was
twelve years old, by which time he had absorbed into his own
character the understanding of himself and his world that Allan
had been at pains to transmit. Taken as a synthesis of meanings,
the family tradition of the Melvills was rich with possibilities;
it embraced a striking diversity of religious attitudes within a
vital coherence of familial affection and pride. Young Herman's
earliest awareness was not engaged by a dead mass of doctrine,
but by a dynamic system of potentially divergent vectors braced
up strongly by mutual loyalty. His heritage was a living thing;

4. Allan Melvill to Maria Melvill, May 18, 1818. GLC. Andrew Melvill
was the subject of a biography in the nineteenth century. See Thomas M'Crie,
Life of Andrew Melvill (Edinburgh, 1855).

it was embodied in the lives of those who surrounded and cared for him in his earliest years, and its theological elements must be understood as they shaped this intimate context, and were themselves shaped by it.

At Herman's baptism assertions of Christian belief were woven into an observance that reflected how the Melvills then thought of themselves and what they expected of their children. The Reverend J. M. Mathews, pastor of the South Reformed Dutch Church of New York City, made an exception to approved church practice in coming to Allan Melvill's home to perform the rite, but the Melvills were an exceptional family and had prepared an impressive occasion.[5] On the day before, the new child's grandmother had purchased the ingredients of a substantial punch, including citron, nutmeg, and four gallons of rum;[6] so there is good reason to believe that it was a festive and possibly quite sizable affair. The service itself was strictly Calvinistic. The pastor asked Herman's parents whether they believed that "children are . . . born in sin, and therefore are subject to all miseries, yea to condemnation itself, yet that they are sanctified in Christ, and therefore . . . ought to be baptized." He asked for their promise to instruct the child in the doctrines of the Dutch Church "to the utmost of your power."[7] These questions were not meant or taken lightly, and Herman assuredly received doctrinal instruction as promised. But this was no litany of gloom. When Herman's parents acknowledged that their new son was "born in sin," it was with the solemn joy of knowing that they had touched one of the sacred principles from which the family had traditionally taken its bearings. The ceremony did not imply that the Melvills had made a wholesale commitment to Calvinism, but represented their intention to perpetuate a tradition of theocentric religiousness as it was carried on in various ways by the new child's welcoming family, a mixed tradition in which Calvinist orthodoxy was important but not supreme.

---

5. For the identity of the pastor see Leyda, I, 4. *The Constitution of the Reformed Dutch Church* (New York, 1815), p. 230, states that the church "discountenanced" baptism in private homes, and demanded that "the same form and solemnity" be used for them as for public baptism in the church.

6. The receipt is in GLC, dated August 18, 1819; cited in Gilman, p. 24.

7. *Constitution,* p. 94.

Neither Allan Melvill nor his wife Maria formally belonged to the Dutch Reformed Church, but Maria had been reared in the church as a member of the mighty Gansevoort clan of Albany. She was the only daughter of General Peter Gansevoort, who was renowned for leading the gallant defense of Fort Stanwix during the Revolution and later became one of Albany's wealthiest citizens.[8] In the traditional manner of Dutch patroons, the Gansevoorts involved themselves in the intricate affairs of municipal life in Albany.

Since devout religious observance was a primary pattern in the fabric of social relations they sought to maintain, the Gansevoorts were staunch supporters of the Dutch Church. There is an interesting congruity between their stubborn commitment to what is intimately known, their tendency to distrust untested outsiders, their shrewd authoritarianism, and the skeptical view of human nature in general that their Calvinist faith expressed.[9]

Catherine Gansevoort, the General's wife, was a gloomy and intensely pious woman. She had wanted very much for Allan and Maria to settle in Albany, and often came to see them in New York.[10] During the visit she made at the time of Herman's birth, Catherine received a letter from her son, Peter Gansevoort, that suggests how the Calvinist emphasis on the evils of life contributed to her besetting fears and suspicions. Peter recommends a trip out to Rockaway for the ocean breeze, hoping it will brighten her spirits, and then gives religious reasons why she should cheer up. Her duty, he states, is "certainly not to cherish those cases nor anticipate those evils which darken the gloom in which our path through life is shrouded — but to relieve your mind of every weight which bends it to the Earth and to claim and direct every ray of light and joy to the illumination

8. Gilman, p. 10.

9. Alice P. Kenney, *The Gansevoorts of Albany, Dutch Patricians in the Upper Hudson Valley* (Syracuse, 1969), discusses the general character of this tradition and traces in detail the family story. She recounts Gansevoort involvement in church affairs on pp. 137-138, 208. Gilman, p. 297, n. 90, gives further evidence of this characteristic patrician activity.

10. Allan wrote to his father from Albany, where he and Maria lived after their marriage in 1814: "I shall go to New York for a few days to ascertain what I could do, as the old Lady is very desirous we should settle there if we must leave Albany where as you may well suppose she would fain keep us." Allan Melvill to Thomas Melvill, May 2, 1816. GLC.

of your course to that 'bourne whence no traveller returns' —
so that in the eternal world you may appear in the full radiance
of a Christian's Glory — I did not intend to have said so much
— however I present it to you as food for reflection. — You
will find it better for body and soul than the composition and
festering of factitious evils."[11] Peter and Maria were not inclined
to morbidity, as their mother seems to have been, but they were
schooled to a sharp awareness of the perils of a transitory human
life.

Very few clues to Maria's piety survive from these early years.
She had been baptized in the Dutch Church, and the task of
teaching Herman Calvinist doctrine in the home doubtless rested on her. Since Peter once chided her piously for reading too
many "foolish and nonsensical novels," it is evident that she
did not confine herself, as the church would have preferred, to
works of orthodox devotion.[12] But her occasional reflections on
the "unsettled state of things earthly" suggest that orthodox
perspectives were a part of her spiritual makeup, and stood ready
to give stability in times of trial.[13]

Allan Melvill would have lived out his days without the slightest association with the Dutch Reformed Church if it had not
been for his marriage to Maria. He came from a distinguished

---

11. Peter Gansevoort to Catherine Gansevoort, July 21, 1819. GLC.

12. Gilman, p. 10.

13. Gilman states that her sentiments "echo Allan Melvill's directly," and
goes on to argue that the religious spirit that prevailed in the Melvill home
"was never darkened by the gloomy theology of Calvin." "The God of the
minister may have stood for Calvin's inexorable justice, but the God of his
parents, with their Unitarian inclinations, was above all else merciful" (pp.
22-27). There are two issues here: the relation of the two traditions, and the
question of "gloom." There is no reason to assume that Maria echoed Allan
any more than he echoed her, as their relationship developed on the common
ground of attitudes they shared. But to absorb her influence entirely into
his "Unitarian inclinations" is to miss the strength of her commitment to
orthodox tradition. If Allan had made his religious views dominant, the family
would have attended a Unitarian church. This does not mean that the Melvills' religious life was "gloomy" at this time. Holding orthodox beliefs and
training children in them does not necessarily "darken" the religious atmosphere, as Gilman assumes. At this stage in the story, Calvinist belief was
not associated with grief or morbidity or gloom for the Melvills, except by
way of Catherine Gansevoort. Peter's effort to cheer her up is sufficient evidence of the fact that an orthodox believer could find grounds for happiness
in his faith, when it suited his temperament and circumstances to do so.

Boston family whose religious sympathies were strongly liberal.[14] His father, like Maria's, had played a heroic role in the American Revolution. He had participated in the Boston Tea Party, and had otherwise acquitted himself so well that President Washington appointed him Collector of the Port of Boston. Major Thomas Melvill's religious interests were as strong as those of the elder Gansevoorts, but the beliefs that he inherited had undergone a decisive change. He had originally intended to enter the ministry, and spent more than a year in Calvinist theological study at the College of New Jersey (now Princeton).[15] But he later broke with Calvinist orthodoxy and became a member of the Brattle Square Church in Boston, under the ministry of the famous Unitarians Joseph Stevens Buckminster and Edward Everett.[16] Allan Melvill was reared, therefore, with an emphatically positive estimate of human nature and of the promise of life in this world, and he retained these liberal attitudes into maturity. Yet he was not openly anti-Calvinist. The potential conflict between his beliefs and those of the Gansevoorts was held firmly in abeyance by a strong and warmly affectionate family pride in which stalwart religious belief could be applauded in general terms as a virtue of men heroic in battle and conscientious in civic duty.

This does not mean, however, that religious belief was incidental to Allan's major concerns, to be routinely invoked on occasions when the traditions of the family were rehearsed. On the contrary, Allan made this aspect of the family tradition a conspicuous feature of his own character. He was selected to lead worship, for example, on the voyage that took him to Scotland. His shipboard meditations, as echoed in his letters to Maria, give ample evidence of his fervor: "if men are ever seriously inclined, or feel their total & immediate dependence on GOD, it must be on an element, where his most wonderful power is displayed, & where his omnipotence alone can save from destruction."[17] When he arrived safe in Scotland, he went as soon as possible to church, "for my heart panted to pour out its grati-

---

14. Gilman, pp. 22-23.
15. *Ibid.*, p. 38.
16. *Ibid.*, p. 22.
17. Allan Melvill to Maria Melvill, May 12, 1818. GLC.

tude in the house of prayer & thanksgiving to the Sovereign
Lord of all, whose wonders had often witnessed in the mighty
deep."[18]

Allan Melvill was flamboyant and bold; he viewed his life
as an arena of heroic enterprise over which God's omnipotence
kept watch. His faith in the "Sovereign Lord of all" was not
self-consoling resignation; it was the talisman of an adventurer.
In launching his business career upon the "mighty deep" of economic vicissitude in New York he spurned the more stable business community in Albany, and found trials aplenty for the testing of his mettle and his faith. The depression of 1819 damaged
him somewhat, but he soon informed his father that "my prospects brighten, & without being over sanguine, I may be allowed
to indulge, under the blessing of Heaven, anticipations of eventual success, my little Barque having weathered the storm which
has wrecked the fortunes of thousands."[19] When Allan checked
the impulse to be "over sanguine," he identified a quality of
his own spirit that was abetted by Unitarian optimism, just as
the Gansevoorts' orthodoxy strengthened their tendency to cau-
tion and skepticism. Allan's ebullience created many anxieties
in Albany, but the clash of personal style and its counterpart
in the realm of religious belief were embraced within strong
family loyalties. Divergent religious attitudes offered no hin-
drance to the gladness of celebration at Herman's baptism, or
at other ceremonies of family piety.[20]

* * *

The "blessing of Heaven" indeed seemed to rest on Allan
in the ensuing years, and permitted him to lay a large foundation
for that piety of family pride in which Herman was brought
up. By 1824, the Melvills moved to a more fashionable house
on Bleecker Street, then in the suburbs, and began to attend
the newly built Dutch Reformed Church on Broome Street.[21]
Despite a later move to a yet more appealing house on Broad-

---

18. Allan Melvill to Maria Melvill, May 17, 1818. GLC.
19. Leyda, I, 6.
20. For example, Thanksgiving celebrations. See Gilman, p. 33.
21. Gilman, pp. 25, 27.

way, they continued to go to church on Broome Street during the balance of their life in New York.[22]

Allan was exceptionally vocal about his faith, so that young Herman would have looked to him as the ultimate authority in religious matters. Herman's earliest religious sentiments would also have been shaped by the pastor who came to Broome Street in 1826, the Reverend Jacob Brodhead.[23] He became an intimate of the Melvill family, his children played with the Melvill children, and his son John Romeyn Brodhead, the historian, remained a friend into later years.[24] Brodhead did not display the cold severity so often ascribed to Calvinistic clergymen in stories of cramped boyhood. He was "affectionately considerate of the young, and delighting to take little children up in his arms."[25]

Far from preaching an emotionally barren faith, Brodhead's spirituality emphasized the struggles of the soul. The Dutch Church in America had a strong tradition of evangelical pietism,[26] and it was receptive in the early years of the nineteenth century to the impulses of the "Second Great Awakening." Led

22. Ibid., p. 32.
23. Edward Tanjore Corwin, *A Manual of the Reformed Church in America,* rev. ed. (New York, 1869), p. 43.
24. Herman Melville wrote to John R. Brodhead in 1846 of "the long-standing acquaintance between our families and particularly that between my late brother Mr. Gansevoort Melville and yourself." Leyda, I, 230. See also Gilman, p. 32.
25. Corwin, p. 43. Drawing upon Abram C. Dayton's recollections of the "Knickerbocker Sabbath," Gilman (pp. 25-26) suggests that young Herman dreaded the Sabbath because strict attention to long abstract sermons was required. Gilman states that reliance on Dayton is "admittedly uncertain"; in this instance better evidence shows it to be quite misleading. Dayton's recollections have a point of view that is often shared by commentators on Melville's exposure to the Dutch Reformed Church. It is defined by the satisfied awareness that Calvinist orthodoxy suffered in America a cultural defeat. If Dayton permits himself the generosity of nostalgia, he carefully includes his own liberal condemnation of the orthodox, citing "their denunciations of all classes and conditions of men who by reason of education had imbibed different views of the paramount duties of poor, weak, erring humanity." See Abram C. Dayton, *Last Days of Knickerbocker Life in Old New York* (New York, 1882), pp. 14-15. The caricatures that survive from the victorious liberal rhetoric have their grain of truth, but are a very uncertain guide to what Melville felt and learned as a child.
26. See James Tanis, *Dutch Calvinistic Pietism in the Middle Colonies: A Study in the Life and Theology of Theodorus Jacobus Frelinghuysen* (The Hague, 1967).

in the Northeast by Timothy Dwight of Yale College, this complex revival movement swept across denominational lines and
produced its crop of sharp theological controversies.[27] The Dutch
Church maintained an unyielding orthodoxy in the midst of
the furor, and as the spirit of the Awakening moved Dutch believers they turned for devotional guidance to time-honored clas-
sics of Calvinist evangelicalism. Catherine Gansevoort's library
contained a typical selection:[28] in addition to the sermons of
Timothy Dwight, she owned the works of John Bunyan, John
Owen, and Philip Doddridge, whose *Rise and Progress of Religion
in the Soul* gave an orthodox statement of the struggles through

---

27. For a good brief statement see H. Shelton Smith, Robert T. Handy,
and Lefferts A. Loetscher, *American Christianity, an Historical Interpretation with
Representative Documents,* 2 vols. (New York, 1960), I 519-525. Perry Miller,
The Life of the Mind in America from the Revolution to the Civil War (New York,
1965), pp. 3-95, gives a detailed interpretation.

28. The "Inventory of the personal property and effects" of Catherine Van
Schaick Gansevoort (June 17, 1831, GLC) contains nineteen entries for religious books. The total list follows, together with some identifications. The
editions cited in brackets are not necessarily those Mrs. Gansevoort possessed.

1 Bible
Sev Religious books, dutch
Newton's Works 4 vols.
Dwight's Sermons 2 vol [Timothy Dwight, *Sermons,* 2 vols. (New Haven:
    Hezekiah Howe and Durrie & Peck, 1828).]
Bunyan's Works 3 vol
Psalm book dutch church
Blairs Sermons 2 vol
Villiage do 3 vol
4 dutch church psalm books
Saints rest
Fullers apeys?
Buck on Experience [Charles Buck, *A Treatise on Religious Experience* (Boston:
    Lincoln and Edwards, 1810).]
Gospel mystery
Owen on Indwelling Sin [John Owen, *On the Nature, Power, Deceit and Preva-
    lence of the Remainders of Indwelling Sin in Believers* (Glasgow: Chalmers and
    Collins, 1825).]
Doddridge rise & progress [Philip Doddridge, *The Rise and Progress of Religion
    in the Soul* (New York: American Tract Society, n.d.).]
Bickenstaff on prayer [Edward Bickersteth, *A Treatise on Prayer* (Richmond,
    Va.: Pollard and Converse, 1828).]
Numbers of National preacher in bound & tracts
1 dutch prayer book silver mounted
1 dutch psalm book silver mounted

which men must pass on the way to redemption.[29] At the heart of his message was the call for regeneration, urging sinners to a crisis of self-awareness in which they would acknowledge and repent their bondage to sin, so as to enter into the joy of salvation.

Jacob Brodhead participated in the revivals of the Awakening; he was famous for a style of preaching that brought on the dramas of regeneration. "In Philadelphia [whence he came to Broome Street] he had control over crowds of hearers, unparalleled in the history of that city and rare in modern times. Thousands hung weeping on his utterances, and hearts long obdurate broke in penitence, as he pleaded with demonstration of the Spirit." Brodhead grounded his abstract theological exposition in the concreteness of scriptural story. "His style was an unusual compound of didactic statement, glowing illustration, and pathetic ardor. . . . He delighted to preach on scriptural narratives, exhibiting the humanity common to us all, and making the hearers feel the applicability of the moral."[30] At the core of Brodhead's passionate appeal was his belief in the transforming power of God's grace. In Calvinistic strictness, he held that man's bondage to sin is so absolute that no significant change in his character can occur until a moral rejuvenation is effected by the Spirit's redeeming work. Brodhead "preached the Gospel only, and that with the greatest simplicity and directness, having no confidence in anything else as a means of salvation or even of moral reform."[31]

This evangelical stress on the dominion of sin, and on the power of the gospel to destroy it, was all too easily taken up by preachers of vindictive temperament as the substance of a harsh and punishing oratory. Brodhead, however, was "free from

29. Philip Doddridge was an eighteenth-century English evangelical. Discussions of the holy life by John Owen and John Bunyan, both Puritans, became popular whenever Calvinists renewed their interest in the personal life of faith. See John T. McNeill, *Modern Christian Movements* (Philadelphia, 1954), pp. 32-33, 72, 76-77. In the early nineteenth century, the term "evangelical" was used in preference to "pietist" to indicate an emphasis on the inner life of faith that recurred in Calvinist tradition.

30. Corwin, p. 44.

31. *Collegiate Reformed Protestant Dutch Church of the City of New York, Her Organization and Development,* ed. William Leverich Brower and Henry P. Miller (New York, 1928), p. 35.

exacting bigotry and petty scrupulosities"; he was remembered, on the contrary, for his "tenderness."[32] Rather than giving evidence of emotional constriction, Brodhead seems to have shown generous and flexible sympathies. "Having that almost instinctive skill to reach the more sensitive chords of the human heart, he could not restrain his emotion while he probed the torpid conscience or applied the balm of Gilead to the bleeding spirit."[33] Disciplined as it was to the absolute claims of the Calvinist gospel, Brodhead's eloquence seems to have moved men by its intense and subtle orchestration of feeling. "He did not claim to be anything but a preacher of Christ, and he was that through and through. His reverence, tenderness and fervor in the pulpit captured the attention of men and swayed their hearts as if by an electric power."[34]

Brodhead's example would have strengthened the impression on young Herman that his father had already created, for he exhibited a style of heroic manliness in which religious devotion was an essential element. In him a major thesis of Christian theocentrism was given manifest embodiment: the moral structure of his character received its shape from a sharply focused and clearly articulated dedication to God.

Such a heroic moral harmony, embracing such a wealth of emotional power, became for Melville a criterion of religious authenticity, and in *Moby-Dick* he shapes Father Mapple's character and his sermon in accordance with the style of orthodox spirituality Brodhead displayed. As he came to repudiate the religious concepts upon which it was founded, Melville continued to be impressed by the personal force that such an integrity can project, dramatizing it at length in Captain Ahab's monomania. Indeed, Melville's own effort to find an ultimate truth perpetuated the style of religiousness at stake here. Melville's quest portrays the heroism of a man without a standard of final belief, who casts himself unreservedly into the search for it. The basic criterion of his quest remains insistently theocentric: he

---

32. Corwin, p. 43. See also p. 44: "Tenderness was especially his characteristic."
33. *Ibid.*, p. 44.
34. *Collegiate . . . Church*, p. 35.

seeks a unified vision of ultimate reality that can gather all
experience into an intelligible and coherent totality.

* * *

Herman was seven years old when Brodhead came to the
Broome Street church, so that he was doubtless not yet capable
of following the intricacies of doctrinal sermons. But it does not
follow that he found them tedious, or that the general bearing
of their interpretation of human experience would have been
lost on him. The abstract issues that fascinated Calvinist and
anti-Calvinist believers in the early nineteenth century may seem
to us as noxious in their bewildering elaborations as the images
and relics of Roman Catholic piety seemed to these Protestants
themselves. Indeed, the passion with which the great canons
of Calvinist belief were studied and debated remains hard to
comprehend until we perceive that, like sacred figurines, they
had a symbolic force. Although we customarily think of a symbol
as the physical or dramatic vehicle of a concept, it is also true
that a concept may have the symbolic power of making present
the reality it describes. An exposition of orthodox belief presented the sacred abstractions in carefully ordered deployments, progressively unpacking the treasures of Truth with an exactitude
that was felt to bring the Truth alive in the soul of the believer.
The colorful pageantry of the Mass could do no more.

The management of a conceptual system thus became a medium of spiritual communication with the essence of reality. Just
as mathematicians, or indeed any attentive reader of philosophy,
may be entranced by the felicity with which stage follows stage
in the unfolding symmetry of proof, so the Protestant rationalists
of the Calvinist tradition responded to an absorbing intellectual
charm and took it as a signal that the divine presence was revealing itself. In Melville's mature writing, and supremely in *Moby-
Dick*, the interplay of thought forms an aesthetic medium. He
exploits traditional religious concepts for the sake of conveying
his own untraditional apprehension of the real. His early introduction to the major issues of Calvinist controversy has an enlarged significance because he was exposed not merely to their
substance but to the reverence with which they were handled.
The believers that Brodhead addressed would have regarded a

distorted treatment of doctrine as a sacrilege, recoiling as a faithful Catholic would recoil at the disfiguring of a Madonna.

When Brodhead was installed at Broome Street, the congregation officially expressed delight in his orthodoxy. "We love to greet such honest, faithful heralds of the cross who, forsaking the new fangled notions of hairbrained theorists, stick to *the good old way.*"[35] Dutch Reformed churchmen believed that their historic doctrines stood as an unshakable rock amid the chronic instability of orthodox tradition.

Calvinist doctrine had been attacked during Calvin's own lifetime on grounds that were to remain troublesome throughout the life of the tradition. Calvin's doctrine of Providence was the crux of the matter; he held that "the world is so governed by God that nothing is done therein but by His *secret counsel and decree.*"[36] Catholic theologians were quick to argue that this theory obliterates the moral freedom of man, and impugns the justice of God Himself. Opponents of Calvin were especially horrified by the decrees of "predestination" by which God "elected" a certain number of men for salvation and "reprobated" the unfortunate remainder.

Not surprisingly, this doctrine disturbed thoughtful believers within the Calvinist tradition, and the Dutch Church never ceased to be proud that the classic controversy over these issues had been settled in Holland. In 1604 Jacobus Arminius, a professor of theology at the University of Leyden, offered a series of lectures on predestination in which he argued that its strictest interpretation made God "the author of sin." The resultant debate swelled until Arminianism became the issue of an extensive ecclesiastical and social turmoil. Finally, an international congress of Calvinists was convened to give the authoritative doctrine.[37] The Synod of Dort (1618-1619) took an exceedingly rigorous Calvinist position, arranging the crucial doctrines into the famous "five points." The first of these concerned "Divine Predestination" and it stated the definition of "reprobation" in

---

35. *Magazine of the Reformed Dutch Church,* 1 (April 1826-March 1827), 130.

36. John Calvin, *Calvin's Calvinism,* trans. Henry Cole (Grand Rapids, 1950), p. 189.

37. For a discussion of the classic form of these problems see *Man's Faith and Freedom, the Theological Influence of Jacobus Arminius,* ed. Gerald O. McCulloh (New York, 1962).

polemical terms: "not all, but some only are elected, while others are passed by in the eternal decree; whom God, out of his sovereign, most just, irreprehensible and unchangeable good pleasure, hath decreed to leave in the common misery into which they have wilfully plunged themselves. . . . And this is the decree of reprobation which by no means makes God the author of sin, (the very thought of which is blasphemy) but declares him to be an awful, irreprehensible, and righteous judge and avenger."[38]

Calvinist believers were quite aware that men in postrevolutionary America were increasingly repelled by the belief that sin and misery are decreed by God but that man is to blame for it. But instead of seeking a theological accommodation, the Dutch Church in America chose a course of heroic resistance; it rejected as Arminian the numerous efforts to dilute this doctrine,[39] and interpreted the popularity of Arminianism as evidence of man's innate hatred of God. Arminianism was regarded as nothing less than a blasphemous effort to convict God Himself for the "common misery into which . . . [men have] plunged

38. *Constitution*, p. 154.

39. The Dutch Church opposed efforts by professed Calvinists to soften the traditional doctrine. In 1824 their General Synod officially condemned "the DOCTRINE commonly called HOPKINSIAN," which was based on the teaching of Samuel Hopkins (1721-1803), a disciple and interpreter of Jonathan Edwards. The Synod objected that "Hopkinsianism" considered the atonement "indefinite," i.e., not restricted to a specific number predestined from all eternity for salvation. See *Magazine*, 3 (April 1828-March 1829), 50-51. The Dutch Church had strong theological sympathies with the Old School Presbyterians (*Magazine*, 2 [April 1827-March 1828], 159) who joined in the attack on Nathaniel William Taylor, who held that men could be damned *only* for freely chosen sinfulness. See Sidney Earl Mead, *Nathaniel William Taylor, 1786-1858, a Connecticut Liberal* (Chicago, 1942), pp. 107, 230. The Dutch Reformed Church sustained an attack from the right in the so-called "Hackensack Insurrection" of 1822, but this rebellion had no effective leadership and was successfully branded "antinomian." See William O. Van Eyck, *Landmarks of the Reformed Fathers* (Grand Rapids, 1922), pp. 166 f. The Dutch Reformed considered all efforts to moderate the doctrines of Dort as a revival of Arminianism: "Call the insubordination of the heart to the sovereignty of God by what name you will . . . it is reproved generally under the name of Arminianism by the orthodox." Although they did not believe that God's truth had changed at all in the centuries since Dort, they knew that men were less disposed to accept it. "The system of Arminianism . . . is very extensively diffused over Christendom. There are very few ecclesiastical communities in which its leaven does not exist." See *Magazine*, 2 (April 1827-March 1828), 307.

themselves." The liberal effort to soften the doctrines concerning redemption, to qualify God's sovereignty so as to give man some measure of direct control over his eternal fate, was taken as an act of defiance against that sovereignty. "Insubordination to the divine sovereignty, displayed in the selection of sinners to be redeemed . . . is the essential heresy of fallen men. . . . [This] error of the natural mind . . . remains in the impenitent forever, unconsumed by the flames of Tophet. . . . The [Arminian] system, as such, is congenial to the enmity of the heart against God and his attributes."[40]

There is a notable resemblance between Captain Ahab and the liberal heretic that Calvinist rhetoric depicts. Filled with a hatred of the divine so profound that all the flames of hell can never consume it, the liberal blasphemously holds God responsible for all the sin and misery of life. The way Calvinists analyzed the liberal estimate of God's relation to man provided Melville a rhetorical arsenal for which he eventually found a use. More important, however, the stance of defiant conservatism that was instilled in Melville contributed to his religious conflict. It directly opposed another set of attitudes and opinions with an equally intimate claim on his allegiance. A bold statement of the Arminian heresy was then being advanced by the Boston Unitarianism to which his father's family was committed.

To William Ellery Channing, Calvinist orthodoxy was a faith for moral cripples. A doctrine so offensive to human dignity, he affirmed, depended for its currency upon the "influence of fear in palsying the moral nature."[41] Man's inherent right to offer or withhold worship in accordance with his own judgments was a major thesis of Unitarian thought. Channing's famous "Moral Argument against Calvinism" (1820) is based on his generous estimate of *"the confidence which is due to our rational and moral faculties in religion."*[42] Refusing to abdicate his rational dignity before the inscrutable glory of a Calvinist God, Channing argues that while God is incomprehensible, he is not therefore unintelligible.

Enough is known of the ways of God that the unknown re-

40. *Ibid.*, p. 308.
41. William Ellery Channing, *Works*, 6 vols. (Boston, 1849), I, 218.
42. *Ibid.*, p. 225.

mainder offers no threat to the confident Unitarian creed. "Should the whole order and purposes of the universe be opened to us, it is certain that nothing would be disclosed, which would in any degree shake our persuasion, that the earth is inhabited by rational and moral beings, who are authorized to expect from their Creator the most benevolent and equitable government."[43]

Channing predicted that Calvinist orthodoxy would soon collapse. He recognized instinctively that the new democratic man would discard the notion of an absolute Divine sovereign as he exercised his right to expect an "equitable and benevolent government."[44] Channing believed that "this silent but real defection from Calvinism is spreading more and more widely .... Calvinism, we are persuaded, is giving place to better views. It has passed its meridian, and is sinking, to rise no more. It has to contend with foes more formidable than theologians, with foes, from whom it cannot shield itself in mystery and metaphysical subtilties, we mean with the progress of the human mind, and with the progress of the spirit of the Gospel."[45]

*　*　*

The Dutch Church was quick to perceive this menace. Aware of the weakening of its general appeal, the church turned with dedication to the nurture of its own, hoping to secure the future by exerting a decisive influence upon children, such as the young Melvills, who were entrusted to it for religious training.[46] In 1828 Jacob Brodhead met with other concerned pastors to develop a plan for a more rigorous education program. The Sabbath School Union that they founded was greeted as a strategic innovation, exactly suited to the church's cultural plight. "Oh! Sir, in the present day when infidelity is stalking abroad through our city, and over our land, with such unblushing effrontery; ... what means or method can be selected, more efficient than this? We lay hold on the minds of the young, and rising generation; and we take care to have them fully and radically indoc-

43. *Ibid.*, p. 228.

44. For a classic discussion of Unitarian thought in its relation to political liberalism see Vernon Louis Parrington, *Main Currents in American Thought*, 3 vols. (New York, 1927), II, 321-338.

45. Channing, *Works*, I, 240.

46. Gilman, p. 25.

trinated in the standards of the Reformation, these bulwarks of our holy religion."[47]

Advocates of the Sabbath School Union insisted that the overwhelming emphasis they placed on doctrinal standards was necessary because of the "moral darkness" in the soul of every child.[48] They warned against giving Biblical instruction independent of orthodox interpretation for fear it "would excite in the minds of children that self conceited, speculative, and *free thinking* spirit, so subversive of all religious instruction "[49]

Herman was nine years old when the Sabbath School Union was started, so he received the full force of its early enthusiasm, and the extent of his exposure to doctrinal teaching may be gathered from the fact that the Sabbath School was by church law forbidden "to interfere with, or take the place of, the regular weekly catechetical instruction by the pastor."[50] Melville's knowledge of the Bible was intimate and extensive (and has been studied at length),[51] but his earliest training insured that Biblical knowledge was acquired under the rubrics of doctrine. In his works, and most decisively in *Moby-Dick*, Melville uses Biblical materials in their doctrinal setting, and he manipulates orthodox motifs with the mastery of one who has been "fully and radically indoctrinated."

Allan wanted Herman to receive his secular schooling in a more liberal atmosphere. He was a trustee and stockholder of the New York Male High School, which actively encouraged intellectual inquiry on a principle flatly opposed to the theory behind the Sabbath School: "what is commonly called a love of mischief in children, is in fact a love of mental occupation."[52] Herman was encouraged at this school to cultivate the independent habits of mind that his Sabbath School teachers sought to restrain. There is no reason to assume, however, that this clash of perspectives now caused Herman any perplexity. He had before him the example of his father, who managed to com-

47. *Magazine*, 4 (April 1829-March 1830), 247.
48. *Christian Intelligencer*, 1 (August 1830-July 1831), 178. This journal replaced the *Magazine of the Reformed Dutch Church* in 1831.
49. *Magazine*, 4 (April 1829-March 1830), 349.
50. *Christian Intelligencer*, 1 (August 1830-July 1831), 159.
51. Nathalia Wright, *Melville's Use of the Bible* (Durham, 1949).
52. Gilman, p. 29.

bine liberal commitments with the belief that an intensive exposure to Calvinism was suitable for the training of a Melvill.
The living transmission of heritage has an intimate chemistry
that cannot be defined merely by reference to the official pro-
nouncements of schools. Allan Melvill, like every true father,
carried a personal authority that transcended the contradictions
young Herman may have sensed in the teaching he absorbed.

During the happy and prosperous years in New York, there
was no reason for Allan Melvill's authority to lose its grip. His
business successes provided a solid basis for the piety of family
pride that made of these opposing elements a rich and engaging
counterpoint. Such pride was uppermost in Allan's mind when
he arranged for his sons, whom he termed "the youthful
Heroes,"[53] to visit the seats of family distinction in Albany and
Boston. In sending Herman to the Gansevoorts for the summer
of 1826 he described him as "an honest hearted double rooted
Knickerbocker, of the true Albany stamp, who I trust will do
equal honour in due time to his ancestry, parentage and
kindred."[54] Grandmother Gansevoort regulated her spirit by
reading such somber works as John Owen's *Indwelling Sin;*[55] and
that fact doubtless took its place in the mosaic of the boy's early
impressions. But an imposing aura of the sacred would also have
attached to the great brass drum that General Gansevoort had
captured from the British.[56] Correspondingly, in the summers
of 1827 and 1829, when Herman visited the Melvill grand-
parents in Boston, he would have grasped that they did not
dread a vindictive divine wrath. The Melvills worshiped a God
who "orders *all* for our *Good* and will not afflict willingly, nor
Grieve the Children of Men."[57] The legacy of Christian devotion
that Herman was expected to make his own had its incompatible
elements, but these were bound in a proud coherence by the
pieties of nation and family. Like the Gansevoorts, the Boston
Melvills preserved sacred tokens of this solidarity. The youthful
hero was permitted to inspect a vial containing tea that had

53. *Ibid.,* p. 21.
54. *Ibid.,* p. 28.
55. See note 28 for complete list.
56. Gilman, p. 49.
57. *Ibid.,* p. 39.

been collected from Major Melvill's shoes after the Boston Tea Party: it was shown "with as much holy reverence as the miraculous robes of St. Bridget by the superstitious believer of the anti-Protestant faith."[58]

58. *Ibid.*, p. 38.

II

A Unitarian Tragedy

The collapse of Allan Melvill's fortunes and his early death shattered the world of Herman's childhood and excluded his immediate family from the realm of wealth and social prominence they had occupied.[1] Describing in *Redburn* the hardships into which this misfortune had cast him, Melville recalls the lost gladness with an expression of continuing grief and perplexity: "I must not think of those delightful days, before my father became a bankrupt, and died, and we removed from the city; for when I think of those days, something rises up in my throat and almost strangles me" (p. 36).

Allan's fall and its consequences posed enigmas that could not be resolved within the system of religious thought that was available to his son. As the paradoxical elements in Herman's religious education ceased to make sense in a coherent totality, he found himself incapable of seeing moral experience intelligibly in theocentric terms. This disaster provided the impetus and the themes for an endless round of agonized meditations in Melville's adult life.

The character of Allan Melvill was of prime importance to the creation of his son's perplexity. Both Freud and Bushnell, as noted, held that a man's adult conception of God is shaped by the impression of his father that he has received in childhood. Sons do not replicate their fathers; but they do form their characters with reference to their fathers, so that a father becomes part of the character of his son, always partly by negation. Allan Melvill did not shape Herman's mentality simply by enrolling him in certain schools, or by packing him off to visit the grand-

---

1. Gilman, pp. 5 f, outlines the partial recoveries that followed Allan's fall.

parents. Allan also lived before him as an example of Christian
faithfulness, presenting an image of what it means to be a man
(and a Melvill) that was absorbed so deeply into Herman's character as to provide a model on which he could form his own
personality.

Inherent in this model was the belief that the character of
a virtuous man is grounded upon faith in God. Allan did not
shrink from the responsibility that Bushnell urged upon parents,
of giving children a pattern of the Christian life and indeed
of the character of God Himself. The psychological processes
by which the image of God the Father is given substance by
the behavior of human fathers were cultivated and reinforced
in the Melvill household.

Allan Melvill's faith assisted him in preserving fatal delusions
about himself and his world. He was guilty of a pervasive religious hypocrisy that lay so deep in his character that it seems
doubtful he was aware of it himself. Interpreting one's experience in religious terms — or in any other terms — is no guarantee
against being wrong, and it sometimes happens that the events
of a man's life unfold in such a way as to refute the way in
which they are being assessed. Melville's mature work reveals
his obsession with such ironic patterns in human experience,
specifically with the way religious delusion prepares for disaster.
His personal religious explorations, furthermore, are characterized by the persistent suspicion that there is some guilty secret
at the heart of reality itself. There is likewise an air of the clandestine surrounding the mysteries that his fictional questers seek
to penetrate: Taji, Ahab, and Pierre attempt to explore something trickier than the "unknown"; the object sought is typically
masked or concealed, so that the quest is balked in part by decep-
tion. But Herman derived more from his father's character and
the disaster that befell him than a generalized suspicion that
things religious are deceptive. Allan's downfall was played out
in the terms provided by specific religious traditions; it was a
tragedy in which liberal belief conspired with moral failure to
bring on bankruptcy, madness, and death.

***

In January of 1827 Allan launched the enterprise that eventually ruined him, a jobbing firm that bought up odd lots of imported goods for resale. He did so with the knowledge that it was at best very risky. Allan's entrepreneurial boldness was supported by his liberal conception of God's benevolence because of the guarantee that benevolence seemed to provide concerning the final outcome of precarious undertakings. He did not abhor worldly evils as infinitely and eternally repugnant to the divine righteousness, but considered them a temporarily discordant feature of the scheme of things, which the divine equity and benevolence would eventually reconcile with universal good.[2]

When he wrote to Peter Gansevoort about the fateful new venture, he framed it in just these terms. "I have now another project in view which I trust will expand ... The event must be left to Providence who sees the end from the beginning & reconciles partial evil with universal good."[3] Allan's Calvinistic brother-in-law was a sober and cautious Albany patroon, whose position as a banker in a decidedly conservative business community made him suspicious of the scramble of investment in New York, where a willingness to engage in speculations was required of anyone who hoped to stay abreast of affairs. He was skeptical

---

2. The pattern of Allan's practical faith corresponds in certain limited respects to the "Protestant ethic" as analyzed by Max Weber and R. H. Tawney, in which Calvinist believers acquired assurance of salvation through their worldly endeavors. See Max Weber, *The Protestant Ethic and the Spirit of Capitalism*, trans. Talcott Parsons (New York, 1958), pp. 109-116; R. H. Tawney, *Religion and the Rise of Capitalism* (New York, 1952), pp. 227-230. But much more striking is the difference between Allan's ebullient confidence in a benevolent God and the strenuous austerities by which the Calvinists discussed by Weber and Tawney sought to rid themselves of the uncertainties of their ultimate fate. Perhaps, the economic order that Weber and Tawney depict as shaped by religious traditions in the sixteenth and seventeenth centuries had in the nineteenth century begun to dominate the interplay between the economic and religious spheres. When the Dutch Calvinist Thomas Vermilye discussed moral excellence as a "requisite to temporal advancement," he plainly violated the orthodox stand, as Weber and Tawney present it, indiscriminately strewing holy water on successful businessmen. (see p. 63).

In addition, it is important to recognize that religious belief in the prosperity of the just and the worldly punishment of the wicked has historical roots as ancient as the Old Testament wisdom literature, where it is avowed in the Book of Proverbs, and by Job's comforters, to be challenged by Job himself and by the writer of Ecclesiastes.

3. Allan Melvill to Peter Gansevoort, January 18 added to January 17, 1827. GLC.

about Allan's new project from the start,[4] so that the letters that passed between them chronicle Allan's effort to provide the most convincing possible reasons for its worthiness.

In a letter of February 10, which more fully reveals the new plan, Allan begins by celebrating the triumphant resolution of a crisis in another of his interests: "The whole affair will pass over *sub rosa*, & in entire confidence among all parties, for I have even now the best grounded assurance, that *all is safe & secret* & with Heaven's Blessing will remain so, while any other course of conduct than the one . . . inspired by HIM who directs all mortal events, could never have accomplished so triumphant a result — to HIM therefore, & to HIM alone, be ascribed all the praise." Allan expresses gratitude to the "divine & gracious Being" for having directed the maintenance of this crucial secrecy, and he thus prepares his brother-in-law for the disclosure that his new undertaking is "entirely *a confidential Connexion* with persons combining every qualification but money." Plans for the jobbing firm are already well under way, Allan reports: "the persons with whom I have associated have left their Employers this eve'g, are now in treaty for a store which . . . [will] be engaged on Monday . . . the articles of agreement are drawn up . . . [and] nothing is wanting but the Funds."[5]

Allan has pledged ten thousand dollars, of which five thousand is due on March 1, less than three weeks from the date of this letter. "To you alone can I look for that sum," he tells Peter Gansevoort, "which you must at all events procure me *in season* as my honour dearer to me than life will be forfeited." Allan insists that the strictest confidence be kept, explaining that "my name will not appear in the firm which will enable them to use my endorsement when necessary."[6] Since his associates had no source of money apart from himself, Allan's signature on their notes would create an illusion of greater financial substance than the firm really enjoyed. This deceit would permit

---

4. Allan opens the subject in his next letter to Peter Gansevoort as follows: "The 'new project' to which you so anxiously allude. . . ." Allan Melvill to Peter Gansevoort, February 10, 1827. GLC.

5. *Idem.* Some of the words italicized in these transcriptions of Allan's letters are underlined twice in the letters themselves. In the expression "*all is safe & secret*," for example, "*secret*" is underlined twice.

6. *Idem.* Here "*season*" is underlined twice.

his associates to secure an extra degree of the credit so necessary
to the speculations of a jobbing firm. But since Allan himself
had to borrow what real funds were available to back the venture, he was moving into a position that was financially vulnera-
ble as well as morally untenable.

Allan's confidence that God helped him keep clandestine deals
safe and secret probably did not reassure Peter Gansevoort. But
Peter now faced a serious dilemma: he was trapped in a choice
between sending the money or forcing an exposure that would
ruin Allan's reputation. Not surprisingly, it appears that Peter
delayed; but a letter of March 2 indicates that he had sent the
requested sum. Allan assures Peter that he may indeed " 'implicitly & confidently rely upon my honour for security' for this
my just pride, and under Providence my chief salvation in all
emergencies, shall never be polluted by a breach of confidence
to a Brother."[7]

It would be an error to suspect the slightest cynicism in this
remarkable declaration; it echoes Allan's most heartfelt convictions. Since Allan believed that worldly success is a just reward
of virtue, he attached great importance to his "honour." He
acquired, we are told, an "international reputation for trustwor-
thiness,"[8] and proud references to his own virtue recur with great
frequency in his letters. In seeking to impress upon Herman
the necessity of maintaining a high standard of pious rectitude,
Allan would have presented himself and his success as an example of justly rewarded virtue. He considered his virtue to be
his "chief salvation" under Providence because a benevolent and
equitable God could not refuse good fortune to the deserving.

Allan knew that he was now embarked on an affair in which
his "honour" was deeply jeopardized. But he seems to have successfully evaded the awareness that only his reputation remained
intact, or that his action was morally indefensible. His boastful
claim to unpolluted honor does not mark him as a conscious
hypocrite, but indicates that he had become a fervent self-de-
ceived hypocrite, who proclaims his innocence the more convinc-
ingly because he is unconsciously seeking to convince himself.

Toward the end of March the date approached on which the

7. Allan Melvill to Peter Gansevoort, March 2, 1827. GLC.
8. Gilman, p. 7.

other half of his ten thousand dollar pledge was due; and other
sources failing, Allan turned once again in desperate straits to
Peter Gansevoort. "I have now to request in the most *urgent
manner,* as equally involving my personal honor & the welfare
of my Family, that you would favour me *by return of Mail* with
your Note to my Order . . . for Five Thousand Dollars." In order
to enforce his request he appealed to Peter's family loyalty: "as
you esteem me, & *love our dear Maria,* do not I conjure you as
a Friend & Brother disappoint me in the *utmost need . . .* $5000
I must have on or before Wednesday next the 4th April, *as all
will be lost even to my honour."*[9] Allan's moral blindness is here
revealed in its frightening extent. If he had been aware that
he, in effect, held Maria hostage against Peter's further investment, he could never have invoked her as he does. Once again
Peter complied with the demand.

If a wealthy brother-in-law could rescue Allan's honor with
five thousand dollars, so could Providence secure it by granting
prosperity to the new firm sufficient to insure backing for its
notes. Thus the "partial evil" of the basic plan could be sub-
sumed into the "universal good" of a divine bounty adequate
to guarantee that everyone involved would make money. As long
as Allan believed that a benevolent God determined the final
outcome, total catastrophe need not be feared. Given the inherent precariousness of the jobbing business, and of this firm in
particular, there were dangers and setbacks aplenty. But there
were periods of great prosperity as well.[10] A letter to Peter Gansevoort at one of these happier times amply demonstrates that
Allan regarded his escape from ruin as an inspiring vindication
of God's justice. "May we unite with equal fervor in ascriptions
of grateful praise to that divine first cause, who always moulds
events to subserve the purposes of mercy & wisdom, often subjects poor human nature to the severest trials, that he may better
display his sovereign power & sometimes would even seem to
interpose his immediate providence, while deducing as by a mir-
acle good from evil & converting an absolute misfortune into

---

9. Allan Melvill to Peter Gansevoort, March 30, 1827. GLC. Here the following words are underlined twice: *"urgent manner," "of Mail," "love," "Maria,"*
and *"need."*

10. Gilman, p. 41.

a positive blessing."[11] Even though God's plan for bringing affairs to a favorable outcome may not be visible when disaster
threatens, yet He has such a plan, molding events so as to extract
in the end a "positive blessing."

Allan's reliance on this divine scheme was the reverse of com-
placent smugness; it was pervaded by a fervor that arose from
profound psychological strain. Schooling Herman in gratitude
for the dispensations of Providence, Allan would have made no
attempt to conceal his fear of spiritual collapse. He declared
quite openly that the struggles through which he had passed
would have crushed him if his personal heroism had not been
girded by religious faith. "My humble yet ardent confidence,
in the constant protection and eventual bounty of our almighty
Parent, has been strong & unwavering, this alone could have
sustained me in a fearful & protracted struggle which would
otherwise have overwhelmed the boldest spirit & the stoutest
heart & will I trust still enable me to meet every future emer-
gency with composure and fortitude."[12] Instead of awakening
him to the seriousness of his moral duplicity, Allan's liberal understanding of "our almighty Parent" gave him the reassurance
that the favorable unfolding of things had vindicated his effort
to quell inward misgivings.

Spiritually as well as financially, Allan had erected a house
of cards, thanking God incessantly for its preservation. When
an uncompromising creditor caught him unprepared, a good
deal more was lost than the jobbing firm. Allan quickly found
himself deep in debt and stripped of the reputation for "honour"
that had made his credit good. Unable to build capital, he could
not make another beginning in New York and moved his wife
and children to reduced circumstances back to Albany in 1830.

There, in the stronghold of the Gansevoorts, he struggled desperately to regain his financial footing. As though incapable of
contemplating the possibility that his financial downfall was
conclusive, Allan drove himself too hard and brought on himself
a truly irreversible disaster. When Peter Gansevoort finally decided that word of his condition should be sent to Allan's
parents, he indicated that Allan was undergoing severe psycho-

11. Allan Melvill to Peter Gansevoort, March 10, 1828. GLC.
12. *Idem.*

logical distress. "He was unwell when he last wrote to you But persisting in giving attention to his business — He devoted himself so closely and assiduously, as to produce a state of excitement, which in a great measure robbed him of his sleep. It is but a few days since he yielded to the wishes of his friends and remained at home."[13]

Allan now turned to a volume of "Buckminster's Sermons"[14] that had been cherished by his parents, seeking in the words of this prominent Unitarian divine some clue to the meaning of his plight. The volume contained a sermon entitled "The Advantages of Sickness," a special favorite of Buckminster's followers,[15] which taught that "Calamities, though they may wear the guise of punishments, are never administered solely for the sake of punishment, but of correction."[16] They are part of God's benevolent plan for the moral improvement of the race. Allan Melvill may well have been moved to pangs of conscience over the unethical arrangement that led to his downfall, although he doubtless knew of businessmen in New York who had made great successes on equally dubious grounds. Yet Buckminster's theory apparently yielded no effective consolation; Peter Gansevoort had to report that "the excitement . . . could not be allayed and yesterday he occasionally manifested an alienation of mind. Last night he became much worse — and today he presents the melancholy spectacle of a deranged man." Instead of achiev-

---

13. Leyda, I, 51.

14. Gilman, p. 59. Before 1831 two volumes of sermons by Joseph Stevens Buckminster, the Melvills' Unitarian pastor, had been published, one in 1814 and another in 1829. Since Thomas Melvill, Jr., referred to the volume Allan read on his deathbed as "much used by my parents" (Gilman, p. 298, n. 97), it is safe to presume that Allan read the earlier edition. This presumption is confirmed by the fact that Allan's mother echoed in a letter to him the language of a sermon found only in the earlier edition. Her letter says that God "will not afflict willingly, nor Grieve the Children of Men" (Gilman, p. 39). The sermon, entitled "The Advantages of Sickness," says that God "does not afflict willingly, nor for sorrow's sake alone grieve the children of men" (p. 58). Hence it is a virtual certainty that Allan read *Sermons by the late Rev. J. S. Buckminster, with a Memoir* (Boston, 1814).

15. Buckminster, *Sermons*, p. xxi, describes the memorable occasion on which the sermon was preached.

16. *Ibid.*, p. 44.

ing the "resignation" that Buckminster advised, Allan became, in his brother's words, "at times fierce, even *maniacal.*"[17]

Before the final madness overcame him, Allan read in his Bible, and marked two verses of Psalm 55: "My heart is sore pained within me: and the terrors of death are fallen upon me. Fearfulness and trembling are come upon me and horror hath overwhelmed me."[18] In the collapse of his pious self-confidence, Allan seems now to have been awash in the horrors of total self-doubt. The faith that had confirmed Allan in his folly was now useless in the crisis that folly had helped bring about, as though its teachings of divine benevolence were consumed in the fires of his frantic and immediate pain. The true source of Allan's madness cannot be identified simply by employing the religious concepts by which he understood his deepest life, but it is quite certain that those concepts had suddenly become inadequate for Allan himself. After more than two weeks of delirium he died, and on the last day of January, 1832, Maria buried him in the Dutch Church section of the common burying ground.[19]

* * *

Melville's response to the death of his father had a far-reaching effect upon his life and work. Although there are differences of interpretation among the critics who have pursued this issue, it is well recognized that a search for the lost security and authority, together with an impulse to indict false "fathers," may be defined as a persistent Melvillian theme.[20] There is agreement that Melville sustained a trauma that he did not overcome by the normal processes of grieving and in the span of time that those processes usually require. The significant fact about the trauma for this argument is that Melville lost a framework in which to understand it. He was unable to manage the emotional

---

17. Leyda, I, 51.
18. *Ibid.*
19. *Ibid.*, p. 52.
20. Gilman, pp. 60-61; Newton Arvin, *Herman Melville, a Critical Biography* (1950; reptd. New York, 1964), p. 23; Edwin Haviland Miller, *Melville* (New York, 1975), p. 71; Sacvan Bercovitch, "Melville's Search for National Identity: Son and Father in *Redburn, Pierre* and *Billy Budd*," *College Language Association Journal*, 10 (1967), 217-228.

cross-pressures for the lack of an acceptable way to make them intelligible.

Viewed from the outside, Allan's fate provided an ironic commentary on the liberal optimism of his creed. But young Herman lived through this experience on the inside. He was not then in a position to contemplate his father's faith objectively as a religious system and to criticize its precepts in the light of the grievous events. What is apparent to us as a contradiction between Allan's optimistic faith and the tragic reality of his fate was suffered by Herman as a conflict between evident features of the real world. God's ordering of human events through Providence was not a debatable hypothesis for him; it was a fact of life so obvious as to require no defense. The problematical issue was not whether God existed, but how His nature expressed itself in human experiences. His father's faith had provided one answer to that question, holding that God's justice is unmysterious; he rewards and punishes men in accordance with their "works," the manifest ethical quality of their actions.

This theory could have sustained its authority for young Herman had he been persuaded that his father was guilty of misdeeds sufficiently drastic to make his fate appear a suitable punishment. But there is good reason to believe that the memory he retained of his father acted, not as a warning against vice, but as a shining example of virtue. In *Redburn* Melville comments on this continuing reverence: "I always thought him a marvelous being, infinitely purer and greater than I was, who could not by any possibility do wrong, or say an untruth" (p. 34). As long as he maintained this conception of his father's character, Herman could hardly have interpreted his father's death within a liberal understanding of Providence. On the contrary, he would have been drawn to the conclusion that Allan had been struck down unjustly, and to the further conclusion that God had indeed betrayed him. We may recall Allan's repeated insistence that God would support him in the face of adversity, would give him the psychic strength necessary to endure all trials, and, through the eventual granting of success, would reveal his divine blessing upon the faithful and virtuous. If these claims were taken at face value, how was Herman to interpret the failure and psychic collapse that in fact rewarded Allan's striving? Her-

man's earliest experience had instilled the impression that his
father was virtuous and that God was just, in a happy con-
gruence of human and divine goodness. But belief in this con-
gruence could not long survive as he came to reflect upon the
religious meanings of his father's fall. The ingredients of a profound skepticism about the liberal conception of God's nature
were present, therefore, in this idealized recollection of his father's virtue.

Herman would not, however, have had to possess exceptional
intuition to sense that beneath Allan's strenuous declarations
of faith there lay a fateful weakness. He may well have experienced his father's collapse as the culmination of a dimly perceived instability, and have clung the more tenaciously to a belief in Allan's moral perfection in order to banish this
disconcerting awareness. As an adult, Melville came to recognize
that the perplexities of his quest for religious truth resulted somehow from the impact of his father's example upon his own life.

In *Pierre* he presents a fictionalized account of this situation,
describing a spiritual distress that ran deeper than the theoretical
incongruity noted. Pierre's family, Melville relates, aided in the
effort to perpetuate an image of his father's exemplary virtue
such as to reduce the true story of his wrongdoing to the status
of a fragmentary rumor. Young Pierre found this rumor all the
more fascinating, however, because of the guilty hush surrounding it. His awakening suspicions about his father's character become overwhelming as the system of pious concealment suddenly
comes unraveled.

Pierre swiftly concludes that his father was guilty of a secret
sin, but this recognition, instead of confirming his religious beliefs about the moral order of human experience, throws him
deeper into confusion. This happens because the image of his
father, as a man whose righteousness partook of the divine righteousness, had become a structural element of his own personality. It was the central feature of a shrine, Melville tells us, "which
supported the entire one-pillared temple of his moral life. . . .
Before this shrine, Pierre poured out the fullness of all young
life's most reverential thoughts and beliefs. Not to God had
Pierre ever gone in his heart, unless by ascending the steps of
that shrine, and so making it the vestibule of his abstractest

religion." (*Pierre,* p. 79). As Pierre's faith in his father is destroyed, so also is his faith in the religious standards by which his character had been shaped. The collapse of this living criterion of religious virtue leaves Pierre disoriented, with a desperate desire to square his life by divine principles but with no trustworthy conception of what those principles might be. Depicting the breakdown of Pierre's confidence in the way he had been taught to assess his most intimate experiences, Melville shows how he makes an appeal to those embracing religious conceptions that were supposed to explain the relationship between daily affairs and a stable reality beyond. The effort is vain, for Pierre finds that these larger standards had somehow become implicated in the general disorientation of his life.

As Pierre moves deeper and deeper into his religious confusions, Melville observes that he "was not arguing Fixed Fate and Free Will," not subjecting these traditional counters of religious controversy to yet another reconsideration: on the contrary, Melville continues, "Fixed Fate and Free Will were arguing him." (*Pierre,* p. 214). Pierre's personal existence becomes subject to the outcome of a debate whose terms are set by the traditions of thought that had structured his mentality. As abstract principles, Fixed Fate and Free Will could act as implements of analysis; but Pierre had moved into a situation in which these conceptions were revealed as aspects of his own mind, having an active power to determine his conclusions. The debate, that is, could no longer be scholastic, and it was not merely a screen behind which more potent psychological forces were at work. It was the form, for Pierre as for Melville, of a dynamic confrontation with the contours of reality itself, a confrontation shaped by conventions of thought that were themselves capable of disposing the course of a young man's life.

III

Child of the Devil

The religious attitudes Herman was exposed
to after Allan's death offered alternative ways of dealing with
that event and its consequences. Twelve years old when Allan
died, Herman was moving into a time of life when he would
begin to find his own way of viewing his experience. He would
now cease to accept adult opinions as direct testimonies to the
reality of the world, and begin to respond critically and selective-
ly in the process of arriving at a distinctive adult character.

His mother Maria, by contrast, was able to call upon the
resources of a fully established identity in coming to terms with
the grief and perplexity of widowhood. Calvinistic religious traditions were available to her as a framework of meanings already
inherent in her character, and she now turned to them with
devout rededication. Within three months of her husband's
death she joined the First Reformed Dutch Church of Albany,
being admitted on "examination and confession of . . . faith."[1]
The terms of her admission show that she had not belonged
to the Dutch Church earlier, but they also indicate that she
gave a good deal of the period after Allan's death to doctrinal
study, enough to carry her through an examination on orthodox
belief. For those who were able to accept it sincerely, and could
live within its account of man's relation to a sovereign God,
Calvinism offered a profound solace. Its doctrines of God's inscrutable Providence could be taken to mean that the justice
of God's dealings may be as obscure to a contemporary believer
as they were to the Biblical Job. Miseries in this world need

---

1. Leyda, I, 53.

not imply rejection in God's kingdom, just as worldly satisfactions certainly do not imply virtue.

Maria's joining the church indicates more than intellectual assent to orthodox doctrine. It shows that she was prepared to "confess" the faith, to declare that she herself had experienced God's saving action. Joining an evangelical orthodox communion was a momentous step, and many devout believers would not take it because of a lingering uncertainty whether they themselves had personally been redeemed. It is evident therefore that Maria had come to regard her miseries as part of God's gracious intention to awaken her to the reality of her fallen state and thus to initiate the stages of her salvation.[2] By acknowledging her helplessness and unworthiness, Maria would have readied herself to accept with joy the remission achieved for God's elect by "the most bitter passion and death" of Christ.[3] In the depths of suffering, God's chosen touch a reality that the blind self-confident world knows not, the ground of a tragic dignity. Since the true meaning of the Christian's life is hidden in the mystery of God's grace, the believer can walk erect amid whatever adversity besets her, without pretending that disaster is not disaster. This clear-eyed toughness of spirit is what was meant in orthodox parlance by "Christian patience."

Even before Maria confessed her full acceptance of orthodox faith, she indicated appreciation for such a spirit. She wrote to her brother that "The Almighty ruler above disposes all things as he sees fit, tis our duty to be resigned & patiently acquiesce in his dispensations — my most earnest prayer is that I may be enabled to do so."[4] During the happier days in New York, Maria may have been attracted by Allan's confidence that fair play in this life will be insured by an intelligible divine benevolence. But now she added a revealing note beside the psalm that Allan had marked on his deathbed: "This Chapter was mark'd a few days before my dear *Allan* by reason of severe suffering was deprive'd of his Intellect. God moves in a mis-

2. Philip Doddridge's *Rise and Progress of Religion in the Soul,* a copy of which Maria's mother owned, makes it clear that such "progress" must pass through a period of deep dismay over sin.
3. *The Constitution of the Reformed Dutch Church* (New York, 1815), pp. 25-27.
4. Gilman, p. 22.

terious way."[5] The bluntness of this comment bespeaks the temper of one who can look catastrophe in the face because of her faith in a God who is beyond human comprehension. That faith now enabled her to draw her suffering into the coherent story of her own salvation.

Maria made a vigorous effort to impress her new religious seriousness upon the children, as may be gathered from the fact that her daughters Helen and Augusta joined the church at the relatively early ages of twenty and seventeen. A letter to her son Allan shows her continuing insistence: "My dear Allan, if you regularly attend the Sabbath School, & thereby obey your Mother's parting injunction, for be assured my beloved Boy the future usefulness of the Man depends much upon the foundation laid in boyhood. The instruction you receive in our Sabbath Schools is very important, *you are away from a Mother's Care.*"[6] Herman was now under pressure to accept the orthodox faith, but as he explored its application to his own experience, he would soon have encountered a painful difficulty.

Seeking empirical support for their version of the doctrine of Providence, according to which God saves some from damnation and abandons the remainder, the orthodox found evidence in the trances of the deathbed, where human powers of self-control are weakened and the presumed consignment to heaven or hell draws near. Deathbed stories were very popular in the Reformed Church; the church publication featured accounts of God's chosen dying in bliss, but gave at least equal space to horrible stories of the damned in convulsions at the foretaste of hell-fire.[7] Such ghoulish tales were not merely a staple of the gossip and periodical literature of popular Calvinism; they were used by learned defenders of the faith. J. M. Mathews' *The Bible and Men of Learning* concedes the "exaggerated importance sometimes ascribed to death-bed scenes" and admits that good Christians have died without giving any memorable testimony. "But notwithstanding all these considerations," he concludes, "the

5. Leyda, I, 51.
6. *Ibid.*, pp. 70, 80, 81.
7. *Magazine*, 3 (April 1828-March 1829), 235; 4 (April 1829-March 1830), 47, 114, 211, 309-310, 312-313. *Christian Intelligencer*, 1 (August 1830-July 1831), 62, 65, 66, 98, 171, 190, 197; 2 (August 1831-July 1832), 9, 197.

value and the power of testimony rendered in a dying hour, no rational man will deny. Every impartial observer must perceive that there is a vast difference between the heaviness that occasionally oppresses the spirit of the dying christian, and the dread horror which . . . distracts and overpowers the dying infidel."[8]

In view of the deathbed ravings of Allan Melvill, it seems likely that this theory would have caught young Herman's attention, however rigorously it may have been excluded from open application to his father.[9] Maria's Christian dignity rested, after all, upon her belief that she was among God's chosen. Yet the torment of Allan's dying corresponded to the pattern of God's way with those who are not elected, and his raving was all too suggestive of the unsolaced horrors of the reprobate. What if Allan were damned?

Herman would have to ask this question in a way that Maria did not, from the point of view of a young man uncertain of the faith to which he would devote himself. And since he had absorbed Allan's style of Christian manliness as a model for his own character, he would have found the effort to assess the meaning of Allan's fate a much more imperative and complex task than did Maria. Holding to the reverent affection that he felt for his father, Herman maintained his grasp on an important part of himself. Energetically confronted by the Reformed belief that God is a "righteous judge and avenger," he was also faced with reasons to believe that his father was one of those "whom God, out of his sovereign, most just, irreprehensible and unchangeable good pleasure, hath decreed to leave in the common misery."[10] He was old enough to understand, furthermore, that his father had never been an orthodox believer, but an Arminian. Allan had been one of those whom the orthodox viewed as expressing an innate hatred of God through the refusal to accept his decrees.

---

8. J. M. Mathews, *The Bible and Men of Learning* (New York, 1855), pp. 164, 167.

9. In his early works Melville twice alludes with revulsion to the theory that the condemned suffer an earthly end that corresponds to the horrors awaiting them in the hereafter. See *Mardi,* pp. 349-350, and *Redburn,* p. 245.

10. *Constitution,* p. 154, giving the language of the Canons of the Synod of Dort.

Since Herman never joined the church, it is evident that he could not humble himself before these decrees. He may, in fact, have been inclined to reverse their moral valuations, holding a divine sovereign responsible for the destruction of a virtuous man. With so striking an example in his intimate memory, Herman may well have come to suspect that an avenging fatality indeed governed human life, and he could hardly conceive that fatality to be "righteous" and "just." On the contrary, his application of the orthodox theory to the fate of his liberal father could have led him to feel a personal hatred, so deep as to seem innate, against the apparent inflictions of an inscrutable God.

Whereas the Calvinistic theory of God's sovereignty offered Maria a way of coping with the loss of her husband because it provided a spiritual basis for continued dignity in the face of worldly reverses, this solace was available only if Allan's death were viewed primarily as a disaster that had befallen Maria and the children. If one felt that the essential misery was that suffered by Allan himself, the same doctrine could arouse furious resentment. It seems plausible that young Herman could have responded in both ways at once. He may well have accepted Maria's example and concluded that his own potential worthiness in God's eyes was not necessarily prejudiced by his current miseries, and that those miseries might themselves form part of a program of his own salvation. But Allan's viewpoint would have retained a spokesman in the heart of his grieving son. Allan had trained Herman to believe that God would make his justice plain. The God of liberal benevolence, unlike the Calvinist God, would not destroy a virtuous father in order to secure the salvation of his wife and children.

The liberal and orthodox pieties that had not clashed within the Melvill family in the happier days of Herman's boyhood were thus forced into mutual opposition. Speaking of the religious "office" that God had ordained for parents to fulfill, Horace Bushnell had asserted that human motherhood and fatherhood were to create a piety that would prepare a child for his mature encounter with the objective doctrines of the faith; they were to establish "a kind of house-religion, that may widen out into the measures of God's ideal majesty and empire."[11]

For young Herman there could be no such continuity between
boyhood piety and mature religious conviction; the traditions
that he had absorbed were themselves contradictory and he had
absorbed them under conditions that made their contradictions
into a living personal conflict. The "house-religion" of the Melvills was now divided against itself.

* * *

The spiritual problems posed by Allan's death were compounded by the economic hardship that followed. While Allan
was alive, it was hardly possible for the family to make a new
beginning, because of the risk that his creditors would get word
of any sizable property he might acquire, and attach it to collect
what he owed them. Within a few months after his death, however, an inheritance of Maria's and a loan from Peter Gansevoort
were put together to form a body of capital, and to protect
it the family changed the spelling of its name to "Melville."[12]
Herman's older brother, Gansevoort, was put at the head of
a fur business, and for a time he prospered; in the spring of
1834 he moved the family into a fine house on Clinton Square,
where they lived in their accustomed patrician style. Although
Herman had to give up his schooling at the Albany Academy
to take a job in the New York State Bank, it probably appeared
from the outside as though little had changed.[13] If this period
of seeming prosperity could have been extended, the family
might have regained its footing, and the taint of disgrace might
have faded. But Gansevoort's business failed in the Panic of
1837, so that the material basis for Melvill family pride was
finally and conclusively destroyed.

The Panic was a classic instance of the "bust" that followed

---

12. Allan Melvill had occasionally used a final *e* in spelling his name. See
Allan Melvill to Catherine Van Schaick Gansevoort, February 5, 1824. GLC.
After the formal change of spelling Maria sometimes dropped the *e*. See Maria
Melvill to Peter Gansevoort, June 26, 1833. GLC. Gilman rightly focuses attention on the business card Gansevoort issued as the crucial *public* use of
the new spelling, and adds that "as the son of a man who had died owing
thousands of dollars to creditors in Albany and New York, Ganesvoort may
well have wished to hide his relationship so that his own business might
escape being strangled at birth" (Gilman, p. 309, n. 74).

13. Gilman, pp. 61-65.

inevitably upon "boom" times in this period of unregulated capitalist enterprise, and if Herman had been equipped to analyze the processes at work, its psychological impact might have been less severe. As it was, the interpretation of this disaster that was represented to him most forcefully was theocentric. He was exposed to an interpretation that claimed to discern moral order in the vicissitudes of the economic arena.

The pastor of the Melville's church at this time was Thomas A. Vermilye, who was soon to leave Albany to join one of the most enviable of Dutch pastorates, at the Collegiate Reformed Protestant Dutch Church of the City of New York (now Marble Collegiate Church).[14] His interpretation of the Panic reveals something of the rhetorical adroitness that helped him to a conspicuous ecclesiastical career: it subtly alters Calvinist teaching in order to accommodate the moral yearnings of those who managed to remain solvent. Addressing the Young Men's Association for Mutual Improvement in December of 1837, Vermilye expounded the thesis that "moral excellence is an important requisite to temporal advancement." Admitting that there are times when the unscrupulous man may succeed, by "cunning, and impudence . . . and vice,"[15] he insisted that such ill-deserved successes always prove to be evanescent in the final unfolding of events.

Vermilye did not quite say that the world rewards men exactly in accordance with their virtue, but he came close: "with few, if indeed there are really any exceptions, every one will ultimately pass, even here [on earth] for what he is, and be estimated much according to his true worth." He anticipated a this-worldly balancing of the scales when "moral integrity and excellence" triumphs and "the opposite character sinks to its proper level: when the vicious and unscrupulous man, even at the high noon of apparent prosperity, if possessed of sensitive feelings will be torn with remorse and anguish." Vermilye then gave numerous

---

14. Edward B. Coe, "Discourse Commemorative of the Reverend Thomas Edward Vermilye, D.D., LL.D." (New York, 1893), pp. 11, 14-15. ARC.

15. Thomas E. Vermilye, "An Introductory Address to the Course of Lectures, before the Young Men's Association for Mutual Improvement in the City of Albany," December 19, 1837, p. 32. ARC.

examples of men whose momentary successes were blighted by guilt and ended in catastrophe.[16]

Vermilye's analysis thus drew a sharp moral distinction between failed and successful businessmen, men who would seem to us differentiated not by moral worthiness, but by economic staying power. The businessman who could keep his creditors at bay, and get through the recession without going bankrupt, might have indulged in as much cunning and vice as his less fortunate neighbor who got caught short. The Panic acquired in Vermilye's discussion a virtually apocalyptic authority, that of separating the virtuous sheep from the unscrupulous goats. Its appeal for those who were surviving the holocaust is not hard to perceive.

Indeed, the cultural force of this commercial piety is manifested by the extent to which it perverted the Reformation theology that Vermilye's church had fought so hard to sustain. Explicit redefinitions of doctrine were instantly detected and excluded by the guardians of Dutch orthodoxy, so that Vermilye's language carefully treads the border of heresy. But his delicate recasting of the austere old faith helped him to notable professional success. The coming of this fashionable revision to the pulpit in Albany can only have compounded Herman's religious difficulties. If, like his mother, he had found any solace in the tragic perspectives of Reformation theology, in which worldly fortune gives no real clue to inner worthiness, he was now faced again with the notion that the one implied the other.

Herman had ample opportunity to sample such teaching, although he was absent from the meeting of the Young Men's Association at which this version of it was given. He and Gansevoort had been active members of the association for some time, but by December of 1837 Gansevoort was bankrupt and they could no longer afford the dues.[17]

The scheme of moral explanations that Vermilye advanced was quite familiar to young Herman, of course, because it was closely analogous to his father's practical creed. But in the life of poverty now inaugurated, Herman was to view this scheme from an unaccustomed social vantage. He certainly knew by

16. *Ibid.*, pp. 33 f.
17. Gilman, pp. 73, 82-83. Leyda, I, 67, 69.

now that many successful men were no better than his father, or than Gansevoort. He was doubtless well acquainted with members of the Young Men's Association to whom surviving the Panic brought increments of moral self-satisfaction and who were eager to claim a religious sanction, like that conferred in Vermilye's discourse.[18] But if he was inclined to reject this piety because his experience had schooled him to its logical defects, he was also forced into opposition because of the adverse moral pressure that it exerted on his own self-respect. He now began to view the piety of the privileged class from beneath, and to learn that the structure of justifications that his father had used to keep himself afloat also worked to keep the unfortunate in their unfortunate place. Just as this system of moral accounting could fortify the morale of the successful, so it could undermine the courage of those who had failed, urging them to believe that they deserved their relative poverty.

Melville found himself passing through an intracultural membrane, much as Alice passed through the looking glass, into a realm where the meanings of his life were strangely reversed. In his mind he was still a young patrician, but now his experiences conspired more and more to insist that he was of the lower class. As he passed through the interface separating privilege and poverty he received new bearings; the general moral reference system, with its theocentric guarantee to represent moral reality itself, came to have a dismaying new significance for his life. He was to feel the sting of a systematic contempt based on assumptions of moral superiority that he knew to be spurious.

Melville came to resent the self-righteous disdain shown him by his social superiors; yet his own character had been shaped by the conventions on which he found himself condemned. The alternative to accepting the verdict was an investigation of something harder to deal with than the imputation of moral unworthiness: the possibility that the suffering he endured made no sense at all within any theocentric scheme of moral order. In *Moby-Dick,* Melville found it possible to articulate such an investigation; but for now he found himself driven into a position

18. H. A. Larrabee, "Herman Melville's Early Years in Albany," *New York History,* 32 (1934), 144-159, discusses the prevalence of such pious arrogance in Albany.

of suppressed revolt. The theocentric system remained in force
as his model of reality; his resentment of its verdicts was all
the more vexatious because he had no independent grounds on
which to make that resentment understandable.

In the spring of 1838 he got into a noisy public quarrel with
a man named Charles Van Loon, who was studying to be a
Baptist minister.[19] The dispute concerned the affairs of a literary
society and was conducted with a great deal of histrionic bluster
on both sides. Despite the huffing and puffing, Melville's line
of attack reveals how readily his belligerence seized upon religious issues. Melville drew Van Loon into the quarrel by publishing a thinly veiled personal attack on him, and then charged
him with hypocrisy. "In all your ribaldry and villification there
lurks a spirit of implacable rancour and hate, which affords the
most delightful commentaries upon the dignity of your christian
character." Melville affects disdainful amusement at Van Loon's
"vindictive nature," but it is clear that he himself was frantic
with anger. Ascribing "implacable rancour and hate" to this
ministerial student, Melville prefigures the idiom that he would
later employ in characterizing Captain Ahab; with the novel
he finally discovered a way to unleash his prodigious anger within a context that would make its religious bearings evident. Melville concludes his public letter with a sarcasm that returns to
the religious theme: "May these truly christian attributes cling
around the sacred lawn with which you are hereafter to be invested, and your angelic nature be a fit illustration of the peaceful spirit of the gospel you profess."[20]

The theocentric system had a set of categories designed to
deal with intractable opposition to its precepts. It had a negative
dimension, so to speak, a realm to which those who were alienat-
ed altogether from its version of reality might be consigned.[21]
For the religious system from which both Melville and Van Loon

---

19. Gilman, p. 91.
20. *Ibid.*, pp. 255-256.
21. Kai Erikson, *Wayward Puritans: A Study in the Sociology of Deviance* (New
York, 1966), describes how deviant members of Puritan society were defined
as representatives of the devil. See also Erik H. Erikson, *Identity, Youth and
Crisis* (New York, 1968), pp. 172-176, 195-196, discussing the attraction of
a "negative identity" for individuals who find no way to define themselves
within the framework of positive values accepted by their community.

drew their rhetoric, the reality of God and his lawful order had its radically antagonistic counterpart in the domain of the devil. When Van Loon discovered that Melville had invoked the "peaceful spirit of the gospel" in order to bring his violent and sarcastic attack to its climax, he called upon this ultimate category of denunciation: "If . . . I have done violence to the spirit of the gospel, most cordially do I recall the objectionable language, and in the meek and charitable spirit of Peter the Apostle, honestly and conscientiously pronounce you Herman Melville, a 'child of the devil, full of all subtility and all mischief.' "[22]

Readers attuned to Melville's adult fascination with the devilish will observe a certain prophetic suggestiveness in Van Loon's insult. As Melville came to explore the religious conflict that lay behind his rage at this smug young Baptist, he found himself more and more attracted by the language of the demonic. It gave him a way to articulate his opposition to the theocentric scheme of understanding. He took the vocabulary of denunciation and transformed it into an idiom of radical defiance. Yet the idea of the demonic offered Melville more than a set of terms; it also provided him a spiritual stance. He became a "child of the devil" with a vengeance, in certain phases of his rebellion, so as to gain leverage against a system that was inherent in his own way of thinking. His cultivation of a demonic consciousness was an effort to break free of theocentric patterns of thought, to find an independent spirituality.

Although the quarrel with Van Loon was an incidental and passing irritation, it permits us to glimpse Melville's response to his religious dilemma. The conflict between the religious beliefs he had inherited was no longer moderated by the secure consciousness of "Melvill" family prominence; instead, that conflict was exacerbated because of the confusion of verdicts on the religious meaning of the family's humiliation. Whereas we now may understand that the fluctuations of credit in an unregulated capitalism trapped many men into the pattern of overextension and collapse that toppled Allan Melvill and his son, such an explanation was not available in their time. The family was reduced to poverty by what must have seemed the dispensa-

---

22. Gilman, p. 259.

tions of an inscrutable fatality, acting like the Calvinistic Providence in total disregard for human calculation, effort, and hope. Melville's family pride, surviving in the midst of outward ruin, prompted fierce outbursts against the smugly self-righteous; but it also animated the deeper levels of his skepticism. He came later to describe his family as one "to whom Providence has brought unspeakable & peculiar sorrows" (*Letters*, p. 32).

During the next few years Melville had little opportunity or reason to explore the agonizing perplexities of his dilemma. He was under heavy pressure to make some material headway in the world, or at least to relieve the burden on his immediate family. The far-flung adventures of his late teens and early twenties supplied the materials that he exploited in undertaking a literary career, but as his career unfolded, his way of treating those materials became increasingly meditative. His attack on the missionaries in *Typee* and *Omoo* indicates his continuing resentment of those whose position of social dominion was girded by religion, and the cogency of the attack reveals that his outrage could find its way to solid ethical insights.[23]

His preoccupation with religious topics came to focus on the most basic issue of all: the question which asked what divine truth could properly be invoked to authorize moral judgments. In order to understand how that issue framed itself, and how it led him to a reconsideration of the religious enigmas that his early experience had posed, we now turn to the period in which these preoccupations came to a head, the period in which he was working on *Moby-Dick*.

---

23. I have given a discussion in "The Force of Prejudice: Melville's Attack on Missions in *Typee*," *Border States*, 1 (1973), 5-18.

IV

Sane Madness

In the spring and summer of 1850, Herman Melville's fortunes seemed definitely on the rise. The success of his South Seas novels had made it seem possible that the hardship of earlier years was behind him. *Mardi's* rhapsodic philosophizings had harmed him somewhat in the public eye, but he had stabilized his reputation with the very acceptable *Redburn.* During the first week of April he learned that the first edition of *White-Jacket* had quickly sold out and that another printing was planned.[1] The self-confidence that this news must have inspired can only have been strengthened by his feeling that he had yet another novel well under way. Toward the end of June he informed Richard Bentley, his London publisher, that he was preparing "a romance of adventure, founded upon certain wild legends in the Southern Sperm Whale Fisheries, and illustrated by the author's own personal experience, of two years & more, as a harpooneer." Melville expected the work to be ready "in the latter part of the coming autumn" (*Letters,* p. 109).

These encouraging prospects prompted Melville, now almost thirty-one years old, to establish the first household he could call his own. Moving his family of three out of his younger brother's house in New York City, where they had crowded in with his brother's family, their mother, and four unmarried sisters, Melville set up housekeeping on a farm near Pittsfield, Massachusetts.[2] He found, however, that he could not complete the whaling book in the time he had allotted himself, and spent

1. Leon Howard, *Herman Melville, a Biography* (1951; reptd. Berkeley, 1967), p. 153.
2. *Ibid.*, pp. 153-154.

the next nine months transforming it into *Moby-Dick*. Beneath
the self-confidence of his letter to Bentley a spiritual conflict
lay in wait, with its portent of creativity and psychic danger.

Various explanations have been offered for the sudden emergence, at this point in his career, of Melville's greatest creative
powers. It has been proposed that his recent reading of Shakespeare inspired him to a new level of achievement; his fast
flowering intimacy with Hawthorne has likewise been proposed
as emboldening him to believe that an American writer could
rival Shakespeare's greatness.[3] These and other circumstances
of external encouragement are mainly important, however, for
having given Melville the strength he needed to come to terms
with something heretofore unmanageable in himself. As a psychic conflict must be held in abeyance until an individual is
ready to sustain its turbulence, so Melville's current sense of
basic well-being enabled him to release thoughts and feelings
that earlier had confounded him.

Just before he returned to work on *Moby-Dick* in the fall of
1850, Melville read Hawthorne's *Mosses from an Old Manse,* and
wrote an essay about it which reveals his own burgeoning ambition, and the conflicts inherent in it. "Hawthorne and His
Mosses" discusses Hawthorne, Shakespeare, and the prospects
for American literature.

* * *

In praising Hawthorne, Melville outlined the exalted literary
mission he had adopted for himself.[4] Exhilarated at having re-
covered from the failure of *Mardi,* Melville permits the prophetic
zeal of that book to express itself once again. He sets forth the
achievement of "Truth" as the criterion of literary greatness.
No true genius can exist, Melville declares, "without also possess-
ing ... a great, deep intellect, which drops down into the uni-

---

3. Newton Arvin, *Herman Melville, a Critical Biography* (1950; reptd. New
York, 1964), pp. 136-141. Charles Olson, *Call Me Ishmael* (San Francisco, 1947),
pp. 35-73. F. O. Matthiessen, *American Renaissance* (1941; reptd. New York,
1968), pp. 413-431. Edwin Haviland Miller, *Melville* (New York, 1975), pp.
19-52, uses the meeting with Hawthorne as the point of departure for a study
of Melville's life.

4. Hubert H. Hoeltje, "Hawthorne, Melville and 'Blackness,'" *American
Literature,* 37 (1965), 41-51, argues that Melville's preoccupations, rather than
valid insights into Hawthorne, predominate in the "Mosses" essay.

verse like a plummet" ("Mosses," p. 539). The essence of Shakespeare's greatness lies in his thought: "it is those deep far-away
things in him; those occasional flashings-forth of the intuitive
Truth in him; those short, quick probings at the very axis of
reality: — these are the things that make Shakespeare, Shakespeare" (p. 541). Insisting that Hawthorne's depth of vision
is a match for the bard's, Melville uses language broad enough
to include himself: "There are minds that have gone as far as
Shakespeare into the universe" (p. 543).

Melville is forced to admit that Hawthorne is not so famous
as Shakespeare, but explains that Hawthorne "refrains from all
the popularizing noise and show of broad farce, and blood-bes-
meared tragedy; content with the still, rich utterances of a great
intellect in repose" ("Mosses," p. 542). In explaining further
the relative obscurity of Hawthorne, Melville makes a startling
comparison between the true artist and Christ. "It is of a piece
with the Jews, who while their Shiloh was meekly walking in
their streets, were still praying for his magnificent coming; looking for him in a chariot, who was already among them on an
ass" (p. 543). Melville is delighted to find that Hawthorne has
anticipated his own thoughts on "The Master Genius," whose
advent Melville hails as "the coming of the literary Shiloh of
America" (p. 550).

Melville suggests that the American experience will enable
the artist to realize large new accessions of Truth, transcending
the wisdom of earlier ages. He conceives the spectacular achievements of the past as a limited frontier beyond which the mighty
spirits of the New World will extend man's vision into the inex-
haustible riches of nature. "Nor has Nature been all over ran-
sacked by our progenitors, so that no new charms and mysteries
remain for this latter generation to find. Far from it. The tril-
lionth part has not yet been said; and all that has been said,
but multiplies the avenues to what remains to be said. It is
not so much paucity, as superabundance of material that seems
to incapacitate modern authors" ("Mosses," p. 544). Melville
envisions the "literary Shiloh" as one whose capacious spirit will
absorb the "superabundance of material" and subdue it to the
purposes of his own voyage into the universe.

Melville attacks the worship of Shakespeare as a kind of "intolerance," scarcely suitable to a democratic culture. "You must believe in Shakespeare's unapproachability, or quit the country. But what sort of a belief is this for an American, a man who is bound to carry republican progressiveness into Literature, as well as into Life?" ("Mosses," p. 543). Instead of idolizing Shakespeare, the American public should "duly recognize the meritorious writers that are our own; — those writers, who breathe that unshackled, democratic spirit of Christianity in all things." Thus the mighty prophet would be honored in his own country, for he would embody the same spirit that "now takes the practical lead in this world" (p. 546). Just as the new America offers a practical challenge, the American prophet would challenge the cultural preeminence of the English tradition, exemplifying "democratic" confidence in the boundless possibilities of the creative intellect. Melville strives to summon support for the American effort in literature on the ground of liberal Christian belief, by implying that in the American dispensation all men have an inherent dignity, and equal access to the deepest secrets of the universe.

The ebullient forward thrust of Melville's literary nationalism is complicated, however, by equally ardent emphases that contradict its religious underpinnings. A reader devoted to the "democratic spirit of Christianity" would in fact have been repelled by the qualities that Melville identified as making Hawthorne and Shakespeare great writers. The "power of blackness" that Melville considers the key to Hawthorne's greatness does not compel the reader because it corresponds to a belief in the spiritual dignity of man; on the contrary, it "derives its force from its appeals to that Calvinistic sense of Innate Depravity and Original Sin, from whose visitations, in some shape or other, no deeply thinking mind is always and wholly free." Despite his claim that Americans are bound to embrace an optimistic "republican progressiveness," Melville finds it necessary to admit, with apparent reluctance, that "in certain moods, no man can weigh this world, without throwing in something, somehow like Original Sin, to strike the uneven balance" ("Mosses," pp. 540-541).

Melville's belief that "perhaps no writer has ever wielded this terrific thought with greater terror than this same harmless Haw-

thorne" ("Mosses," p. 541) carries him directly into the comparison of Hawthorne with Shakespeare. For the "blackness" that
"furnishes the infinite obscure of [Hawthorne's] . . . background"
is the same "background, against which Shakespeare plays his
grandest conceits, the things that have made for Shakespeare
his loftiest, but most circumscribed renown, as the profoundest
of thinkers" (p. 541).

The renown of Hawthorne and Shakespeare at its "loftiest"
is also "most circumscribed" precisely because the "terror" with
which they wield the concept of original sin makes up that prophetic vision which gives them true greatness. Shakespeare
plumbs the "blackness" with such daring as to achieve insights
that threaten to derange the basis on which Christian liberalism
rests, suggesting that man's quest for spiritual truth may lead
to madness. His probings at the axis of reality are conveyed
"through the mouths of the dark characters of Hamlet, Timon,
Lear, and Iago"; through them Shakespeare "craftily says, or
sometimes insinuates the things, which we feel to be so terrifically true, that it were all but madness for any good man, in his
own proper character, to utter, or even hint of them" ("Mosses,"
pp. 541-542). Shakespeare himself was driven to obscure the living essence of his religious insight, disclosing it only when "tormented into desperation, Lear the frantic King tears off the
mask, and speaks the sane madness of vital truth" (p. 542).

Although Melville advances progressivist and liberal considerations as the grounds upon which American writers ought to
be celebrated in America, he is aware that the vision that makes
a writer truly great will endanger his popularity. "The sane
madness of vital truth" is unfit for public consumption. Even
Shakespeare discovered that "in this world of lies, Truth is forced
to fly like a scared white doe in the woodlands; and only by
cunning glimpses will she reveal herself " ("Mosses," p. 542).
Melville came to believe that Hawthorne had chosen to hide
the real meaning of his sketches behind apparently trivial titles
"directly calculated to deceive — egregiously deceive — the su-
perficial skimmer of pages" (p. 549). Melville would seem to
imply that unless he obscures his true message, the coming
American literary Shiloh may be greeted with something like
a crucifixion.

Melville tells the American public to adore American writers for the wrong reasons, but this fact does not convict him of duplicity; nor does it lead him to a systematic program of concealing his spiritual discoveries.[5] It reflects a deep-running tension in his own mind about the nature of the Truth to which the American artist should aspire, and about the spiritual capacities required to achieve it. He felt the artist should yield himself to the "power of blackness," pursuing a Calvinist apprehension of the world even to the point of apparent madness. This enterprise yields a statement of "vital truth" when it culminates in tormented frenzy. But Melville also shows enthusiasm for a serene amplitude of spirit that is congruent with the liberal belief that human powers of religious insight can achieve truth directly, without undergoing such agonized distortions. He praises Hawthorne for his "contemplative humor," "a humor so spiritually gentle, so high, so deep, and yet so richly relishable, that it were hardly inappropriate in an angel." This "very religion of mirth" reveals a "boundless sympathy with all forms of being," which by its scope and flexibility approximates an "omnipresent love" ("Mosses," pp. 538-539).

Melville wanted to believe that these contrasting aspects of prophetic genius were complementary, and presents a series of images to suggest the harmony between them. He proposes that the heavenly sunlight illuminates one side of Hawthorne's soul, while "the other side — like the dark half of the physical sphere — is shrouded in a blackness." Likewise he invokes the bright fringes of a thundercloud to symbolize divine radiance playing

---

5. Lawrance Thompson, *Melville's Quarrel with God* (Princeton, 1952), contends that well before the composition of *Moby-Dick* Melville's spiritual confusions were at an end, so that he confronted the problem of expressing an obsessive and unwavering hatred of God in a way that would permit him to make a living as a writer. Melville was compelled, Thompson argues, to devise procedures for veiling his real meanings. In the course of making this argument, Thompson rightly observes thematic inconsistencies; but he goes on to claim that the passages that suggest positive religious aspirations or beliefs form a surface intended to conceal Melville's heartfelt blasphemies. My researches indicate that Melville was not nearly so self-possessed in his dealing with religious matters as Thompson implies, and that his struggle included a sincere yearning to achieve a positive faith. The divergent impulses evident in Melville's work do not represent mere stylistic manipulations; they are a sign of inner uncertainty.

upon the "blackness of darkness" ("Mosses," pp. 540-541). When
he says that "Original Sin" must be thrown into our estimate
of the world to correct an uneven balance, he insists on the
achieved equilibrium, a judiciously poised Truth. However well
this description fits Hawthorne's temperament, it invokes the
issues of a fundamental conflict in Melville's own mind.

The logical discontinuities in "Hawthorne and His Mosses"
correspond to subsurface dislocations in his earlier work. The
tensions that run through his evocations of madness and inspira-
tion, of human dignity and depravity, emerge from Melville's
inability to place his insights within a framework of basic religious belief. He found, in fact, that his preoccupations led him
more and more to doubt that a system of Truth could be formulated on the terms that were available to him.

***

Melville's desire to achieve a vision of Truth through the exercise of a joyous and sympathetic spirituality is clearly evidenced
in *Mardi*, where he allegorically represents such fulfillment in
the Island of Serenia. The religion of Serenia asserts the dignity
of man and his inherent capacity to perceive spiritual reality;
this religion is sharply distinguished from the faith that teaches
that Christ (under the figure of "Alma") brought a "revelation
of things before unimagined, even by the poets" (*Mardi*, p. 626).
William Ellery Channing had declared that "revelation does
not find the mind a blank . . . but finds it . . . in possession
of great principles . . . which are derived from itself."[6] In maintaining that Christianity is a "rational religion," he claimed that
revelation only makes clear to man what he already knows in
the depths of his moral and rational nature. Likewise the Seren-
ians: "But are Truth, Justice, and Love, the revelations of Alma
alone? Were they never heard of till he came? Oh! Alma but
opens unto us our own hearts" (*Mardi*, p. 626).

Channing's confidence in man's reason and moral sense
brought him to maintain that Christianity is truly valuable because "it enlarges, invigorates, exalts my rational nature. If I
could not be a Christian without ceasing to be rational, I should

6. William Ellery Channing, *Works*, 6 vols. (Boston, 1849), IV, 38. Subsequent references to this edition appear in the text.

not hesitate as to my choice. . . . Christianity wages no war with
reason, but is one with it, and is given to be its helper and
friend" (*Works*, IV, 32-33). Reason has two functions, and with
the invigoration that Christianity provides, it performs them
with the fullest independence. These are the search for universal
truths and the reduction of these truths to consistency and unity.
In the wide circuits of its quest, reason "must collect and weigh
the various proofs of Christianity. It must especially compare
this system with those great moral convictions, which are written
by the finger of God on the heart, and which make man a law
unto himself. A religion subverting these, it must not hesitate
to reject, be its evidences what they may" (IV, 41). Channing's
view conforms to the historic conception of right reason; he holds
that Christianity elevates man's rationality to an exalted communion with the divine, where the vital truth of God's nature
and the authenticity of human reason are reciprocally confirmed.[7]

This sentiment is echoed as the spokesman for Serenia answers
the charge that "in your faith must be much that jars with
reason." "No, brother! Right-reason, and Alma, are the same;
else Alma, not reason, would we reject. The Master's great command is Love; and here do all things wise, and all things good,
unite. Love is all in all. The more we love, the more we know;
and so reversed" (*Mardi*, p. 629). Moral law and the sovereign
reason are harmoniously attuned in the spiritual fulfillment of
Serenia. The "omnipresent love" that Melville praised in Hawthorne seems to be at one with the judgments of an intellect
which strives for Truth.

Although Melville was strongly attracted by the religious felicity of Serenia, his way of shaping the allegory suggests an equally forceful recoil. The four allegorical questers who accompany
his protagonist accept the humane and liberal faith, but the

---

7. Melville also encountered the concept of right reason in Seneca and
Sir Thomas Browne, whose works he read during the composition of *Mardi*.
See Sir Thomas Browne, *Religio Medici*, ed. James Winny (Cambridge, 1963),
p. 11, and *Seneca's Morals by Way of Abstract, To Which Is Added, A Discourse,
under the Title of An After-thought*, by Sir Roger L'Estrange (Philadelphia, 1845),
pp. 82-86. These pages are in the essay "Of a Happy Life," to which Melville
refers in *Mardi*. See *Mardi*, p. 388. For Melville's readings of Browne at this
time see Leyda, I, 273.

protagonist himself refuses. As he is urged by the other questers
to make Serenia his spiritual home, a desperate frenzy over-
whelms him. "Then, then! my heart grew hard, like flint; and
black, like night; and sounded hollow to the hand I clenched.
Hyenas filled me with their laughs; death-damps chilled my
brow; I prayed not, but blasphemed" (*Mardi*, p. 639). Melville
does not give his hero's blasphemy any explicit intellectual content, and the meanings of the quest for which he forsakes Serenia
remain ambiguous. But the presentation of Serenia itself is arranged to suggest that a contradiction lies at the heart of its
claim to honor untrammeled rationality.

The Serenian oracle is asked what fate the rational paradise
has in store for those "who have no aptitude for . . . thought,"
lead "thoughtless lives of sin," and "die unregenerate." The oracle replies that "Sin is death."

" 'Ah then,' yet lower moan made I; 'and why create the germs
that sin and suffer, but to perish?'

" 'That,' breathed my guide; 'is the last mystery which underlieth all the rest. Archangel may not fathom it; that makes of
Oro [God] the everlasting mystery he is; that to divulge, were
to make equal to himself in knowledge all the souls that are;
that mystery Oro guards; and none but him may know' " (*Mardi*,
pp. 634-635).

Profound reflection on the fact that "Oro" creates many souls
that "sin and suffer, but to perish" might lead to a mad conclusion indeed, the conclusion that the "mystery Oro guards" con-
ceals a drastic moral inadequacy. Channing argued that religious Truth must be tested against "those great moral
convictions, which are written by God upon the heart"; he did
not foresee the confusion that results when this procedure leads
to the conviction that God himself is morally tainted. How can
man's innate moral consciousness be God-given if it indicts the
God who gave it? Channing felt that a man in search of Truth
could be a "law unto himself," because of his fundamental assumption that man's moral nature and the nature of the divine
were embraced in a cosmic harmony. Melville earnestly wanted
to share that assumption, to believe that a "boundless sympathy
for all forms of being" in the seeker for Truth would bring him
to the discovery of an omnipresent love in the character of Being

itself. But he could not silence doubts that appeared to suggest
an ultimate discord. An untrammeled spiritual quest for Truth
is deranged from its ontological basis when it encounters reasons
to believe that the divinely ordained structure of things is morally faulty; it runs mad in doubts of the divine nature and corresponding doubts of its own authenticity.

When these radical implications of the "mystery Oro guards"
are followed up, the quester loses his grip on the criterion of
ultimate moral reality; the Truth itself disintegrates as a standard by which the values of madness and rationality may be
determined. Instead of being absolute opposites that are defined
in relation to a final Truth, madness and right reason become
two extreme modifications of an essentially uniform activity, the
autonomous effort of the mind to read the character of the
Beyond in the evident meanings of experience.

After completing *Mardi,* Melville made a notation that indicates he had glimpsed this disconcerting conclusion: "Madness
is undefinable, it & right reason extremes of one."[8] His way

---

8. This remark appears among a number of jottings in Melville's copy of
William Shakespeare, *The Dramatic Works,* 7 vols. (Boston, 1837), VII, 3d rear
fly. Sealts, No. 460. Since this volume contains *King Lear,* it has been argued
that the remark was prompted by his reading of that play; it is clear, however,
that the idea at stake was already implicit in Melville's own meditations.
Luther Mansfield and Howard P. Vincent argue persuasively that Melville
made these jottings after the completion of *Mardi* and before he finished *White-
Jacket.* See Herman Melville, *Moby-Dick or, The Whale,* ed. Luther Mansfield
and Howard P. Vincent (New York, 1962), p. 643.

There is a difference of opinion about this notation. Charles Olson, *Call
Me Ishmael* (San Francisco, 1947), p. 52, and Mansfield and Vincent use the
form I have given: "It and right reason extremes of one." But in the Davis
and Gilman edition of the *Letters* the quotation is presented as "it and right
reasons extremes of one" (p. 133). An examination of the flyleaf on which
Melville made the notation reveals that the handwriting is ambiguous.

"It and right reason extremes of one" bears a meaning that is consistent
with meanings Melville is known to have intended elsewhere. When "Hawthorne and His Mosses" first appeared, his phrase "the sane madness of vital
truth" was printed as "the same madness of vital truth." Melville explained
to Sophia Hawthorne that he had prepared the copy in haste, and had not
read the proofs. See Eleanor Melville Metcalf, *Herman Melville, Cycle and Epicycle* (Cambridge, Mass., 1953), pp. 91-92. Possibly, the editor or typesetter was
not attuned to Melville's strange meaning and tried to correct what he found.
But Melville was perfectly capable of conceiving that madness might be sane,
and that madness and right reason might be extreme modifications of an
essentially uniform mental activity.

of treating Serenia suggests that the apostles of right reason maintain a safe distance from madness only by evading basic questions about evil. Hence although the Unitarian paradise is paraded as the expression of man's moral and spiritual independence, it is really a peculiar form of subservience, in which the quester is forbidden to demand of "Oro" the reason for undeserved suffering. Since this mystery "underlieth all the rest," the liberal optimism of Serenia might be said to rest upon a bomb, whose hidden fuse could be ignited by a fearless inquiry into the mad meanings of radical evil.

Melville did not want to arrive at so devastating a conclusion. These implications of his spiritual probing in *Mardi* remain entirely provisional; he does not openly denounce Serenia, or charge God with wrong. But he continued to be fascinated by the metaphysical significance of undeserved suffering, and extended his speculations in the two books that followed. *Redburn* and *White-Jacket* reveal the intensifying cross-pressure into which these speculations drew him. His desire to believe that the essential structure of reality is determined by divine benevolence is inreasingly threatened by an opposing vision whose logic and emphases are Calvinistic, but whose substance is insane.

In *Redburn* his reflections upon unredeemable human misery come to a focus in Jackson, who is trapped permanently in a hellish existence and possessed by a contagious spirit of blasphemy. "He was a Cain afloat; branded on his yellow brow with some inscrutable curse; and going about corrupting and searing every heart that beat near him" (*Redburn*, p. 104). Although Melville's youthful hero is horrified by this bearer of the divine curse, he cannot finally condemn him. "There seemed even more woe than wickedness about the man; and his wickedness seemed to spring from his woe; and for all his hideousness, there was that in his eye at times, that was ineffably pitiable and touching; and though there were moments when I almost hated this Jackson, yet I have pitied no man as I have pitied him" (p. 105). Melville interprets the suffering of Jackson, not as the punishment for his sin, but as the reason for it. He glances at Calvinistic doctrine, proposing Jackson as the victim of an inscrutable curse, to suggest that he cannot be held accountable for his own wickedness.

In *White-Jacket*, Melville once again employs Calvinistic ideas as he ponders the wretchedness of a woman whose countenance was horribly disfigured by a horn: "The horn seemed the mark of a curse for some mysterious sin, conceived and committed before the spirit had entered the flesh. Yet that sin seemed something imposed, and not voluntarily sought; some sin growing out of the heartless necessities of the predestination of things; some sin under which the sinner sank in sinless woe" (*White-Jacket*, p. 249). Melville's brooding on the horned woman arouses intimations of an ultimate heartlessness, as evident in the facts of experience as any omnipotent benevolence. He proposes the character of Bland as revealing an aptitude for evil-doing which arises as naturally from the inherent nature of things as all the love in Serenia. Bland was a treacherous informer, but not in defiance of God-given impulses to shun wickedness and seek the good. Melville reports that "a studied observation of Bland convinced me that he was an organic and irreclaimable scoundrel, who did wicked deeds as the cattle browse the herbage, because wicked deeds seemed the legitimate operation of his whole infernal organization" (p. 188). Thus if Channing could discover benevolence as the essential attribute of man's moral nature, and maintain that it was rooted in the character of the divine, so Melville, drawing upon the "Calvinistic sense of Innate Depravity and Original Sin," glimpses a mutual correspondence of divine and human malignity. Behind these suggestions loomed the vision Melville wanted to fend off, that of a universe governed by hate, whose essence is known in madness.

He sought to formulate a positive religious hope sturdy enough to subdue such nightmarish intimations. Since the root issue for him was that of undeserved human suffering, he was passionately eager to believe that it could somehow be ended. Whereas the religion of Serenia had decreed that there would always be souls that "sin and suffer but to perish," Melville expresses the belief in *Redburn* and *White-Jacket* that the American nation has a messianic destiny that would make the universal fatherhood of God a historical reality. Acknowledging that the condition of the common sailor appears at present to indicate divine indifference, Melville insists that "Time must prove his friend in the end; and though sometimes he would almost seem

as a neglected step-son of heaven . . . yet we feel and we know
that God is the true Father of all, and that none of his children
are without the pale of his care" (*Redburn,* p. 140). A universal
redemption will come about, Melville claims, as America fulfills
her historical mission: "On this Western Hemisphere . . . there
is a future which shall see the estranged children of Adam re-
stored as to the old hearth-stone in Eden" (p. 169).

Melville's enthusiasm for this prospect became increasingly
fervent. *Redburn* gave no tangible indication of the way in which
the fatherhood of God would manifest itself in an American
paradise. But in *White-Jacket* Melville ardently espoused a social
cause, whose object was to ban flogging in the United States
Navy. Melville denounces it on American principles as "opposed
to the essential dignity of man . . . [and] utterly repugnant to
the spirit of our democratic institutions" (*White-Jacket,* p. 146).
The strength of the antiflogging movement, which succeeded
in outlawing the practice shortly after *White-Jacket* was published,[9] could be taken as evidence that history was on the move,
bringing in a new order that would vindicate faith in "the democratic spirit of Christianity." To Melville the proposed abolition
of flogging was an earnest of the messianic destiny of America.
He reached the climax of his declamations on the subject with
a strenuous evocation of the American future as a realm in which
human dignity would receive divine confirmation: "we Americans are the peculiar, chosen people — the Israel of our time;
we bear the ark of the liberties of the world. . . . God has predestinated, mankind expects, great things from our race; and great
things we feel in our souls. . . . Long enough have we been sceptics
with regard to ourselves, and doubted whether, indeed, the political Messiah had come. But he has come in *us,* if we would
but give utterance to his promptings" (p. 151).

Melville had already contemplated the religious meaning of
evils that could never be remedied by political reform, but he
felt the promptings of the democratic spirit of Christianity within himself. He determined to give it utterance in order to quell

9. There is a legend that *White-Jacket* had great influence on the final decision of the Congress to outlaw flogging, but the most thorough historian of
the controversy gives good reasons to doubt the validity of the legend. See
Harold D. Langley, *Social Reform in the United States Navy, 1798-1862* (Urbana,
1967), pp. 194 f.

certain other promptings that seemed to lead to madness. His comments in "Hawthorne and His Mosses" on the "literary Shiloh of America" reveal that he expected the redeemer nation to have its artistic harbinger, and hoped that he himself might take up that role. But it is equally evident that the quest for Truth that the American prophet was to conduct presented severe unresolved problems. How could the "heartless predestination" that had cursed the horned woman be reconciled with the benign predestination that had ordained triumph for the democratic spirit? How could the dignity of man be affirmed as a divine principle when certain living men appeared to manifest Calvinistic depravity? How could the prophetic spirit act independently as a "law unto itself," making its way into the secrets of the universe, if the secrets it must reveal are tantamount to madness?

* * *

Melville had far too much social insight to believe for long that America was a political Messiah,[10] and he soon discontinued his flirtation with the idea that he would act as a literary Christ. But these fantasies had a strong grip on him because they forestalled the conclusion that undeserved suffering was a permanent feature of human experience. That conclusion would lead him to a religious quandary in which the harmonious relation of divine truth to human moral experience would become deranged. The coherence of Melville's mental universe, at its deepest levels, depended upon that harmony. For the time being it made better sense to identify himself and his nation as Christ than to lose the system of understanding by which "making sense" was possible.

The issues Melville faced in writing *Moby-Dick* were not pieces of a puzzle that could be laid aside if no way could be found of fitting them together. Gabriel Marcel distinguishes a "problem" from a "mystery" by observing that it is possible to separate a problem from the person who is looking for its solution, whereas a mystery everywhere pervades the attempt to reflect

---

10. Ernest Lee Tuveson, *Redeemer Nation: The Idea of America's Millennial Role* (Chicago, 1968), notices Melville's interest in this idea, in the course of a fine study of its historical and intellectual relations.

upon it.[11] Mysteries will not stand clear in the mind because
they have formed the mind. Although intellectual mysteries may
concern scientific or philosophical issues, they always have a
religious dimension. They touch the question of whether the
meaning on which a given human life depends has a secure
purchase on the real world. That question arouses anxieties that
problems never give us; it reminds us that our existence is staked
on questionable propositions. Coping with a mystery requires
techniques for dealing with the attendant anxiety; it requires
the capacity for meditation.

The letters Melville wrote to Hawthorne during the composition of *Moby-Dick* reveal the intellectual issues of his struggle
with the enigmas of Truth, and also reveal the psychic distress
amid which that struggle was conducted. He tells Hawthorne,
indeed, that a perverse and stubborn conflict is inherent in meditative quest, calling it "the tragicalness of human thought in its
own unbiassed, native, and profounder workings" (*Letters,* p.
124). Praising Hawthorne for the courage to face this conflict,
Melville celebrates his "intense feeling of the visable truth," a
resolute truthfulness that can only be sustained through heroic
struggle. "By visable truth, we mean the apprehension of the
absolute condition of present things as they strike the eye of
the man who fears them not, though they do their worst to
him" (p. 124). Rather than believing that the intellectual quest
is welcomed by the reality toward which its searches extend,
Melville propounds a tragic opposition: intellectual integrity can
only be maintained against cosmic resistance. The quester must
contend with divine powers, like the God of Serenia, who will
not submit to exhaustive inquiry.

Struggling to gain leverage against conceptions outside of
which thought about ultimate questions hardly seemed possible
at all, Melville desperately insists on the metaphysical sovereignty of his own nature. He celebrates "the man who, like Rus-
sia or the British Empire, declares himself a sovereign nature
(in himself) amid the powers of heaven, hell, and earth. He
may perish; but so long as he exists he insists upon treating

---

11. Gabriel Marcel, "On the Ontological Mystery," in *Philosophy in the
Twentieth Century,* ed. William Barrett and Henry D. Aiken, 2 vols. (New York,
1962), I, 364-386.

with all Powers upon an equal basis" (*Letters,* pp. 124-125). Melville resumes his speculations on jealously guarded divine secrecy, now proposing that it amounts to a momentous fraud. "If any of those other Powers choose to withhold certain secrets, let them; that does not impair my sovereignty in myself; that does not make me tributary. And perhaps, after all, there is *no* secret. We incline to think that the Problem of the Universe is like the Freemason's mighty secret, so terrible to all children. It turns out, at last, to consist in a triangle, a mallet, and an apron, — nothing more!" (p. 125).

Melville's notion that divine powers resist the spiritual inquiries of men is analogous to Calvinistic belief in the sovereign holiness of God, but his claim to absolute self-sovereignty in the face of such transcendent opposition is uniquely Melvillian. It is an evidence of the deadly salience with which he sought to turn the tables on the traditions he had inherited. In the face of an eternal divine omniscience, liberal and Calvinist believers were alike prepared to accept their own mortality and failures of understanding as an inducement to reverence. Fighting to break clear of this ingrained spiritual habit, Melville scoffs at the divine jealousy. There is a prohibition upon human inquiries, he maintains, because God is embarrassed at not being able to answer them. "We incline to think that God cannot explain His own secrets, and that He would like a little information upon certain points himself. We mortals astonish Him as much as He us" (*Letters,* p. 125).

But even as he uttered this defiant assertion Melville became aware that his meditations were being clogged by something more basic than the habit of reverence before the Godhead. Merely to rearrange the relationship between his own nature and God's nature, to place them on a democratic level, would not escape the constriction of thought that resulted from dealing in the systematic terms by which the nature of man and the nature of God had to be defined. "But it is this *Being* of the matter"; Melville continued; "there lies the knot with which we choke ourselves. As soon as you say *Me,* a *God,* a *Nature,* so soon you jump off from your stool and hang from the beam. Yes, that word is the hangman. Take God out of the dictionary, and you would have Him in the street" (*Letters,* p. 125).

Like so many of Melville's profoundest utterances, this one is cryptic because its meaning is very condensed; yet it immediately conveys the spiritual quandary in which Melville found himself. He was struggling to avoid being enmeshed in a complex pattern of thought that somehow monopolized the territory over which he wanted to move. The concepts of "God," of "Me," of any given "Nature," were defined within a framework that came into play as soon as one of the concepts was invoked. When one metaphysical wire was tripped, the whole interworked system began to vibrate, and then it became necessary to talk somehow with reference to those vibrations. It was the system itself that was inimical to the kind of thinking and writing that Melville wanted to do.

For this reason it was finally not suitable to insist on metaphysical democracy, because that was nothing more than a rearrangement of the terms. Removing God from the dictionary, where he receives his customary reverential definition, only causes him to show up in the street. The street is obviously a more vital and democratic setting, but that only makes it clearer that the root problem is not one of reverence or lack of reverence: "it is this Being of the matter." The knot that chokes off meditative inquiry is ontological analysis itself, as conducted within theocentric coordinates. "God" was by definition the ultimate abstract essence from which every other abstract definition finally had to take its bearings. An assertion of self-sovereignty translated automatically into a definition of "Me," which included assumptions and implications on the plane of "Being." But ontology was unthinkable without "God," so that what began as an effort to displace him merely plays back into the system of which he is the center. Melville's problem was to find somehow a language — or a dramatic framework — that would permit him to deal with ultimate questions in a manner truthful to his radical insights, in such a way as to avoid having them digested by the very presuppositions he wanted to assail. His image of himself as perched on a stool with a rope around his neck suggests the precariousness of his work. A lapse into conventional modes of religious expression would be suicide.

Melville knew by now that his radical investigations would not be welcomed by the reading public. When he next wrote

Hawthorne, he cast himself in the role of a religious reformer who must suffer rejection by the world for the sake of his visionary integrity. "Try to get a living by the Truth — and go to the Soup Societies. Heavens! Let any clergyman try to preach the Truth from its very strong-hold, the pulpit, and they would ride him out of his church on his own pulpit bannister. It can hardly be doubted that all Reformers are bottomed upon the truth, more or less; and to the world at large are not reformers almost universally laughingstocks? Why so? Truth is ridiculous to men" (*Letters,* p. 127).

Melville believed that his spiritual quest had carried him to the depth of reality on which all great reformers had founded their intransigence; but he now clearly perceived that such prophetic austerity included a disdain for the general populace sharply at variance with the appeal he had made in "Hawthorne and His Mosses." Having boldly pursued his individual sovereignty, he correctly anticipated the hostility his conclusions would arouse and scolded "the world at large" in advance for its refusal to listen to the Truth. Melville became uneasily aware that his way of interpreting democratic principle involved a contradiction. "It seems an inconsistency to assert unconditional democracy in all things, and yet confess a dislike to all mankind — in the mass. But not so — But it's an endless sermon, — no more of it" (*Letters,* p. 127). Although his endless sermon might have achieved a theoretical resolution of these opposites, he knew that he faced a grim dilemma. "Though I wrote the Gospels in this century, I should die in the gutter" (p. 129).

As Melville labored over the whaling book, the prospect of financial ruin added yet another element to his psychic struggle. His literary successes had made it appear that his long effort to find his footing in the world might be coming to an end. He had acquired a house of his own, now, which could be maintained and made a comfortable home if he could continue to market his books. The practical meaning of failure spurred him to write a book that would sell, but the religious conflict drove him deeper and deeper into unmarketable profundities. Melville wondered whether he could stand the strain. "Dollars damn me; and the malicious Devil is forever grinning in upon me,

holding the door ajar. My dear Sir, a presentiment is on me,
— I shall at last be worn out and perish, like an old nutmeg-
grater, grated to pieces by the constant attrition of the wood,
that is, the nutmeg. What I feel most moved to write, that is
banned, — it will not pay. Yet, altogether, wrote the *other* way
I cannot. So the product is a final hash, and all my books are
botches" (*Letters*, p. 128).

In a further anticipation of psychic collapse, he employs an
image that shows that his present struggle is forcing deeper and
deeper layers of his personality to open up, revealing configu-
rations established in a time that now seemed infinitely remote.
"I am like one of those seeds taken out of the Egyptian Pyramids,
which, after being three thousand years a seed and nothing but
a seed, being planted in English soil, it developed itself, grew
to greenness, and then fell to mould. So I. Until I was twenty-
five, I had no development at all. From my twenty-fifth year
I date my life. Three weeks have scarcely passed, at any time
between then and now, that I have not unfolded within myself.
But I feel that I am now come to the inmost leaf of the bulb,
and that shortly the flower must fall to the mould" (*Letters*, p.
130). Melville here explains the vertiginous speed of his literary
and intellectual development as resulting from an interruption
in the normal schedule of growth; thoughts and feelings of his
deepest life flourished now with hectic luxuriance because they
had been held too long in abeyance. The long-buried issues of
his early religious training came to him now with that atmosphere of the archaic which accompanies repressed early memo-
ries making their way into consciousness. But Melville's allusion
to Egypt suggests more than great antiquity; he was aware that
Egypt had been identified as the source of European monotheism. "I shudder at idea of ancient Egyptians," he later wrote.
"It was in these pyramids that was conceived the idea of Jehovah. Terrible mixture of the cunning and awful."[12] Melville
was now in a position to challenge the "Egyptian" heritage of
theocentric spirituality; the seed buried within him now reached
the climax of its flowering.

* * *

12. Herman Melville, *Journal of a Visit to Europe and the Levant*, ed. Howard
C. Horsford (Princeton, 1955), p. 118.

As he worked his way deeper and deeper into himself, Melville discovered more than a warfare of blind psychic forces; he found a wealth of elaborated intellectual traditions, the conventions of Calvinistic controversy, whose characteristic themes and motifs were generic to his psychological turmoil.[13] His quest for a Truth that would harmonize the conflicts within himself was equally an effort to come to terms with his cultural heritage. In writing *Moby-Dick* he found a way to take up the elements of this heritage and to reframe them in terms that were faithful to his intuition of their essential significance. Just as traditions of thought were inherent in his perplexity, so they were available to carry the burden of his insight. Acute psychic conflict is a domain of silence because no way has been found to set the elements of the conflict in an intelligible order. Melville was enabled to speak because he found an aesthetic framework that permitted him to explore the possibility that the theocentric interpretation of moral experience was unworkable. Now enabled to utter what had been locked in silence, Melville endowed his story of the whale hunt with meanings that bear upon the deepest spiritual problems of the age.

Edward Beecher's *Conflict of Ages,* which appeared in 1853, treats the "great debate on the moral relations of God and man" in accordance with his recognition of certain characteristic spiritual quandaries. The most extreme and dangerous of these dilemmas he calls "the fifth experience" or "the eclipse of the glory of God."[14] In terms that recall Melville's reflections on the "power of blackness," Beecher discusses a state of mind in which "the scene of human existence, from the beginning to this hour . . . appears a most mysteriously awful economy, over-

---

13. Thomas Werge, *"Moby-Dick* and the Calvinist Tradition," *Studies in the Novel,* 1 (1969), 484-593, gives a sensitive and learned study. He stresses the grand issues of the Augustinian-Calvinist-Edwardsean tradition in which Melville was steeped, to the exclusion, however, of the Pelagian-Arminian-Unitarian challenge to that tradition. As a result he does not consider the traditions of popular Calvinistic controversy that Melville knew well. Werge's treatment skillfully evokes the larger spiritual dimensions of *Moby-Dick;* yet it moves at a level rather remote from the shaping of specific passages, which can be analyzed when Melville's use of specific controversial issues is recognized.

14. Edward Beecher, *The Conflict of Ages; or, The Great Debate on the Moral Relations of God and Man* (Boston, 1854), p. 184. Subsequent references to this edition appear in the text.

spread by a lurid and dreadful shade" (p. 184). Citing Channing's claim that Calvinism "spreads over . . . [some minds] an
impenetrable gloom" (p. 122), Beecher explains that this spiritual distress arises when the Calvinistic perception of man's condition is combined with the liberal belief that God should deal
with man in accordance with "the principles of honor and
right": "a conviction of the radical facts as to the ruin of man,
as clear and unwavering as the belief of one's own existence;
and, at the same time, to have an equally unwavering belief
of the principles of honor and right, and of the demands made
by them on God with reference to new-created beings" (p. 188).
When these two convictions merge, God's glory is eclipsed and
the excruciating contradictions "present to the mind a malevolent God" (p. 189).

Beecher affirms that although "no Christian will ever, in fact,
believe God is dishonorable and unjust in his dealings with his
creatures, yet his alleged acts may be such that he cannot rationally be seen in any other light" (*The Conflict of Ages,* p. 189).
Thus Beecher recognizes, as Melville had, that in the question
of God's justice the pursuit of rational implications may bring
the pursuer to an apparently mad conclusion. He cites Channing's warning that Calvinism "sometimes shakes the throne of
reason" by plunging the universe in gloom. "If it be believed,
I think there is ground for a despondence bordering on insanity"
(p. 122). Beecher insists that "the fifth experience" reveals the
essence of the age-long theological conflict he seeks to resolve.
But in citing expressions of this dire state he relies mainly on
private correspondence; Beecher is forced to concede that "how
many ever pass in fact into this dark valley, I have no means
of determining. It is not an experience that men are disposed
to make public" (p. 189).

Melville knew quite well the dangers of publishing the visions
of such a consciousness, but unlike the "religious leaders," Melville did not shape his reflections upon them in accordance with
the desire to produce an arguably "Christian" conclusion. He
was willing to consider that the convictions of an apparent
madness did in fact cut deeply into the very axis of reality,
and was propelled into a realm of speculation in which every
religious authority was opened to radical doubt. The liberals

located religious authority in reason, but Melville understood that reason turned into madness when the facts of evil were fully recognized. The orthodox considered revelation authoritative, but Melville felt that the God of orthodox revelation was unfit for worship, however much the arbitrariness attributed to him might seem to be vindicated by the facts of experience.

Melville's radical questioning brought him to doubt the principle that liberal and orthodox controversialists agreed on, namely their implicit belief that a morally compelling scheme of truth could be organized around the concept of "God." He advanced his explorations by concentrating on themes that distressed spokesmen for both sides of the controversy. Liberal and orthodox leaders were acutely concerned about the breakdown of theocentric authority, and they perceived each other as embodiments of the resultant spiritual decay. Although they quarreled violently about the source of religious Truth, they agreed in their analysis of the perversions that result from the lack of it.

Without a guide to Truth, men become either bigots or infidels: they commit themselves to falsehoods and maintain them stubbornly in the face of all resistance, or they find it impossible to settle upon any religious belief at all. Controversialists developed these figures of the bigot and the infidel as typical of the situation in which divine Truth is absent, in order to arraign each other for preaching false conceptions of theocentric authority. Melville commandeers the same figures for purposes of his own; he juxtaposes Ahab's "intense bigotry of purpose" ("The Quarter-deck," p. 141) with the ranging skepticism of Ishmael in order to arraign the notion of theocentric authority itself.

William Ellery Channing, speaking for the liberal tradition, argued that reason should be the final arbiter of religious belief, and objected to the Calvinistic contempt of reason, "because it leads, we believe, to universal skepticism" (*Works,* III, 66). "The worst error in religion," Channing noted, "is that of the skeptic, who records triumphantly the weaknesses and wanderings of the human intellect and maintains, that no trust is due to the decisions of this erring reason" (I, 225). Thus Calvinistic bigots "forge the deadliest weapon for the infidel" (I, 227), and the truly faithful are threatened with despair. Channing clearly enunciated this connection between bigotry and skepticism: "It is worthy of remark, how nearly the bigot and the skeptic approach. Both would annihilate our confidence in our faculties, and both throw doubt and confusion over every truth" (III, 66).

The orthodox employed the same rhetorical artillery in defending the citadels of Revelation. J. M. Mathews stated that "The two great enemies of Divine Revelation are Superstition on the one hand, and Infidelity on the other." Fixing the Catholics and the Unitarians with a single glance, he declared that superstition "professes to believe in Christianity, but obscures and often buries it beneath the inventions and traditions of men." On the strength of its fraudulent claim to divine knowledge apart from revelation, superstition "generally makes its assaults openly and without disguise, 'going about as a roaring lion, seeking whom it may devour.'" The infidel, by contrast, lacks a false standard of positive belief beneath which to march against the faithful, and resorts instead to sneak attacks. Behind disarming appeals to rationality and common sense, infidelity "masks its earliest attacks, and approaches like the tiger, crouching; but when it makes its spring, the bound is the more dangerous and fatal."[15] Channing's analysis of bigotry and skepticism thus has its orthodox analogue in "superstition" and "infidelity." These correlative spiritual distortions were perceived by liberal and orthodox leaders alike as resulting from the loss of religious authority.

Melville achieved a major creative synthesis in presenting Ahab and Ishmael as the figures of a consciousness for which the moral authority of religious Truth has collapsed. Using them, he found it possible both to bring forward from the depth of memory his bitter religious perplexities and to refashion the themes and motifs of theological tradition in a compelling aesthetic idiom. There is ample evidence that his reading during the composition of *Moby-Dick* included religious works, and at points he uses passages from books at hand. But his way of using tradition does not confine itself to such borrowings; he had fuller sources in himself.[16] In this personal culmination he discovered

15. J. M. Mathews, *The Bible and Men of Learning* (New York, 1855), pp. 13-14.
16. C. Hugh Holman, "The Reconciliation of Ishmael: *Moby-Dick* and the

a way to correlate materials with which he had long been familiar and to exploit their potential for art, employing them with
the same independence of spirit he celebrated so grandly. Setting
forth Ahab as a heroic embodiment of the madness which perceives God's evil, Melville progressively reveals that such
heroism is monstrous. Ishmael's skepticism contains layer beneath layer of meaning because Melville's messianic spiritual
aspirations implicitly provide the criteria of Ishmael's skeptical
commentary, and are sometimes set forth in qualified expressions
of positive hope. Ishmael joins for a time in Ahab's sharply focused hatred of the divine; his resignation from Ahab's quest
is presented as the ultimate skeptical discovery that no coherent
vision of the Truth is possible. Ishmael passes beyond Ahab's
madness into the larger sanity to which its moral implications
lead him, discovering that no unified structure of divine authority can be reconciled with the evident moral realities of experience.

Book of Job," *South Atlantic Quarterly,* 57 (1958), 477-490, observes that "the
Bible, absorbed in his childhood, was a portion of his unconscious patterns
of thought and properly can be called an experiential source as opposed to
a literary source; but it is also, a work to which he turned with close attention
while he was writing *Moby-Dick,* so that it is a significant conscious literary
source" (p. 479). This good statement needs to be modified in light of the
fact that Melville absorbed the Bible in childhood according to the formulas
of orthodox belief, and that such unconscious patterns became available for
the purposes of conscious art in *Moby-Dick.*

Part Two

V

Ishmael as Spiritual Voyager

The opening passages of *Moby-Dick* do not present the inauguration of Ishmael's meditative quest in tones of triumph or even of hopeful expectation. Ishmael's jocular self-introduction suggests a state of spiritual distress in which the sufferer sees no advantage in taking himself too seriously. He describes a vaporous uneasiness, in which he finds himself "involuntarily pausing before coffin warehouses" ("Loomings," p. 12); the image of a wholesale business servicing death provides a momentary focus for the wearisome restlessness of his spirit. But he reports no earnest vow to search the depths of this mortal dismay, as though a forthright inquiry would only increase his vexations. In the midst of explaining how "meditation and water are wedded" (p. 13), Ishmael declares his doubt that the deeper meanings can be fathomed. The "image of the ungraspable phantom of life" (p. 14), he observes, is given in the fact that when we look into the water we see the image of ourselves. Ishmael's sardonic tone is determined by the fact that he is describing himself in retrospect, presenting an ingenuous earlier self from the vantage he has achieved by passing through the physical and spiritual terrors of the *Pequod's* doom. The Ishmael who addresses us has adopted a rueful skepticism about the prospects of spiritual quests because he has himself pursued one.

As he makes jokes about his earlier naïveté, he characterizes his initiation into the quest, defining the conventional views he repudiated, and the positive hopes that led him forward. The greenhorn misgivings that are exploited in the comical story of his encounter with Queequeg receive an increasingly complex definition. They represent the very earliest stage of Ishmael's spiritual education, the stage he transcended in becoming a spiritual quester. Dismayed that he must share a bed for the night, Ishmael is further dismayed as the whimsical innkeeper informs him that his prospective· bedfellow is trying to sell a shrunken head that night: "cause to-morrow's Sunday, and it would not do to be sellin' human heads about the streets when folks is goin' to churches" ("The Spouter-Inn," p. 26). These two emphases remain central to the comic development. The innkeeper teases Ishmael by playing upon his squeamishness about sleeping with a man, and by exciting his pious dismay over the information that his bedfellow engages in heathenish enormities.

Ishmael's dual abhorrence is extended as Melville sets before us his initial confrontation with Queequeg. Ishmael approaches the bed with considerable hesitation. He climbs in only after reassuring himself with the thought that the head-peddler might not come home that night at all. When Queequeg does arrive, Ishmael sees his outlandish tattoos and pities him, thinking he must have been disfigured by cannibals. When it becomes apparent that Queequeg is himself a cannibal and a pagan, who offers worship before a polished ebony idol, Ishmael's horror is redoubled. The confrontation reaches its uproarious climax as the savage leaps into bed: "I sang out, I could not help it now; and giving a sudden grunt of astonishment he began feeling me" ("The Spouter-Inn," p. 31). Prohibitions against heathen practice and against physical intimacy between men are thus confirmed as the premise of Ishmael's comical plight.

Ishmael specifically repudiates these prohibitions as his friendship with the savage develops, so that they form a pivot on which he turns from conventional attitudes toward the outlook that underlies his further meditations. Melville defines the inner connection of these issues and their significance for Ishmael's religious quest by interrupting the progress of his acquaintance with Queequeg to present Father Mapple as an embodiment of Calvinist authority.

Ishmael shows great enthusiasm for Father Mapple, whose spiritual authority is symbolized by the fact that he is unapproachable in his lofty pulpit after he draws up the rope ladder by which he ascends to it. This "act of physical isolation . . . signifies his spiritual withdrawal . . . from all outward worldly ties and connexions" ("The Pulpit," p. 43). Melville knew from his boyhood exposure to Calvinism that orthodox pastors claimed to have unique access to God's truth as interpreters of his sacred word. Observing that the pulpit was shaped like the prow of a ship, Ishmael reads its meaning like a true child of the orthodox: "What could be more full of meaning? — for the pulpit is ever this earth's foremost part . . . the pulpit leads the world . . . From thence it is the God of breezes fair or foul is first invoked for favorable winds" (pp. 43-44). Ishmael clearly enunciates orthodox judgment when he associates the impregnable authority of the pulpit with the fact that it contains the holy book: "Yes, for replenished with the meat and wine of the word, to the faithful man of God, this pulpit, I see, is a self-containing strong-hold — a lofty Ehrenbreitstein, with a perennial well of water within the walls" (p. 43).

Ishmael's ascription of "self-containing" authority to the pulpit bears directly on the unfolding definition of his own character as a spiritual quester; it invokes a belief that categorically denies all human capacity for independent religious insight. The orthodox held that no vision of spiritual truth is possible apart from God's sovereign disclosure of himself in scripture. Because of his innate spiritual blindness, man's "natural" religious life is an affront to the Godhead: unredeemed men typically offer worship to some object of the creation rather than to the creator. These themes are subtly extended as Ishmael returns from the Chapel to discover that Queequeg left before the service was complete, and now is intently at work with a penknife, rectifying his deity's nose. Explaining the universal prevalence of such idolatry, orthodox commentators elaborated Saint Paul's claim that God had made knowledge of his own nature available to men by giving evidences of it in the creation. Melville marked in his Bible Paul's central assertion in Romans 1: "Because that which may be known of God, is manifest in them; for God hath shewed it unto them. For the invisible things of him from the creation of the world are clearly seen, being understood by the things that are made, even his eternal power and Godhead; so that they are without excuse" (Romans 1:19-20).[1]

Men are without excuse because despite the evidences of the

1. *The New Testament . . . The Book of Psalms* (New York, 1844). Sealts, No. 65.

Godhead in the created world, they do not glorify him in worship
as the creator. This universal failure did not mean for the orthodox that the evidence for God's activity is inadequate. Calvin
insisted that "the manifestation of God, by which he makes his
glory known in his creation, is, with regard to the light itself,
sufficiently clear; but that on account of our blindness, it is not
found to be sufficient."[2] The signs of the creator are adequate
only to relieve God of blame: "It is not necessary to maintain
that this revelation is competent to supply all the knowledge
which a sinner needs," a nineteenth-century commentator explained. "It is enough that it renders men inexcusable."[3] God's
revelations of himself in the created order are emphatically real,
and are crucial to the life of man's spirit; they are the grounds
upon which the infinite Holiness takes offense at the promiscuous
worships of his creatures. But these revelations, however definitive for the true nature of things, are an enigma to man's darkened understanding. This frame of reference is important to
Ishmael's extended spiritual broodings, for he also explores the
possibility that behind the natural order there is a reality of
supreme importance, with potentially absolute claims upon his
life, but concludes that its nature must remain an unfathomable
mystery. Ishmael, however, does not interpret this situation as
a sign of man's "inexcusable" depravity. Despite the affinity
between his somber conclusions and the pessimistic orthodox
estimate of man's spiritual capacities, Ishmael neither begins
nor ends his quest in obedience to orthodox belief.

He begins with a gesture of defiance. Melville specifically
parodies Calvinist teaching as he describes the growing intimacy
between Ishmael and Queequeg. In order to condemn the spiritual emptiness of man-made idols, orthodox believers asserted
that "the heathen formed their gods after their own imagina-
tions."[4] Thus when Queequeg puts his penknife to the nose of
his little deity, he exemplifies what the Calvinists considered

---

2. John Calvin, *Commentaries on the Epistle of Paul the Apostle to the Romans*,
trans. and ed. John Owen (Grand Rapids, 1948), p. 71.

3. Charles Hodge, *A Commentary on the Epistle to the Romans* (1836; reptd.
Philadelphia, 1870), p. 34.

4. "The Character of the Heathen," *Magazine of the Reformed Dutch Church*,
4 (1831), 335.

man's disastrous spiritual folly. With its emphasis on the holiness of God, orthodox tradition revived from Hebrew monotheism a proud contempt for any worship except that of the true God. That a man should abase himself in worship before the product of merely human effort was considered tantamount to the utmost depravity. Claiming that men "changed the truth of God into a lie," Saint Paul noted the consequence: "For this cause God gave them up unto vile affections . . . the men, leaving the natural use of the woman, burned in their lust toward one another; men with men working that which is unseemly" (Romans 1:25-27). The orthodox believed that God had ordained a connection between homosexuality and the idolatrous workings of man's vain imagination, and they confirmed this belief by observing that "the most moral of the Greeks, and even the *'martyred Socrates'* practised . . . without shame, abominations which we christians cannot name."[5]

Now, however, Ishmael finds "a Socratic wisdom" in the "calm self-collectedness of simplicity" which characterizes his savage friend. Forced into unconventional associations, Ishmael finds that the ways and worship of Queequeg begin to redeem his spiritual restlessness. In direct allusion to his Biblical namesake, whose "hand will be against every man" (Genesis 16:12), Ishmael says "I felt a melting in me. No more my splintered heart and maddened hand were turned against the wolfish world. This soothing savage had redeemed it" ("A Bosom Friend," p. 53).[6] Relaxing into an unwonted intimacy, Ishmael now accepts the signs of friendship offered by the savage and enters with him into a marriage that joins them in worship and in bed.

As Melville brings this development to its head, the values of the orthodox frame of reference become the object of a specific and deliberate travesty. The offhand mockery audible in Ishmael's declaration that he was "born and bred in the bosom of the infallible Presbyterian Church" ("A Bosom Friend," p. 54) is given point as he deduces from his orthodox upbringing an imperative directly contrary to orthodox teaching. To wor-

5. *Ibid.,* p. 339.
6. Lawrance Thompson, *Melville's Quarrel with God* (Princeton, 1952), pp. 152, 165, notes this correspondence of the Biblical Ishmael with Melville's.

ship the idol Yojo would be to violate the First Commandment; and the Westminster Catechism, a copy of which Melville acquired in the later stages of his work on *Moby-Dick,* elaborated the commandment with emphasis: "The first commandment forbiddeth the denying or not worshipping and glorifying the true God . . . and the giving that worship and glory to any other which is due to him alone. . . . God, who seeth all things, taketh notice of, and is much displeased with the sin of having any other God."[7] In an unmistakable parody of the catechetical singsong of question and answer, Ishmael rattles off his justification for joining with "this wild idolator in worshipping his piece of wood": "But what is worship? — to do the will of God — *that* is worship. And what is the will of God? — to do to my fellow man what I would have my fellow man to do to me — *that* is the will of God. . . . And what do I wish that this Queequeg would do to me? Why, unite with me in my particular Presbyterian form of worship. Consequently, I must then unite with him in his; ergo, I must turn idolater" (p. 54).

The violation of monotheistic exclusivism is immediately linked with Ishmael's acceptance of physical intimacy with Queequeg; "So I kindled the shavings; helped prop up the innocent little idol; offered him burnt biscuit with Queequeg . . . kissed his nose; and that done, we undressed and went to bed. . . . But we did not go to sleep without some little chat. . . . Thus, then, in our hearts' honeymoon, lay I and Queequeg — a cosy, loving pair" ("A Bosom Friend," p. 54). The orthodox connection between homosexuality and idolatry is thus presented most clearly as its meaning is repudiated. Melville endows Ishmael's personal explorations with an independence of spirit abhorrent to orthodox thought, arranging his departure into the wonderworld of meditation with a deliberate scoff at Calvinist doctrines of man's spiritual blindness.

This burlesque prepares for Melville's elaboration of the positive values implicit in Ishmael's relationship with the generous savage. He uses that relationship to develop the religious outlook

---

7. *The New England Primer; Containing the Assembly's Catechism,* pp. 39-40. Sealts, No. 384.

that Ishmael expresses in his refusal to believe "that the magnanimous God of heaven and earth — pagans and all included
— can possibly be jealous of an insignificant bit of black wood"
("A Bosom Friend," p. 54). The strenuous austerity of Father
Mapple's service contrasts with the relaxed intimacy of this
friendship in a way that indicates the difference in spirit between
the worship of a holy God who tolerates no rivals, and a magnanimous God who is too wealthy in spirit to be jealous.

Melville extends the religious meanings of the friendship between Ishmael and Queequeg as he emphasizes the hostility it
aroused. When a bumpkin jeers at him, Queequeg flips the of-
fender over in a somersault as though he were a child, arousing
cries of "devil" and "cannibal." Melville thus identifies the attitudes of the mockers with the same context of value that had
controlled Ishmael's initial reaction to Queequeg, and he then
arranges for the brawny savage to rescue from drowning the
man he had just chastized. To Ishmael, Queequeg's unassuming
heroism reveals his conviction that "It's a mutual, joint-stock
world, in all meridians. We cannibals must help these Christians" ("Wheelbarrow," p. 61). The vision of an ideal mutuality
of fellow beings which transcends the separations between Christian and idolator, civilized and savage, is implicit in the friendship of Ishmael and Queequeg.

Ishmael further explains the religious meaning he sees in
Queequeg's humanity when he is directly challenged by Christian exclusivism. Before signing Queequeg on to the *Pequod,* Captain Bildad insists that he "must show that he's converted. Son
of darkness . . . art thou at present in communion with any Christian church?" Ishmael seeks to stave off the inquiry by counter-
ing that Queequeg is a member of "the First Congregational
Church." But Bildad presses his questions home, and forces Ishmael to make himself clear: "I mean, sir, the same ancient Catholic Church to which you and I, and Captain Peleg there, and
Queequeg here, and all of us, and every mother's son and soul
of us belong; the great and everlasting First Congregation of
this whole worshipping world; we all belong to that; only some
of us cherish some queer crotchets noways touching the grand
belief; in *that* we all join hands" ("His Mark," p. 83).

Ishmael dreams of a universal religion that does justice to

what is genuine in the diverse pieties of the "whole worshipping world." The hope that men could join hand to hand in a common reverence is prompted by Ishmael's belief that all men worship; this common experience indicates the possibility of a non-exclusive faith. The meaning of the reverent commonalty thus envisioned would appear to support Ishmael's refusal to recognize a monopoly of religious truth in the "queer crochets" of any particular piety. Ishmael expresses his contempt for exclusivist communities as he arrives at the fullest declaration of this "democratic faith." "Men may seem detestable as joint stock-companies and nations," he declares, but man in the ideal is the bearer of a "democratic dignity which, on all hands, radiates without end from God; Himself!" It is man's relation to this "great democratic God" which makes him "so noble and so sparkling, such a grand and glowing creature." "The great God absolute!" Ishmael exclaims, "The centre and circumference of all democracy! His omnipresence, our divine equality!" ("Knights and Squires," p. 104).

Melville appeals to this god as he declares his intention to "ascribe high qualities" to the renegades and castaways of his tale. With evident reference to Ahab, he prays "if even the most mournful, perchance the most abased, among them all, shall at times lift himself to the exalted mounts . . . then against all mortal critics bear me out in it, thou just Spirit of Equality" ("Knights and Squires," pp. 104-105). But his doubt concerning the ultimate warrant for his faith in human dignity receives expression even in the midst of this grand celebration. He invokes the "spectacle of a valor-ruined man" as so shameful that "piety itself " cannot "completely stifle her upbraidings against the permitting stars" (p. 104). This comment recalls Melville's ambiguous reflections on the "democratic Spirit of Christianity" in "Hawthorne and His Mosses" and points forward to his analysis of Starbuck's moral collapse. Melville's ardent desire to believe in the "great democratic God" here contends with the skeptical resistance aroused by his awareness that human dignity can be destroyed by the cruelties of fate. Correspondingly, his presentation of Queequeg is complicated by a skeptical crosscurrent that qualifies further the definition of Ishmael as a searcher for Truth.

Having developed Queequeg as a figure of what is genuine in man's religiousness, Melville uses his practices as a vehicle for religious satire. Queequeg comes to believe that his wooden god Yojo has chosen a whaleship upon which employment will be found and that if Ishmael is sent out alone he will "infallibly light upon [it], for all the world as though it turned out by chance" ("The Ship," p. 66). Queequeg believes very firmly in the good and merciful ways of Yojo's providence, despite dismaying evidences to the contrary. He believes in him "as a rather good sort of god, who perhaps meant well enough upon the whole, but in all cases did not succeed in his benevolent designs" (p. 66). Melville's evident target is Christian liberals, whose effort to maintain that benevolence is God's supreme attribute encountered serious difficulties with the "problem of evil." That Yojo's dispensations lead to the embarkation of Ishmael and Queequeg upon the *Pequod* is Melville's earliest exploitation of the story of that fated craft as an attack upon Christian liberalism. But if Queequeg's faith shares the fatuity of liberalism, it also displays the rigidness of orthodoxy.

When Ishmael returns from his interview on the *Pequod,* he finds Queequeg in the midst of his Ramadan. Ishmael is so dismayed by the sufferings required by the long fast that he gives Queequeg a lecture on comparative religion in order to show that such observances are "stark nonsense; bad for the health; useless for the soul; opposed, in short, to the obvious laws of Hygiene and common sense" ("The Ramadan," p. 81). Ishmael's speech is founded on his belief that a man's religion should not be permitted to become a "positive torment to him," and that when it "makes this earth of ours an uncomfortable inn to lodge in," it should be corrected. But Queequeg does not believe that religion is meant to serve human comfort; like the orthodox of more familiar persuasions, he regards divine truth as the measure of man, not *vice versa.* Thus Ishmael states that Queequeg "thought he knew a good deal more about the true religion than I did. He looked at me with a sort of condescending concern and compassion, as though he thought it a great pity that such a sensible young man should be so hopelessly lost to evangelical pagan piety" (pp. 81-82).

This evident satire against orthodox "evangelicals" extends

a parody on the doctrine of original sin given earlier in this exchange, when Ishmael informs Queequeg that "hell is an idea first born on an undigested apple-dumpling; and since then per-petuated through the hereditary dyspepsias nurtured by Rama-dans" ("The Ramadan," p. 82). But despite Melville's use of Queequeg to direct satire against remoter targets, like the "he-reditary dyspepsias" of orthodox dogma, it is quite evident that he also intends to bring Queequeg's personal religiousness under fire. Queequeg's "condescending concern and compassion" be-tray the same ludicrous complacency that Captain Bildad evinces when he gives Queequeg a tract entitled "The Latter Day Coming; or No Time to Lose" ("His Mark," p. 85).

In the midst of his admiration for Queequeg, Ishmael remains alone in his skeptical tolerance, his determination to "cherish the greatest respect towards everybody's religious obligations, never mind how comical." He argues that "we good Presbyterian Christians should be charitable in these things, and not fancy ourselves so vastly superior to other mortals, pagans and what not," but not on the ground that the non-christian religions of the world are innocent of nonsense. On the contrary he asserts that Queequeg's piety is filled with "half-crazy conceits," and "absurd notions," and he extends this awareness to make a fur-ther observation about man's religiousness. Not only are all men at one in their instinct for worship, they are also universally subject to religious folly. "Heaven have mercy on us all — Pres-byterians and Pagans alike — for we are all somehow dreadfully cracked about the head, and sadly need mending" ("The Rama-dan," p. 78). If there is something genuine in all human worship, there is equally a pervasive absurdity, something approaching madness in the "somehow dreadfully cracked" religiousness of man. Innate to this spiritual liability is the impulse to assume a stance of self-righteous superiority over any who do not share one's own beliefs.

In a work so "broiled" in "hell-fire" (*Letters*, p. 133) as *Moby-Dick*, many meanings are conveyed through concepts of the "dev-ilish," but in the sections that portray Ishmael's embarking there is a considerable degree of consistency in the use of such terms. "Devilishness" is imputed to the outsider by those who are trapped by a limited religious and cultural outlook. Ishmael first

perceives Queequeg as devilish, as does the bumpkin who insults
Queequeg, and also the pious Bildad, who was so rigidly enclosed that "all his subsequent ocean life, and the sight of many
unclad, lovely island creatures . . . had not moved this native
born Quaker one single jot" ("The Ship," p. 72). The provincia-
lism that disdains the "outlandish" corresponds to a religious
impulse that claims universal validity for limited truths, brand-
ing alien pieties as damnable. Melville implies that an authentic
religious quest will transgress the intellectual and spiritual
boundaries thus created, so that the searcher must accept the
stigma of "devilishness"; he must seek Truth in realms considered the domain of the Evil One. Ishmael's friendship with the
frightful head-peddling cannibal, and his acceptance of the deri-
sion it invites, confirm this aspect of his definition as a searcher
for Truth.

But the glimpses of a "magnanimous god" that Melville
derives from the friendship of Ishmael and Queequeg do not
amount to the assertion that human fellowship is the avenue
to an adequate vision. On the contrary, Melville's estimate of
man's communal intolerance led him to consider the relinquish-
ment of fellowship an essential of the quest. Such considerations
account for the peculiar blend of irony and sympathy with which
Melville presents Father Mapple. The juxtaposition of Queequeg's worship with Mapple's is not intended to obliterate the
appeal of the preacher's staunch integrity. Melville celebrates
Mapple's lonely and heroic fidelity because he recognizes it as
a virtue required for any quester who proposes to transcend the
limitations imposed on the search for Truth by the exclusivist
folly in which even Queequeg participates.

Several converging patterns of allusion strengthen Ishmael's
identification as one whose isolation is forced upon him by religious exclusivism. The Biblical Ishmael was not only a wanderer;
he was an outcast. God promised Abraham that Sarah, his aged
wife, should bear him a son, and that this child should found
a people who would be God's chosen. When the child of promise
arrived, Ishmael and his mother, Hagar, were driven out of the
holy family because Sarah did not want them to share the inheritance with her own child (Genesis 21:10). Melville's Ishmael
seeks employment among the Quakers of Nantucket, whom the

Puritans drove out of New England as they sought to preserve
the purity of their sacred community.[8] He chooses, under the
providence of a wooden idol, to set out on a ship named for
"a celebrated tribe of Massachusetts Indians, now extinct as the
ancient Medes" ("The Ship," p. 67). The Pequods (Pequots)
had been rendered extinct by the Puritans, who waged a war
of total extermination against them. The Puritans justified this
action on Biblical grounds, citing the wholesale massacres Joshua conducted to eliminate the idolatrous tribes who occupied
the promised land before the arrival of God's chosen from
Egypt.[9] And finally the mad sea captain, whose "quenchless
feud" Ishmael for a time wholly shares, is named for an Old
Testament king whose major crime was that he reinstated the
worship of the excluded Canaanite divinities in the midst of
the holy land. All these allusions invoke cases in which God's
self-styled historical darlings banished or destroyed those whose
divergent character appeared to threaten the claims of the sacred
group. Because the exclusiveness of particular religious communities necessitates hostility against those who disagree, the one
who seeks a comprehensive vision must be an Ishmael.

The effort to transcend the "queer crotchets" of parochial
faiths reveals a criterion of Ishmael's quest; he seeks a universal
Truth that acknowledges the innate human dignity shared by
Christian and cannibal alike. His quest therefore is inherently
theocentric, aiming toward the realization of a single divine reality which is conceived to lie at the heart of moral Truth. He
wants to vindicate his faith in the "great God absolute! The
centre and circumference of all democracy!" ("Knights and
Squires," p. 104). The possibility of squaring such a vision of
ultimate reality with the experiences of life is a topic of his continuing inner debate.

As he pursues his meditations, Ishmael continues to display
a flexibility of imagination in which cultural boundaries are de-
nied the status of ultimate boundaries; he goes on sympa-

---

8. Lydia S. Hinchman, *Early Settlers of Nantucket* (Philadelphia, 1901), pp.
15 f. See also Charles Frederick Holder, *The Quakers in Great Britain and America*
(New York, 1913), pp. 465 f.

9. Roy Harvey Pearce, "The 'Ruines of Mankind': The Indian and the
Puritan Mind," *Journal of the History of Ideas,* 13 (1952), 205.

thetically exploring the essential humanity shared by men of
sharply differing character and conviction. He is likewise receptive to the intimations of spiritual meaning that he receives in
contemplating the world of nature, and although those intimations finally refuse to compose themselves in a unitary religious
vision, Ishmael does not impose his private desire for coherence
upon them. Even as the prospects of his quest darken, he remains
unceasingly hospitable to new impressions; his consciousness remains open to the abundant possibilities of meaning that are
suggested to him in "the watery part of the world."

VI

The Dignity of Man: Mapple and Bulkington

W hen he invoked the "just Spirit of Equali-
ty," Melville voiced the religious vision he derived from his fundamental moral commitment to the dignity of man. Like others
who sought to conceive a God who respects the liberal estimate
of man's dignity, Melville was forced to recognize that the spectacle of worldly evil created an anomaly, a body of undeniable
fact that could not be digested within any scheme of supernal
benevolence. But Melville also knew that this "problem of evil"
does not arise within an orthodox frame of reference. His meditations upon the meaning of human suffering are immeasurably
deepened because he explores the implications of Calvin's belief
that man cannot suffer unmerited affliction.

Father Mapple's sermon arises directly from that orthodox
piety which liberals considered an insult to human dignity. He
presents the whale's attack upon Jonah as an instance of God's
wrath against the original sin in which all men live. There can
be no unjustified worldly suffering, in the orthodox view, since
all the miseries of this mortal life cannot satisfy God's indignation against the innate refusal of men to obey him.

Mapple points out that "all the things that God would have
us do are hard for us" because "if we obey God, we must disobey
ourselves; and it is in this disobeying ourselves, wherein the
hardness of obeying God consists" ("The Sermon," p. 45). The
Calvinist God does not seek compliance by appealing to reason
and the moral sense; man must be brought to violate the dictates
of his fallen nature. Thus Father Mapple observes that God "of-

tener commands us than endeavors to persuade" (p. 45). He
offers Jonah's story as an example of God's way with human
recalcitrance; because of Jonah's disobedience, "God came upon
him in the whale, and swallowed him down" (p. 50).

Mapple orders his treatment of Jonah in accordance with the
doctrine of man's depravity, as it was applied to spiritual life
in the evangelical tradition, whose emphasis on "rebirth" had
influenced the Dutch Church from its earliest period in America.[1] Doddridge's *Rise and Progress˙ of Religion in the Soul* (which
Melville's orthodox grandmother owned) traced a turbulent spiritual regeneration in which the sinner is "awakened," "sen-
tenced," "struck with the terror of his sentence," and then receives "news of salvation."[2] In introducing the Jonah story,
Father Mapple declares: "As sinful men, it is a lesson to us
all, because it is a story of the sin, hard-heartedness, suddenly
awakened fears, the swift punishment, repentance, prayers, and
finally the deliverance and joy of Jonah" ("The Sermon," p.
45).[3] The hymn sung in the Whaleman's Chapel, a close adapta-

---

1. James Tanis, *Dutch Calvinistic Pietism in the Middle Colonies: A Study in
the Life and Theology of Theodorus Jacobus Frelinghuysen* (The Hague, 1967), pp.
111 f. The theme of "rebirth" has been recognized as central to *Moby-Dick*,
but the shape Melville gives it through his use of pietist teaching has not.
For a good discussion see William Rosenfeld, "Uncertain Faith: Queequeg's
Coffin and Melville's Use of the Bible," *Texas Studies in Literature and Language*,
7 (1966), 317-327.

2. Philip Doddridge, *The Rise and Progress of Religion in the Soul* (New York:
American Tract Society, n.d.). The terms quoted are from the outline in the
Table of Contents.

3. Nathalia Wright, *Melville's Use of the Bible* (Durham, 1949), pp. 82-89,
observes rightly that Mapple's presentation of the Jonah story does not correspond closely to the Biblical account. In accordance with her thesis that Old
Testament "patterns of prophecy" inform *Moby-Dick*, Wright argues that Melville shaped Mapple's version of Jonah to "the story of another Old Testament
prophet: Jeremiah." Lawrance Thompson argues that Melville creates a
"Mapple-sermon trap which encourages a certain kind of reader to make his
ultimate interpretation in terms of Christian doctrine." Thompson asserts that
Melville achieves an "equivocal insinuation ... by arranging to let Father
Mapple illuminate the Christian doctrine of repentance, submission, obedience, in terms of querulous Jonah. The total action of the Jonah story,
in the Old Testament, provides us with a picture of a headstrong, recalcitrant,
God-challenging prophet, whose one supreme moment of surrender to God's
will occurred only after God had scared poor Jonah witless." See Lawrance
Thompson, *Melville's Quarrel with God* (Princeton, 1952), pp. 163-164, 428. Recognizing Calvinist interpretations of Jonah as the source of Melville's treat-

tion of a hymn used by the Dutch Reformed Church,[4] stresses
the central transaction of this "progress," the acute crisis in
which the sinner comes to an awareness of his own total helplessness and calls upon God for rescue:

I saw the open maw of hell,
    With endless pains and sorrows there;
Which none but they that feel can tell —
    Oh, I was plunging to despair

In black distress, I called my God,
    When I could scarce believe him mine,
He bowed his ear to my complaints —
    No more the whale did me confine. (p. 44).

When Channing asserted that the Calvinistic system had persisted because of the influence of fear on men's minds, he struck
at the vital center of orthodox piety. The primal dread inherent
in man's awareness of the holy was given a decidedly moral
cast in the devotional tradition of Protestant orthodoxy.[5] The
radical contingency of mortal existence was experienced as helplessness in the midst of deadly moral depravity, a helplessness
which demonstrated the absolute need for a savior. Melville's
profound appropriation of this tradition extended beyond a
knowledge of its doctrinal outworkings; in Father Mapple's sermon God's righteous judgment operates through the textures
of Jonah's intimate life.

Melville subtly depicts the writhings of conscience suffered
by one who can neither escape or relieve his own guilt. "Like
one who after a night of drunken revelry hies to his bed, still
reeling, but with conscience yet pricking him, as the plungings
of the Roman race-horse but so much the more strike his steel
tags into him; as one who in that miserable plight still turns
and turns in giddy anguish, praying God for annihilation until

ment gives us a more fruitful explanation of Melville's deviations from the
Biblical story and of his stress upon Jonah's terror.

4. David Battenfield, "The Source for the Hymn in *Moby-Dick*," *American
Literature*, 27 (1955), 393-396.

5. Rudolf Otto, *The Idea of the Holy*, trans. John W. Harvey (1923; reptd.
New York, 1963), pp. 12-30.

the fit be passed; and at last amid the whirl of woe he feels, a deep stupor steals over him, as over the man who bleeds to death, for conscience is the wound, and there's naught to staunch it; so, after sore wrestlings in his berth, Jonah's prodigy of ponderous misery drags him drowning down to sleep" ("The Sermon," pp. 47-48). This sentence, with its blending images of torment and deadly exhaustion, with its periods suspended until the parallel of sleep and dying is fully established, and resolved in the funereal sonority of "drags him drowning down," has a dynamic structure that is perfectly suited to its place in Father Mapple's Calvinistic exhortation. It conveys the futile strivings of the depraved heart. Putting out phrase after phrase as though resisting the inevitable conclusion in death, this sentence expresses the religious desperation felt by a man whose sin is innate, so that all his efforts to escape it are themselves infected and only worsen his plight.

But Jonah in the horrors of guilt is not yet truly repentant; God's righteous vengeance against sin has not displayed its full terrors. The awesome might and presumed ferocity of the whale were a symbol in the conventions of orthodox interpretation for the wrath of God. In the famous retort by which God had silenced the rebellious questions of Job, Leviathan was adduced as a manifestation of divine power aroused against human impudence. Calvin published sixty-five sermons on the Book of Job, and in the tradition that he established, the Leviathan was typically identified as the whale, and was invoked to terrify impudent sinners. God "can destroy us, sooner than Leviathan can crush us, were we between his teeth. The consideration of the terribleness that is in any Creature; should lead us to consider how terrible the Lord is to those who provoke him. Are the teeth of a Leviathan ... terrible? ... How terrible then is the wrath of God!"[6]

When this terror inspires a proper repentance, the sinner recognizes that God has been righteous in his dreadful inflictions. The doctrine of total depravity implies the requirement of total self-abhorrence from the convicted sinner. As sinful men, we must "be willing to own the vengeance of Almighty God, and

6. Joseph Caryl, *An Exposition with Practical Observations upon the Book of Job*, 2 vols. (London, 1676-1677), II, 2249.

to judge ourselves, to justify him that may condemn us, and
be witnesses against ourselves."[7] Accordingly, Father Mapple
celebrates Jonah's eventual submission: "Jonah does not weep
and wail for direct deliverance. He feels that his dreadful punishment is just ... And here, shipmates, is true and faithful repentance; not clamorous for pardon, but grateful for punishment.
And how pleasing to God was this conduct in Jonah, is shown
in the eventual deliverance of him from the sea and the whale"
("The Sermon," p. 49).

Jonah's strenuous passage under the wrath of God leads finally
to his redemption; he emerges reborn from the belly of the
whale, entirely reshaped to serve his Master's purposes. The
hymn, whose pattern corresponds to the emotional direction of
the sermon, ends with an exultant celebration of God's rescue.
Melville says that Mapple started reading it in "prolonged solemn tones" and in the closing lines "burst forth with a pealing
exultation and joy" ("The Sermon," p. 44). Likewise, Mapple
concludes the sermon with an excited evocation of the fulfillment that belongs to him who, by learning to disobey himself,
becomes a true child of God: "And eternal delight and deli-
ciousness will be his, who coming to lay him down, can say
with his final breath — O Father! — chiefly known to me by
Thy rod — mortal or immortal, here I die. I have striven to
be Thine, more than to be this world's, or mine own" (p. 51.).

* * *

Calvinism taught that joyous reconciliation with God and
adoption into his service must be achieved by way of submission
to his wrath as it manifests itself in everything that crosses the
natural man and awakens his fear. Calvin himself, discussing
the Leviathan in Job, declared that God "allureth us to him,
to the intent that we should find all joyfulness there, but yet
can we not come at him, till we have been utterly beaten down.
Therefore there must first go a fear before."[8] Man must humble
himself before God's awful majesty, and when the correcting

---

7. Edward Reynolds, *Works*, 6 vols. (London, 1826), I, 111. This reissue
of the works of Reynolds, a seventeenth century English divine, was greeted
with enthusiasm by the Dutch Reformed. See *Magazine of the Reformed Dutch
Church*, 4 (April 1829-March 1830), 61.

8. John Calvin, *Sermons ... upon the Book of Job*, trans. Arthur Golding (London, 1574), p. 803.

rod is applied, must kiss it. When Melville encountered in his Bible the statement that "the patient in spirit is better than the proud in spirit," it seemed to him a paradigm of Christian teaching; "Christianity this," he noted in the margin.[9]

Despite the appealing burliness of the masterful Father Mapple, Melville gives evidence of having felt that the practical lesson implicit in his teaching undercut manliness. He says that the "soft, curled, hermaphroditical Italian pictures" of Christ most successfully embody "his idea," and that "destitute as they are of all brawniness, [they] hint nothing of any power, but the mere negative, feminine one of submission and endurance, which on all hands it is conceded, form the peculiar practical virtues of his teachings" ("The Tail," p. 315). If a man must abhor every impulse by which he may resist the infliction of punishments when they come from God, then it is hard to see how he is to resist any impositions upon his person. Carried to one logical extreme, the doctrine of total depravity would seem to imply an unceasing abjectness.

If the "feminine" virtue of submission is an apparent implication of Father Mapple's doctrine, it is not at all characteristic of his person. This pastor preached humility to God with all the force of his "own inexorable self "; his formidable manfulness had been sanctified by a regeneration such as his treatment of Jonah commends. In describing Mapple, Melville alludes to the text on which the rebirth doctrine was founded, in which Nicodemus asked Jesus how a man could be born again when he is old (John 3:4); he tells us that Mapple had entered "that sort of old age which seems merging into a second flowering youth, for among all the fissures of his wrinkles, there shone certain mild gleams of a newly developing bloom" ("The Pulpit," p. 42). We find in Mapple that harmonious blend of humility and manliness which characterized Jacob Brodhead, the pastor in whom Melville first encountered the heroic orthodox spirituality that Mapple displays.

Melville presents a contrasting style of manliness in the aloof and sober Bulkington. With "noble shoulders, and a chest like a coffer-dam," Bulkington is idolized by his fellow sailors, and

9. *The Holy Bible . . . Together with the Apocrypha* (Philadelphia, 1846). Sealts, No. 62. Ecclesiastes 7:8.

considerately accepts their admiration; but his face bears the mark of "some reminiscences that did not seem to give him much joy" ("The Spouter-Inn," p. 23). He always puts back out to sea as soon as his voyages end, and Melville offers this peculiar habit as the image of a desperate effort to maintain intellectual independence. When a storm threatens to drive a ship against the shore, it must fight the winds to stand clear; so Bulkington in his tumult of remembered woe struggles to maintain his self-possession. Father Mapple had taught that salvation comes through being overwhelmed, through accepting the fury of nature as divine fury against sin; but Melville establishes Bulkington as the figure of a manliness that pits itself against the storm. He invokes the orthodox belief that an inveterate hostility exists between human striving for self-sufficiency and God's sovereign power, but he reverses its valuations. Bulkington becomes a symbol of that "mortally intolerable truth; that all deep, earnest thinking is but the intrepid effort of the soul to keep the open independence of her sea; while the wildest winds of heaven and earth conspire to cast her on the treacherous, slavish shore" ("The Lee Shore," p. 97).

Melville expresses utter contempt for the cowardice of submission. "Better is it to perish in that howling infinite, than be ingloriously dashed upon the lee, even if that were safety! For worm-like, then, oh! who would craven crawl to land!" ("The Lee Shore," p. 97). Against the background of Father Mapple's sermon, Bulkington's struggle is thrown into relief as an effort to maintain his masculine self-sufficiency in the face of a God who raises storms in order to humiliate his creatures. The pride of physical honor is joined with spiritual pride in the contemptuous refusal to submit.

In Father Mapple heroic manliness and humility before the manifestations of God's wrath were at one. The interior of the Whaleman's Chapel was decorated with a large painting of a "gallant ship beating against a terrible storm off a lee coast of black rocks and snowy breakers" ("The Pulpit," p. 43), while an angel's face beams down encouragement through a rift in the clouds. Using the plight of a ship off the lee shore as the figure of opposed spiritual stances, Melville points the contrast between the heroism of orthodox faith, which braves the disdain of men under the favor of God, and the heroism which braves hostility from man and God alike in the effort to maintain total self-sufficiency and independence. No angel smiles on Bulkington, for Bulkington seeks to achieve godhood himself in deadly contention with the storm. "Bear thee grimly, demigod!" Melville exclaims, "Up from the spray of thy ocean-perishing — straight up, leaps thy apotheosis!" ("The Lee Shore," p. 98).

The opposing styles of spiritual heroism that Melville presents in Bulkington and Father Mapple provide a matrix of intellectual and spiritual issues in which the grander heroism of Captain Ahab can be defined. Melville was aware that he faced the problem of giving his old whale-hunter the stature of a tragic hero, that his protagonist lacked the impressive royal trappings that distinguished Shakespeare's tragic monarchs. "Oh, Ahab! what shall be grand in thee, it must needs be plucked at from the skies, and dived for in the deep, and featured in the unbodied air!" ("The Specksynder," p. 130). Ahab's heroism is distinctively spiritual; it stands upon his relationship to a set of vitally significant ideas. Melville endows his quest with meanings that go to the heart of the liberal-orthodox controversy concerning the moral relations of God and man; he uses Ahab to explore the fate of human dignity in a world seemingly controlled by an enraged Calvinist God.

VII

Ahab Reprobate

We receive our first impressions of Ahab from Captain Peleg, a crusty Nantucketer who shares ownership of the *Pequod* with Captain Bildad. Melville intimates a great deal about the unseen Ahab through his portrayal of the relations between Peleg and Bildad. Bildad's name recalls the pious "comforter" who sought to bully Job into a confession of sins he had not committed, on the ground that Job's affliction must be a just punishment from God (Job 8:2-22; 18:1-21; 25:2-6). Melville's Bildad, similarly, tries to intimidate Peleg with threatening references to God's judgment, hoping to elicit a coward's penitence: "as thou art still an impenitent man, Captain Peleg, I greatly fear lest thy conscience be but a leaky one; and will in the end sink thee foundering down to the fiery pit, Captain Peleg." To which Peleg replies: "Fiery pit! fiery pit! ye insult me, man; past all natural bearing, ye insult me. It's an all-fired outrage to tell any human creature that he's bound to hell" ("The Ship," p. 75).

This exchange gives substance to the comparison Peleg makes shortly afterward between Ahab and himself. "I know what he is — a good man — not a pious, good man, like Bildad, but a swearing good man — something like me" ("The Ship," p. 77). Peleg's bluster foreshadows Ahab's cosmic fury; Ahab is enraged by what it means to be "bound to hell." Perceiving the "outrage" of his own damnation, Ahab is obsessed by its implications, so that his entire nature is absorbed in metaphysical revolt. "Gifted with the high perception, I lack the low, enjoying power; damned, most subtly and most malignantly! damned in the midst of Paradise!" ("Sunset," p. 147).

Melville establishes an elaborate antithesis between Mapple's Jonah and the mad sea captain. Whereas Jonah accepts the whale's attack as divine correction, Ahab takes it as a cosmic affront: Jonah yields to the dread power in fear; Ahab resists it in unceasing fury. Jonah is reduced to total self-abhorrence; Ahab recoils in a gigantic self-assertion. Jonah moves on from his experience to do his Lord's bidding; Ahab sets out upon an "audacious, immitigable, and supernatural revenge" ("Moby Dick," p. 162). Behind this antithesis lies a contrast of types with which Melville had become familiar as a child. Mapple's Jonah is a paradigm of the relations between the Calvinist God and his elect; Captain Ahab is a paradigm of the relations between the Calvinist God and the reprobate, the natural man left in his sin. Thomas Robinson's *Scripture Characters,* an early nineteenth century orthodox commentary for use in families, explains that while the sacred records "relate chiefly to those, who were 'redeemed,' " they also bring before us examples of "our nature in a state of awful degeneracy." King Ahab is proposed as "a sinner of peculiar infamy, depraved beyond the common measure of his species."[1] This popular interpretation of Ahab reflects a tradition descending from Calvin himself, in which the Old Testament king is used as a prime example of the way God deals with the worst of sinners. Melville draws heavily on this tradition in portraying Ahab's refusal to be awed by the divine anger that he perceives in the whale's attack upon himself.

Robinson discusses King Ahab as stubbornly persisting in his wickedness despite the punishments God inflicted upon him. "Ahab himself felt the distress, but was not humbled by it." God's efforts to chasten Ahab had an effect which showed that God's saving grace was not at work in Ahab's heart: "Some bold offenders become the more obdurate under the divine corrections. Such is the hardness and impenitence of the human heart, that neither mercies nor judgments will of themselves, soften or subdue it."[2] The reprobate cannot repent because the grace required to redeem his hard heart is not supplied; but

1. Thomas Robinson, *Scripture Characters, or a Practical Improvement of the Principal Histories in the Old and New Testaments,* 4 vols. (London, 1808), II, 240.
2. *Ibid.,* p. 244.

God nonetheless punishes him. In the story of the ten plagues of Egypt, Calvinists found evidence for their view that repeated applications of divine judgment against such a man will produce a steadily escalating fury. "What desperate and horrible rage did the heart of Pharaoh swell into, when, in the midst of those fearful judgements, he hardened his heart, and exalted himself."[3]

Melville traces in Captain Ahab just such a mounting pattern of resistance to the divine inflictions. The earliest description of Ahab's appearance indicates that he had already been exposed to penal fires, but that they had only hardened him. "He looked like a man cut away from the stake, when the fire has overrunningly wasted all the limbs without consuming them, or taking away one particle from their compacted aged robustness" ("Ahab," pp. 109-110). Melville explicitly associates Ahab's "infinity of . . . unsurrenderable wilfulness" with the "crucifixion in his face," and declares that Ahab stood before his crew "in all the nameless regal overbearing dignity of some mighty woe" (p. 111).

Calvinistic writers recognized clearly that natural disaster might stir a man to anger against the God who ordained it, since they considered enmity against God an essential impulse of the depraved heart. They insisted that such anger must be turned against the self, so as to make for repentance. "Do not repine at God's providence, nor quarrel with the dumb creatures; but let thine indignation reflect upon thine own heart."[4] After Ahab reveals to the crew his wild plan to take revenge on the whale, Starbuck objects in terms that invoke this admonition: "To be enraged with a dumb thing . . . seems blasphemous." But Ahab replies in a frenzy: "Talk not to me of blasphemy, man; I'd strike the sun if it insulted me" ("The Quarterdeck," p. 144).

God's "Mene, Mene, Tekel Upharsin" of electric fire in the *Pequod's* cordage so awes the crew that Starbuck brings them to the point of giving up the chase: "God, God is against thee, old man; forbear!" ("The Candles," p. 418). But Ahab seizes his harpoon all glowing with the fires, terrifying the crew by

---

3. Edward Reynolds, *Works,* 6 vols. (London, 1826), I, 158.
4. *Ibid.,* p. 76.

his own rage and boldness so that they obey him rather than
the apparent divine will. The rage of Ahab comes to its height
as the "god-bullied hull" of the *Pequod* is settling into the deep,
and he darts his harpoon into the whale crying, "from hell's
heart I stab at thee; for hate's sake I. spit my last breath at
thee. . . . *Thus,* I give up the spear! " ("The Chase—Third Day,"
p. 468).

The context of orthodox belief that gives cosmic meaning to
Ahab's rage bears also upon the terror that he faces down in
pursuing his quest. Orthodox teachers claimed that all human
fears testify to the vengeance of God that is implicit in every
worldly menace: "the consciences of all mankind concur to cor-
roborate this truth." From this source "every word of dire meaning and evil omen, as *terror, horror, tremor* . . . have derived their
origin. Conscious to themselves of their wickedness, and convinced of the divine dominion over them . . . [sinners reveal]
that he with whom they have to do is supremely just, and the
avenger of all sin."[5] Ahab's rebellion against "divine dominion"
requires him to suppress this terror in himself. As he approaches
the Straits of Sunda through which he must pass in order to
find his albino quarry, he encounters whales and chases them
through the straits. It soon appears that he himself is pursued
by pirates at his rear. When Ahab "bethought him that through
that gate [the straits] lay the route to his vengeance, and beheld,
how that through that same gate hs was now both chasing and
being chased to his deadly end; and not only that, but a herd
of remorseless wild pirates and inhuman atheistical devils were
infernally cheering him on with their curses; — when all these
conceits had passed through his brain, Ahab's brow was left
gaunt and ribbed, like the black sand beach after some stormy
tide has been gnawing it, without being able to drag the firm
thing from its place" ("The Grand Armada," p. 321).

The orthodox considered such conscious resistance to divine
warnings an example of reprobate fury in its distinctively intellectual aspect: reprobate madness. When the wickedness of man

5. John Owen, "A Dissertation on Divine Justice," in *Works,* ed. William
H. Goold, 16 vols. (London, 1967), X, 519. Owen's works were a durable
staple of Calvinist teaching. The *Magazine of the Dutch Reformed Church,* 3 (April
1828-March 1829), 141, referred to him as the "prince of theologians."

"rises up to rage or madness, it will also condemn all these [signs], even the rod, and him that hath appointed it." God ordains the insanity of rage to confound the reprobate, to check his potential destructiveness, and to bring about his ruin in a way that will provide a salutary lesson for the faithful. The destruction of the reprobate, while it is fully ordered and controlled by God, is nonetheless arranged so as to make it evident that the reprobate has brought his destruction upon himself. Thus, "sinners that are wholly under the power of this rage, are said, to 'run upon God, and the thick bosses of his buckler' . . . that wherein he is armed for their utter ruin."[6] God brings the reprobate to his end by working upon the inmost fabric of his person, crazing his mind and hardening his heart. As Calvin himself stated, God "knows how to shatter the wickedness of our enemies in various ways. For sometimes he takes away their understanding so that they are unable to comprehend anything sane or sober, as when he sends forth Satan to fill the mouths of all the prophets with falsehood in order to deceive Ahab."[7] Melville marked in his Bible the verse that declares God's sovereign freedom in this matter: "Therefore hath he mercy on whom he will have mercy, and whom he will he hardeneth."[8]

A notable symptom of reprobate madness is the failure to recognize how magnificent a display of God's justice this is. Fallen men, in their deluded pride of reason, typically perceive this arrangement as unjust. But the orthodox taught that as God's law requires infinitely more than man can perform, so his truth presents an impenetrable mystery to unaided understanding. To Calvinist interpreters, man's dissatisfaction with God's decrees was the primary evidence for the weakness of mortal reason before the ineffable mysteries of the divine being.

Calvin was asked how he could possibly affirm that God decreed the fall of Adam, and hence the doings and miseries of all the resultant damned souls, without reflecting adversely on

---

6. John Owen, *The Nature, Power, Deceit and Prevalency of Indwelling Sin in Believers* (Philadelphia, n.d.), p. 91.

7. John Calvin, *Institutes of the Christian Religion*, ed. John T. McNeill, trans. F. L. Battles, 2 vols. (Philadelphia, 1960), I, 219.

8. *The New Testament . . . The Book of Psalms* (New York, 1844). Sealts, No. 65. Romans 9:18.

God's justice. But Calvin did not give reasons that conceded
the validity of the question. The very suggestion that God might
be the "author of sin" was evidence enough for Calvin that his
disputants were in no condition to discuss questions of the nature
of God. Calvin warned them, rather, against impious madness:

> "Although, therefore, I thus affirm that God did ordain
> the Fall of Adam, I so assert it as by no means to concede
> that God was therein properly and really the *author* of that
> Fall. . . . I solemnly hold that man and apostate angels *did,*
> by their sin, *that* which was *contrary* to the will of God, to
> the end that God, by means of their *evil will,* might effect
> that which was *according·* to His *decreeing will.* If anyone should
> reply confess the same. But why should we wonder that the
> *infinte* and incomprehensible majesty of God should surpass
> the narrow limits of our *finite* intellect? So far, however, am
> I from undertaking to explain this sublime and hidden mystery
> by any powers of human reason, that I would ever retain
> in my own memory that which I declared at the commence-
> ment of this discussion — that those who seek to know more
> than God has revealed are *madmen!* Wherefore, let us delight
> ourselves more in wise ignorance than in an immoderate and
> intoxicated curiosity to know more than God permits."[9]

Because Calvin took refuge in God's "incomprehensible majesty" when taxed as to his justice, the term "inscrutable" became a catchword of orthodox polemic. It is twice echoed, signif-
icantly, in the famous passage wherein Ahab expounds his
hatred of the whale. "I see in him outrageous strength, with
an inscrutable malice sinewing it. That inscrutable thing is chiefly what I hate" ("The Quarter-deck," p. 144).

The thrust of intellect in Ahab is the madness of one who
refuses to submit to the "inscrutable." Just as Father Mapple
had presented the fear of Jonah as the key to the supernal mysteries, so Captain Ahab determines to follow his rage in the
effort to penetrate them. He intends to discover what lies behind
the visible objects of his mortal experience by an act of total

---

9. John Calvin, *Calvin's Calvinism,* trans. Henry Cole (Grand Rapids, 1950),
pp. 126-127. This volume contains Calvin's polemical treatises, "The Eternal
Predestination of God" and "The Secret Providence of God."

intellectual aggression. He conceives the "reasoning thing" behind the objects of experience as shielded by a "mask" no
tougher than "pasteboard." Hence Ahab is confident that with
a plunging intellectual attack, like the darting of his harpoon,
he will be able to "strike through the mask," and liberate himself
from the prison of his intellectual mortality. Since to Ahab the
white whale is the wall of that prison, his quest becomes the
figure of a spirituality that finds its own limitations intolerable.
By killing the whale, he intends to vindicate himself as one who
enjoys in his own person the sovereignty of Truth. "Who's over
me?" he shouts at Starbuck. "Truth hath no confines" ("The
Quarter-deck," p. 144).

Calvinist theory proposed a universe in which independent
thought is tantamount to madness, since the truths of God infinitely transcend man's earthly reason. Accepting that estimate of
the cleavage between the earthly and the heavenly, Melville
proposes that a metaphysical quester might cross the chasm so
as to proclaim "the sane madness of vital truth." He takes the
Calvinist warning against the "madness" of questioning God's
justice and builds it into a celebration of Ahab's spiritual
heroism; a man can discover that God is unjust if he is prepared
to pursue his insights resolutely, beyond that meridian at which
he plunges into madness.

* * *

In order to claim that Calvinism slandered God's justice, liberal theologians conjured up a hypothetical image of divine malignity that Melville uses to define Ahab's vision of the whale.
It was claimed that the doctrine of God's absolute sovereignty
makes him responsible for all misery and evil, and implies that
he created the majority of men for no other destiny than to
suffer. One of Calvin's contemporaries declared that "No beast
is so cruel (to say nothing of man) that it would desire to create
its young to misery."[10] John Taylor's *Scripture Doctrine of Original
Sin* (1740), which Melville read during the composition of *Moby-
Dick*, stated that Calvinist teachings "represent the Divine
Dispensations as unjust, cruel and tyrannical."[11] In nine-

10. *Ibid.*, pp. 264-265.
11. John Taylor, *The Scripture Doctrine of Original Sin, Proposed to a Free and*

teenth-century America, the tide of outrage reached its height as a Methodist theologian declared that if such doctrines were true, the final judgment would turn into a protest rally where "heaven and hell would equally revolt at ... [God's plan], and all rational beings conspire to execrate the almighty monster."[12]

Considering himself damned, Ahab believes that he is contending with just such an almighty monster. In the chapter that explains Ahab's hatred, we are told that the rumors of this whale "did in the end incorporate with themselves all manner of morbid hints, and half-formed foetal suggestions of supernatural agencies" ("Moby Dick," p. 156). Moby Dick is invested with ubiquity and immortality. He exhibits such an "infernal aforethought of ferocity, that every dismembering or death that he caused, was not wholly regarded as having been inflicted by an unintelligent agent" (p. 159).

These statements prepare for the expression of Ahab's vision in language which invokes the specter of a malignant God who, according to an "infernal aforethought of ferocity," created the race of men in order to consign a majority to Satan, and as a means of doing so decreed the fall of Adam. The whale became for Ahab an incarnation of "That intangible malignity which has been from the beginning; to whose dominion even the modern Christians ascribe one-half of the worlds. ... All the subtle demonisms of life and thought; all evil, to crazy Ahab, were visibly personified, and made practically assailable in Moby Dick." The wrath of Calvin's God is suffered by those of his human creatures who do not enjoy the sovereign favor of his grace. According to Calvin's opponents, this procedure involves a "subtle demonism" indeed. Calvin's God damns the reprobate by decreeing that they shall hate him, and thereby displays an

---

Candid Examination (London, 1746), p. 256. Sealts, No. 496. This book, by the Englishman John Taylor of Norwich (1694-1761), was of considerable importance in American religious thought. Jonathan Edwards attacked it extensively in *The Great Christian Doctrine of Original Sin* (1758). See Perry Miller, *Jonathan Edwards* (Cleveland, Ohio, 1959), pp. 273-278. Its repute in Melville's time is indicated by Edward Beecher's reference to it in 1853 as a "celebrated work against original sin" which had an important influence on the New England theology. Beecher viewed *Scripture Doctrine* as a precursor of Unitarianism. See Edward Beecher, *The Conflict of Ages* (Boston, 1853), pp. 333-343.

12. R. S. Foster, *Objections to Calvinism* (Cincinnati, 1849), p. 54.

incalculable (and hateful) hatred of his own. This complex of meaning is invoked in Melville's ambiguous summary sentence. "He [Ahab] piled upon the whale's white hump the sum of all the general rage and hate felt by his whole race from Adam down" ("Moby Dick," p. 160). This rage and hate is felt by the race as an infliction of the rage and hate of God himself. The story of this impacted, reciprocating malevolence begins precisely with Adam.

Ahab's crazy hatred of this whale and his vision of its meaning are strongly akin to "wild rumors" generally abroad in the sperm-whale fishery, a fact which makes it possible for Ahab to secure his crew's agreement to join in the fiery quest. Having gone beyond the "modern Christians" in recognizing that the whole race is subjected to divine rage, Melville places Ahab's reaction in the context of mankind's general disposition toward the Beyond. In "The Quarter-deck" he describes the "magnetic" attraction that springs up between Ahab and the crew as Ahab begins to voice his immitigable hatred. Ahab touches a vein of feeling within his men that has been buried so deep that they themselves were scarcely aware of it. As Ahab's peculiar vitality stimulates them, the men "began to gaze curiously at each other, as if marvelling how it was that they themselves became so excited" (pp. 141-142).

The view of the whale shared by Ahab and his crew is confirmed and extended as Melville invokes characteristics of Calvin's "monster God" in the reports concerning Moby Dick that accumulate as the quest goes on. In "The Town-Ho's Story," a sailor who plans a murder is relieved of the task when his intended victim is killed by Moby Dick. Several times marking the doomed man as "predestinated," Melville archly observes that the story "seemed obscurely to involve with the whale a certain wondrous, inverted visitation of one of those so called judgments of God which at times are said to overtake some men" (p. 208). The mad Shaker Gabriel declares the white whale to be "no less a being than the Shaker God incarnated" ("The Jeroboam's Story," p. 267). The Shakers, as Melville knew, renounced sexual relations because of their fanatical preoccupation with original sin.[13] In summarizing what was learned about

13. Leyda, I, 381.

Moby Dick from the ships the *Pequod* encountered, Melville uses
terms that distinctly recall the Calvinist view that election has
nothing to do with the virtues of the elect: "all his successive
meetings with various ships contrastingly concurred to show the
demoniac indifference with which the white whale tore his hunt-
ers, whether sinning or sinned against" ("The Hat," p. 437).

Melville's use of these Calvinistic motifs gives Ahab's mad
purpose a logically integrated force, conforming it to a Calvinist
account of the relations between God and those of his creatures
who live under the decree of reprobation. But Melville presents
the various elements of that account in accordance with his stubborn commitment to the liberal conception of what is required
by human dignity. The concept of the inherent rights of man,
noted as the criterion of Ishmael's hopeful religious vision,
operates in the characterization of Ahab to turn the Calvinist
system on its head. Melville evokes the image of a positive cosmic
evil by dramatizing the efforts of a noble spirit to maintain its
dignity and to resist the divine inflictions. Although this structural and thematic development is complicated by Ahab's moral
deterioration, it remains central to Melville's interests and comes
to a head in the description of Moby Dick's final attack. There
Melville combines specific elements of the charge that Calvin's
God displayed an eternal malice through predestination, against
which mortal effort is futile. Moby Dick "from side to side
strangely vibrating his predestinating head, sent a broad band
of overspreading semicircular foam before him as he rushed.
Retribution, swift vengeance, eternal malice were in his whole
aspect, and spite of all that mortal man could do, the solid
white buttress of his forehead smote the ship's starboard bow,
till men and timbers reeled" ("The Chase — Third Day," p.
468).

VIII

The Infidel's Cosmic Resentment

M elville uses the figures of Ahab and Ishmael to evoke the spiritual situation in which divine Truth has disintegrated as a standard by which the validity of earthly morals may be measured. Ahab's insanely coherent world view and Ishmael's inability to discover any embracing system of spiritual truth represent alternative responses to the crisis that arose within the theocentric interpretation of moral experience. The two figures are not static, however; each passes through dramatic struggles that reveal ever broader and more subtle ranges of the essential attitudes they represent. Ishmael's most significant discoveries emerge from his relationship to Ahab. It is not a personal relationship, to be sure, since the two never exchange a word in the long course of the voyage; it is a relationship of thought. Ahab stimulates Ishmael to radical new investigations, based on an absorbing preoccupation with evil that may come as a surprise when compared with the amplitude of spirit with which Ishmael sets out on his spiritual voyage. Yet our early introduction to Ishmael lays a firm basis for his vehement allegiance to Ahab and to his ferocious quest: the essence of Ishmael's allegiance is a deep resentment aroused by the perception that his desire to achieve a comprehensive vision of divine Truth cannot be satisfied.

Ishmael does not share Ahab's vision of the whale; he develops a vision of his own as he is prompted by Ahab's magnetic excitement to see "naught in that brute but the deadliest ill" ("Moby Dick," p. 163). The eerie dread awakened in Ishmael by the whiteness of the whale yields a complex spiritual meaning that compels Ishmael powerfully for a time, and then loses its force. Ishmael's participation in Ahab's quest is temporary; it is a stage on his journey toward final skepticism. But it is a critically important stage, since it dramatizes the way in which a world without final religious Truth appears to a consciousness that expects such Truth to be discoverable. Ishmael, as his earlier ambitions make clear, demands that life should somehow yield itself to a theocentric formulation. "The Whiteness of the Whale" chapter reveals what happens when that demand is frustrated.

Ishmael protests that the "vague, nameless horror" aroused by the whale's whiteness is "so mystical and well nigh ineffable" that he nearly despairs of "putting it in a comprehensible form" ("The Whiteness of the Whale," p. 163). This apology is the first of three that Melville employs in concerting the rhetorical strategy of this chapter. Instead of stating abstractly the meaning of Ishmael's angry consternation, he seeks to convey the experience in which it is rooted. Melville arranges this chapter, correspondingly, to tire his reader's capacity to follow imaginative impressions. In presenting Ishmael's entry into the "wonder world" of spiritual adventure, he had piled up numerous instances of the connection between water and meditation; now he organizes the associations of whiteness into five massive clusters.

Melville's first two clusters establish the connection of whiteness with objects that suggest, respectively, sacredness and panic. His third seeks to indicate that the thing of whiteness exerts a fearful sorcery even when "stripped of all direct associations calculated to impart to it aught fearful" ("The Whiteness of the Whale," pp. 166-167). Whiteness is thus distinguished as having a spectral meaning in itself, independent of the meaning of any given white object. Now asking the reader to sense the tenuous intimations of whiteness alone, Melville begs indulgence through the second of his apologies: "in a matter like this, subtlety appeals to subtlety, and without imagination no man can follow another into these halls. And though, doubtless, some at least of the imaginative impressions about to be presented may have been shared by most men, yet few perhaps were entirely conscious of them at the time" (p. 167).

Melville's fourth cluster returns to objects that are terrible in themselves and also white, to deepen the contrast between what is evident to the "common apprehension" and the mean-

ings that imagination conceives at a level beneath routine consciousness. He declares that unimaginative men are instinctively
horrified by whiteness, but do not understand why, so that imagination becomes the means through which "the instinct of the
knowledge of the demonism in the world" ("The Whiteness of
the Whale," p. 169) can be appropriated for consciousness and
become true knowledge. Melville progressively heightens the importance of this imaginative inquiry as he intimates the porten-
tous secret it will uncover. But he is quite aware that the blizzard
of examples places a heavy strain on his reader's sympathy. His
third apology anticipates a growing impatience: "But thou
sayest, methinks this white-lead chapter about whiteness is but
a white flag hung out from a craven soul; thou surrenderest
to a hypo, Ishmael" (pp. 168-169).

Just as this last apology seeks to forestall the reader's exasperation, so Melville's final cluster of instances exploits it. The "in-
cantation of this whiteness," so long continued, reveals its central
meaning in the discovery of a world that baffles the imaginative
quest. The rhetorical structure of the chapter serves Melville's
desire to convey this discovery as a betrayal.

> Is it that by its indefiniteness it shadows forth the heartless
> voids and immensities of the universe, and thus stabs us from
> behind with the thought of annihilation. . . ? Or is it, that
> as in essence whiteness is not so much a color as the visible
> absence of color, and at the same time the concrete of all
> colors; is it for these reasons that there is such a dumb
> blankness, full of meaning, in a wide landscape of snows —
> a colorless, all-color of atheism from which we shrink? And
> when we consider that other theory of the natural philoso-
> phers, that all other earthly hues — every stately or lovely
> emblazoning . . . all these are but subtile deceits, not actually
> inherent in substances, but only laid on from without; so that
> all deified Nature absolutely paints like the harlot, whose al-
> lurements cover nothing but the charnel-house within; and
> when we . . . consider that . . . the great principle of light,
> for ever remains white or colorless in itself, and if operating
> without medium upon matter, would touch all objects, even
> tulips and roses, with its own blank tinge — pondering all

this, the palsied universe lies before us a leper ("The Whiteness of the Whale," pp. 169-170).

The disgust implicit in the images of the harlot, the charnel-house, and the leper registers Ishmael's response to a peculiar spiritual treachery; it suggests something quite different from that narcissism of the mind's relation to nature he noted earlier. In this appalling whiteness, the mind does not see its own reflection, but is thrown back into itself by the spectacle of a world indifferent to its life and probings. The beckoning appeal of the "wonder-world" is laid bare as a revolting deceit, and the searcher after the Truth becomes a "wretched infidel [who] gazes himself blind at the monumental white shroud that wraps all the prospect around him" ("The Whiteness of the Whale," p. 170). In the most strenuous exercise of his spiritual powers, the quester enters an experience that destroys those powers. Resentment of this betrayal joins Ishmael with Ahab in his vengeful campaign to destroy the hated symbol of man's "intellectual and spiritual exasperations." Ishmael's interpretation of the whiteness closes with a reassertion of its controlling purpose: "Wonder ye then at the fiery hunt?" (p. 170).[1]

In its exemplary use of fact to convey spiritual meaning, "The Whiteness of the Whale" chapter has been taken as a triumph of the "symbolic imagination" by critics who have recognized the analogy between Melville's procedures and the aesthetic theories current during the second quarter of the twentieth century.[2] The Puritan background of Melville's practice has been studied, but without sufficient appreciation of the way Ishmael's developing meditation reflects the orthodox mistrust of imagina-

---

1. Howard C. Horsford, "The Design of the Argument in *Moby-Dick,*" *Modern Fiction Studies,* 8 (1962), 233-251, presents *Moby-Dick* as "the response of a powerful imagination to the intellectual disintegration of faith" (p. 234). His excellent discussion traces to David Hume the epistemological skepticism that split the symbolic bond between the "creation" and any conceivable "creator," and notes Melville's participation in this skepticism as contrasted with the transcendentalists' refusal to reckon with its implications. But for Melville, as for his contemporaries, the moral issues discussed here were more immediate and distressing; accordingly, I have placed Melville's epistemological doubts in their moral context.

2. The most extensive study of this aspect of Melville's art may be found in Charles Feidelson, Jr., *Symbolism and American Literature* (1953; reptd. Chicago, 1966), pp. 27-35, 162-212.

tion as a guide to action. In his earliest commentary, Ishmael reported that "the overwhelming idea of the great whale himself " was chief among "the springs and motives which being cunningly presented to me under various disguises, induced me to set about performing the part I did, besides cajoling me into the delusion that it was a choice resulting from my own unbiased freewill and discriminating judgment." Ishmael's capacity for symbolic interpretation becomes the means by which he is conformed to "The grand programme of Providence that was drawn up a long time ago." "By reason of these things, then, the whaling voyage was welcome; the great flood-gates of the wonderworld swung open." Ishmael views his entry into the "wonderworld" as the exercise of the "wild conceits that swayed me to my purpose" ("Loomings," p. 16), not as the discovery of reality.

Opponents of Calvinist doctrine in Melville's time charged that the orthodox concept of Providence could not be true, because it would imply that self-deception was characteristic of the human mind. Since man experiences his own will as free, the idea that his decisions were in fact decided before Creation cannot be consistent with a benevolent deity, who would never "sport with the understandings of his creatures."[3] Correspondingly, Ishmael's resentment results from his implicit demand that imagination produce more than an idiosyncratic delusion, which is ordered so as to induce him to perform unwittingly that part in the grand program of providence that has been ordained for him. His skeptical inquiries cannot be satisfied until a truth has been discovered by which action can be guided; and the apparent betrayal of such inquiries contributes to his disgust at the "harlot" world. The requirement that imagination achieve a comprehensive spiritual vision that yields moral validity marks a sharp contrast between Melville's view of symbolism and that of later theory. Melville was suspicious of radically private meanings, and sought a fuller truth than that given in the coherence of the mind with its own objects. He was not content with a wry celebration of the perishing moment in which meanings and fact are one. Thus Ishmael rebounds from his

---

3. William Ellery Channing. *Works,* 6 vols. (Boston, 1849), III, 68.

failure to achieve a positive theocentric vision and ardently embraces its obverse. He is inspired by the heroic scope of Ahab's cosmic rebellion, and by the sharply focused vision of divine malignity by which it is animated. Spurred by Ahab, he finds it possible to formulate a visionary ground for action from the suggestions of his own frustration. He takes the discovery of a world indifferent to his religious yearnings as a cue for religious anger, and asserts that for a time "Ahab's quenchless feud seemed mine" "Moby Dick," p. 155).

* * *

Ishmael's further commentary on the whale and on whaling often carries a blasphemous edge appropriate to his cooperation in Ahab's vengeful quest. We have observed that Ahab sees in the whale an "almighty monster" whose essential features are implicit in liberal attacks on the Calvinist God. The subtleties of Ishmael's commentary can be explained if we bring to bear orthodox conceptions concerning "fact" and "symbol." Although the orthodox tradition stimulated the symbolizing imagination by encouraging the pious "improvement" of the acts and objects of daily life, it also sought to regulate the actions of the spirit by Calvinist doctrine.

Orthodox respect for the power of the imagination was as evident in the attempt to contain its restless strivings, to prune back its wanton luxuriances, as in the efforts to train it along the pathways of sacred truth. Early exponents of the Calvinist tradition had sought to give a precise doctrinal meaning to every object mentioned in the Bible,[4] so that the world of nature, considered the "second book" of God's revelation, could be glossed as thoroughly as the Bible itself, and in accordance with Biblical doctrine.

Ahab's mad vision perversely accepted the doctrinal meaning that the orthodox attached to the whale; likewise Ishmael's cetological taxonomy picks up blasphemous meanings as Melville sets it in relation to orthodox teaching. "To grope down into the bottom of the sea after them; to have one's hands among the unspeakable foundations, ribs, and very pelvis of the world;

---

4. See Benjamin Keach, *Tropologia, a Key to Open Scripture Metaphors* (London, 1682). The continuing influence of this book is suggested by the fact that a revised edition was brought out in 1779.

this is a fearful thing. What am I that I should essay to hook
the nose of this leviathan! The awful tauntings in Job might
well appal me. 'Will he' (the leviathan) 'make a covenant with
thee? Behold the hope of him is vain!' " ("Cetology," p. 118).

To the orthodox, the leviathan in Job was an image not only
of God's power but of his transcendent mystery, an image
proposed to humble man's pride of knowledge. God's first questions to Job had been, "Who is this that darkeneth counsel by
words without knowledge? . . . Where wast thou when I laid
the foundations of the earth?" (Job 38:2-4). Now, however, Ishmael declares his intention to delve into these "unspeakable
foundations" in order "to project the draught of a system-
atization of cetology" ("Cetology," p. 118). His division of
whales into folios, quartos, and duodecimos suggests that man's
power to analyze nature, that great "second book" of God's revelation, offers a challenge to the claim advanced by the "first

---

5. Studies of Melville's use of the Book of Job have not reckoned with
his response to Calvinistic interpretation. Nathalia Wright, "Moby Dick:
Jonah's or Job's Whale?" *American Literature*, 37 (1965), 190-195, argues for
a sharp distinction between Jonah's whale as an instrument of punishment
in a moral creation, and Job's whale as symbolizing a universe that is "not
only amoral but inscrutable," so that Ahab rebels against the morality inherent in the Jonah story, whereas Ishmael "bypasses the whole problem of evil
. . . and describes a natural world that is neither good nor evil but sheerly
marvelous" (pp. 192-193). Together with its plausible elements this analysis
has shortcomings that can be remedied when we recognize the influence of
Calvin's view that Job's whale was likewise an instrument of punishment.
Then Ishmael's sharing in Ahab's hatred of the whale becomes intelligible,
as does his resentment of "the awful tauntings in Job." Janis Stout, "Melville's
Use of the Book of Job," *Nineteenth-Century Fiction*, 25 (1970), 69-83, takes a
position close to Wright's, and acknowledges that her reading of Job largely
follows "a recent book by Robert Gordis" (p. 69). Twentieth-century interpretations of the Bible are of limited value to an understanding of how Melville
himself read Job.
    C. Hugh Holman, "The Reconciliation of Ishmael: *Moby-Dick* and the Book
of Job," *South Atlantic Quarterly*, 57 (1958), 477-490, asserts that Job provides
"the most informing single principle of the book's composition" (p. 477). The
Lord's speech referring to Leviathan is intended to teach Job humility, and
Holman argues that Ishmael at length learns just this lesson. "There is necessity that he survive [the wreck of the *Pequod*] inherent in the moral order
of the universe in which Melville puts him — the primitive, pre-Christian
universe of Job. In that universe he has learned, as man must if he is to
live in his world, the lesson of acceptance" (p. 490).
    Ishmael's skeptical parodies at this stage of his participation in Ahab's quest
cannot be understood if their rationale is not distinguished from his final

book" that God's mysteries cannot be penetrated.[5]

In the Bible Melville had at hand during the composition of *Moby-Dick* he marked and underlined a passage from "the awful tauntings in Job" that .brings into focus another of his skeptical parodies: "Shall thy companions make a banquet of him? Shall they part him among the *merchants?*"[6] Stubb, one of Ishmael's "companions," has his supper from the first whale that the *Pequod* kills. As sharks gather to feed on the whale, Melville presents the occasion as a comment on the sharkishness of man,[7] pointing the likeness between Stubb and the sharks in language that clearly echoes the Biblical passage: "Nor was Stubb the only banqueter on whale's flesh that night" ("Stubb's Supper," p. 249).

As Stubb eats whale, whose might is the image of God's, he bullies the cook into preaching a sarcastic sermon to the sharks. This brutal charade, with its raucous mockery of divine threatenings, is not merely fanciful. Melville emphasizes the fact that it is grounded upon the practice of whalemen. The technical mastery represented by nineteenth-century whaling, in which leviathan was in fact parted among the merchants, gave Melville an opportunity to parody orthodox doctrine, and to present the operations of the trade as inherently impious.[8]

He invokes the orthodox understanding of "whale," as defined by God's word in the Book of Job, in order to suggest that God's power is routinely mocked in the whale fishery. In discussing

view, just as his final view cannot be fully appreciated without a study of how he reaches it. Wright's judgment that Ishmael ultimately reckons with an "amoral" world that is "sheerly marvelous" is preferable to Holman's belief that a "moral order" finally prevails; but Ishmael scarcely "bypasses" the moral issues that attract him to Ahab's quenchless feud. Melville's preoccupation with the conflict between the Calvinistic assertion of God's inscrutable sovereignty and the liberal definition of human dignity brought these issues to the center of his thematic concerns.

6. *The Holy Bible . . . Together with the Apocrypha* (Philadelphia, 1846), Sealts, No. 62. Job 41:6.

7. Stuart C. Woodruff, "Stubb's Supper," *Emerson Society Quarterly,* No. 43 (1966), 46-48, presents this incident as "an instructive paradigm of the coalescence of theme and technique" and analyzes carefully Melville's "man-shark analogy" (p. 46).

8. Thornton Y. Booth, *"Moby-Dick:* Standing up to God," *Nineteenth-Century Fiction,* 17 (1962), 33-43, observes in general terms that the technical proficiency of nineteenth-century whalers conflicts with the Joban claims of human incapacity.

the terrified deep dive of an "unspeakably pitiable" old whale Melville further emphasizes this connection:

> Is this the creature of whom it was once so triumphantly said — 'Canst thou fill his skin with barbed irons? or his head with fish-spears? The sword of him that layeth at him cannot hold, the spear, the dart, nor the habergeon: he esteemeth iron as straw; the arrow cannot make him flee; darts are counted as stubble; he laugheth at the shaking of a spear!' This the creature? this he? Oh! that unfulfilments should follow the prophets. For with the strength of a thousand thighs in his tail, Leviathan had run his head under the mountains of the sea, to hide him from the Pequod's fish-spears! ("The Pequod Meets the Virgin," p. 300).

Melville's practical experience largely contradicted what he had been taught and was for that reason inherently loaded with philosophic and religious meanings. He had only to tell what he had seen and done in the whaleship in order to question orthodox beliefs. Melville sardonically denies that his tale is "a hideous and intolerable allegory," claiming to offer only the "plain facts . . . of the fishery" ("The Affidavit," p. 177). But the plain facts which he offers were of the kind that created much confusion in orthodox religious circles.

Melville exploited a situation in which the distinction between "fact" and "allegory" had become problematic. Orthodox Biblicists took Biblical "fact" to have doctrinal meaning and resisted new "fact" which seemed to undermine its sacred moral bearing. The orthodox did not defend the Biblical stories about Job and Jonah as "allegory," but they implicitly used them as such. Hence the discovery that no whale could possibly swallow a man had a moral impact.[9] Because it disturbed the general symbolic frame of reference, it took on symbolic overtones. Melville's symbols gain peculiar equivocal bearings from this situation: he is both a product of the orthodox practice of symbolization and a highly sensitive register of its disruption. He sensed that

---

9. Melville exploits the philosophical significance of this discovery. He presents the arguments of an old whaleman to the effect that the Jonah story could not be factual, and concludes sardonically that these arguments "only evinced his foolish pride of reason" ("Jonah Historically Regarded," p. 308).

"fact" and "symbol" were shifting into a new and uneasy relation. In orthodox theory the "fact" or "truth" for which the symbol stood was the item of sacred insight visible through the physical object. But in increasing numbers of cases it became evident that the physical object in question did not have a nature amenable to the "truth" it was supposed to symbolize. Whales, it was discovered, are not invincible. Hence the "fact" of the physical nature of the object came into conflict with the "fact" of divine truth, and its potency as "symbol" began to decline as it was detached from the system in which the disparate meanings of objects were coalesced into a meaningful world. Because of such intellectual and moral conflict, the advance of scientific knowledge in the nineteenth century had a cultural impact that it no longer enjoys.

* * *

Ishmael's most amusing skeptical sallies are directed against "natural theology," which was a liberal effort to accommodate new scientific fact to the received religious traditions of the West. This ambitious program attempted to deduce the essential attributes of "the Christian God" from his manifestations in the world of nature. Its best-known exponent in Melville's time was William Paley, whose work Melville studied in youth,[10] and whose *Natural Theology* is quoted among the excerpts that precede the text of *Moby-Dick* ("Extracts," p. 7). The bulk of Paley's work presents detailed examples that conform to a single argument, based on the presumed analogy between the processes of nature and the workings of man-made machines.

The machine Paley typically cited in this connection was the watch. He was convinced that if a watch were found and examined, its evident design would immediately establish the existence of a watchmaker. To Paley, all examples of "contrivance" in nature prove the existence of a contriver, an "artificer" whose characteristics are apparent in his works. The proof that such an artificer exists is greatly strengthened when contrivances of great variety and complexity are discovered. Thus Paley believed that as science perceives the cunning mechanisms in nature,

---

10. Gilman, pp. 54, 58.

greater validation is given to the religious claim that "an intelligent being" is the creator of the world.[11]

Demonstrating the intelligence of the deity did not satisfy Paley's ambition, however, and he struggled hard to deduce "benevolence." But he could only bring himself to claim a "plurality of instances in which contrivance is perceived, [where] the design of the contrivance is *beneficial*."[12] To strengthen his case, Paley asserted that no train of contrivance had been discovered with an evil effect as its end. Melville ridicules this assertion in a parody of Paley's form of argument, elaborately explaining "the battering ram" of the sperm-whale's head. He details its great mass, its resiliency and buoyant lightness, as characteristics all cooperatively tending to a single effect: its implied capacity to sink ships. "Now, mark," he warns portentously. "Unerringly impelling this dead, impregnable, uninjurable wall, and this most buoyant thing within; there swims behind it all a mass of tremendous life . . . all obedient to one volition, as the smallest insect. . . . Unless you own the whale, you are but a provincial and sentimentalist in Truth" ("The Battering-Ram," pp. 285-286).

For one who had been trained in the belief that nature bears witness to God's wrath against the human race, the sentimentalism of "natural theology" was rather easy to detect. In defense of the doctrine of original sin, the orthodox hymnist Isaac Watts wrote a lengthy treatise which reverses Paley's technique and argues for natural "proofs" of the divine displeasure. "Would there have been any such creatures in our world as bears and tygers, wolves and lions, animated with such fierceness and rage, and armed with such destructive and bloudy teeth and talons, if man the supreme creature in it had not sinned?"[13] The learned fatuity of "natural theology" comes in for satire as the physician aboard the *Samuel Enderby* seeks to dissuade Ahab from his dark convictions about Moby Dick's ferocity: "Do you know, gentlemen, that the digestive organs of the whale are so

11. William Paley, *Natural Theology; or Evidences of the Existence and Attributes of the Deity, Collected from the Appearances of Nature* (Hallowell, 1826), pp. 5-13.

12. *Ibid.*, p. 241.

13. Isaac Watts, "The Ruin and Recovery of Mankind," in *Works*, ed. D. Jennings and P. Doddridge, 6 vols. (London, 1753), VI, 195.

inscrutably constructed by Divine Providence, that it is quite impossible for him to completely digest even a man's arm? And he knows it too. So that what you take for the White Whale's malice is only his awkwardness" ("Leg and Arm," p. 368).

Paley was compelled to admit that there are natural phenomena that are hard to reconcile with an altogether benevolent creator. Conceding the existence of scorpions, sharks, poison ivy, and the like, he answered that the "plurality" of benign evidences should govern the final decision as to God's morals. "When we cannot resolve all appearances into benevolence of design, we make the few give place to the many."[14] While granting that there may appear to be debits against the Lord's account, Paley insisted that the credits far outweighed them, thus trivializing the question at stake in a way which makes quite understandable Melville's "revulsion from the counting-room philosophy of Paley."[15] The most succinct crack at Paley's argument for "benevolence" is given as the muscular spasm of a dead shark's jaw slashes Queequeg's hand. " 'Queequeg no care what god made him shark,' said the savage, agonizingly lifting his hand up and down; 'wedder Fejee god or Nantucket god; but de god wat made shark must be one dam Ingin' " ("The Shark Massacre," p. 257). At the moment when the undeserved agony is inflicted, considerations concerning the "plurality" of more agreeable experiences do not adequately sustain belief in the "benevolence" of the powers beyond.

Although the influx of new scientific knowledge disrupted the orthodox faith, it was not successfully absorbed into a new basis for the moral life by those more liberal interpreters of the Christian tradition who sought to arouse the moral spirit to the standard of "benevolence." For Melville, at least, the liberal creed was inadequate. The "facts" which had such extraordinary power to demolish the old faith did not seem to him endowed with constructive, synthetic tendencies of a kind that would per-

---

14. Paley, p. 246.
15. Gilman, p. 58. Gilman gives information that confirms my suggestion as to the reason for Melville's revulsion. "Melville read in Madame de Stael's *Germany*: 'A man, regarded in a religious light, is as much as the entire human race.' Beside this he wrote: 'This was an early and innate [?] conviction of mine, suggested by my revulsion from the counting-room philosophy of Paley.' "

mit man to find moral sanction and guidance in them. The evidences of mechanism appeared to support the view that the Creator of the visible world was intelligent, but they suggested no more than an amoral intelligence. In terms which recall Paley's famous argument, Melville expressed his misgiving to Hawthorne: "The reason the mass of men fear God, and *at bottom dislike* Him, is because they rather distrust His heart, and fancy Him all brain like a watch" (*Letters*, p. 129).

The significance of personal existence is as severely threatened in a world of amoral order as it is in a world wholly governed by God's decrees. Ahab's obsession with the necessitarian processes of his own damnation prompts him to exclamations that resemble those of a man caught in a universe of impersonal natural law. This is a further element of the deep kinship between Ishmael and Ahab, although Ahab under the tyranny of God believes that he has an adversary against whom to contend, whereas Ishmael is threatened by paralyzing, annihilating indifference. Ahab begins in outrage and sometimes expresses the belief that there is "naught" beyond the white wall against which he hurls himself ("The Quarter-deck," p. 144).[16] Ishmael is equally dismayed by the wanton misleadings of the imagination and the barren impersonality of the world of "fact," and comes to the conviction that Ahab's quenchless feud is indeed his own.

These two aspects of Ishmael's distress are indicated by the correlated portents he reads into the roundness of the planet itself. Expressing the futility of imagination when it is not given a definite course by some reliable guide to what is real, Ishmael muses:

> Were this world an endless plain, and by sailing eastward we could for ever reach new distances ... then there were promise in the voyage. But in pursuit of those far mysteries we dream of, or in tormented chase of that demon phantom that, some time or other, swims before all human hearts; while chasing such over this round globe, they either lead us on

---

16. This impulse finds momentary expression also in "The Candles": "In the midst of the personified impersonal, a personality stands here" ("The Candles," p. 417).

in barren mazes or midway leave us whelmed ("The Alba-
tross," p. 204).

This is no world for self-generating speculations; its roundness
brings the imagination back upon itself. Under the same figure,
Ishmael expresses the barrenness of a world in which there is
no purchase for fancy. "And some certain significance lurks in
all things, else all things are little worth, and the round world
itself but an empty cipher, except to sell by the cartload, as
they do hills about Boston, to fill up some morass in the Milky
Way" ("The Doubloon," p. 358).

IX

Ahab Transfigured

I t is clear from the first revelation of his purpose that Ahab is a "monomaniac"; with his energies and intellect focused on a single object, Ahab stands as a figure of theocentric piety run mad. He is enclosed by the vision that defines his furious quest, and his encapsulated self-sustaining world view becomes more evidently obsessional as his commitment to it increases in force. The awesome violence of his quest for the white whale corresponds to an inner violence, the torture that he suffers as his personality is wrenched to fit the object to which he has devoted it. Ahab's spiritual condition, as well as his way of interpreting the outer world, becomes perversely multilayered, self-contradictory as well as self-confirming. It is as though his once large and brilliant character has suffered an implosion, like a collapsing star, so that fantastic energies are concentrated at the center. Instead of casting light outward, Ahab's mind draws his experiences into a pattern that corresponds to its lurid inner life. Melville brings Ahab's agony to a crisis in which the coherence of his purpose is sustained even as its moral legitimacy is undermined. The terms in which Melville defines Ahab's torment and his transfiguration are crucial to his final meanings, for they spell out the dilemma Ishmael comes to face and pose the issues he must finally resolve.

Ahab makes of his own damnation a gigantic defiance against the divine malice that decreed it. By vindictively redoubling his madness and fury, he strikes back at the source of his fate. If the white whale is a sign of the ultimate malevolence directed against him, it can equally become the means of his revenge. The presence of God in the whale makes it sacramental, a theophanic object. Just as the fire had burned Ahab in "the sacra-

mental act" ("The Candles," p. 416), so the whale had maimed
him, giving him an opportunity to assert the integrity of his
own being in a conscious act of desecration. Ahab explains this
curious reciprocation to Starbuck, claiming that he would strike
the sun if it insulted him: "For could the sun do that, then
could I do the other; since there is ever a sort of fair play herein"
("The Quarter-deck," p. 144).

Ahab understands why Starbuck interprets his hatred of the
whale as blasphemous madness, but declares that his is "madness
maddened," and musters the intention to "dismember my dis-
memberer" ("Sunset," p. 147). The Biblical Ahab was destroyed
in a military mission that had no relevance to the fact of his
damnation except as the agency by which his death was accomplished. Melville's Ahab, by contrast, sets out on a quest that
directly confronts the dread powers that seek his end. He taunts
his cosmic adversaries, asserting that they cannot evade his vengeance because they themselves have decreed it: "come and see
if ye can swerve me. Swerve me? ye cannot swerve me, else
ye swerve yourselves! man has ye there." Thus Melville locates
an ambiguity at the heart of Ahab's defiant self-assertion: Ahab's
own purpose is simultaneously his predestined course. "The path
to my fixed purpose is laid with iron rails, whereon my soul
is grooved to run" (p. 147).

The Calvinistic frame of reference in which Melville elabo-
rates Ahab's quest permits him to portray this ambiguity with
extraordinary depth and subtlety. The God of Calvin's theology
was not only arraigned as the "author of sin." Under such a
God, it was also charged, man could not be a moral agent. If
a man's eternal destiny and his everyday actions are determined
by decrees set forth before the world was created, then human
life becomes a "mere mechanical" working out of what has already been decided. The liberal protest in favor of human "freedom" gained its force from the recognition that the Calvinistic
view of God's sovereignty bleaches all the meaning out of human
activity, that it dissolves the moral tangibility of the self. Melville
depicts Ahab's self-assertion so as to engage the question whether
Ahab's action is really his own; what is dramatized is Ahab's
struggle to lay claim to his own life.

Calvin found the Old Testament story of Ahab especially use-

ful because Ahab's victimization by the devil could be taken
to confirm Calvin's theory of God's sovereignty.[1] Calvin invoked

---

1. John Calvin, *Calvin's Calvinism*, trans. Henry Cole (Grand Rapids, 1950),
pp. 195, 240, 288, 321. *Institutes of the Christian Religion*, ed. John T. McNeill,
trans. F. L. Battles, 2 vols. (Philadelphia, 1960), I, 176, 219, 230, 620; II,
1170. The relation between Melville's Ahab and the Old Testament King
Ahab has been interpreted in differing ways, which turn on differences concerning the way in which Melville himself might have taken the Biblical
story. Nathalia Wright, *Melville's Use of the Bible* (Durham, 1949), argues for
an "essential duality" in the character of Ahab, and finds that duality in
the Biblical account. "For the picture of King Ahab which emerges in I Kings
is a composite of two points of view: that of the sources, according to which
he was an able and energetic ruler, and that of the didactic compiler, who
saw him also as a dangerous innovator and a patron of foreign gods" (pp.
61-62). The theory that I and II Kings is a composite, containing materials
from "sources" arranged by a "compiler" of the Deuteronomic [didactic]
school, is a product of late nineteenth-century Biblical scholarship. Its most
influential exposition in English was given by S. R. Driver, who wrote in
the 1880s. Driver cites German scholarship as early as 1873 in presenting
this theory, which is itself an outgrowth of the advanced studies of the Penta-
teuch carried out in Germany in the 1860's. See S. R. Driver, *An Introduction
to the Literature of the Old Testament* (Edinburgh, 1897), pp. 185 f., and Robert
H. Pfeiffer, *Introduction to the Old Testament* (New York, 1941), pp. 47-49, 139.
It is possible that Melville noticed the evidences that led to this discrimination
between "sources" and "compiler," but his use of the Biblical figure is more
complex than this possibility would suggest.

Lawrance Thompson, *Melville's Quarrel with God* (Princeton, 1952), argues
that the "conventional reader" would recall that Ahab was an evil king who
deserved an evil fate. The reader better attuned to Melville's dark meanings,
Thompson continues, would recall a more sinister correlation between the
two Ahabs:

"Each of them is seduced to his death by a prophet, and Captain Ahab's
misleading prophet is Fedallah, whose symbolic values are complex. Consider,
however, the hint in First Kings as to how it happened that King Ahab
was similarly victimized: 'I saw the Lord sitting on his throne. . . . And the
Lord said, Who shall persuade Ahab, that he may go up and fall at Ramoth-
gilead? . . . And there came forth a spirit, and stood before the Lord, and
said, I will persuade him. And the Lord said, Wherewith? And
he said, I will go forth, and I will be a lying spirit in the mouth of all his
prophets. And the Lord said, Thou shalt persuade him, and prevail also:
go forth and do so.' " Thompson argues that "for Melville's anti-Christian
purposes, that passage lends itself nicely to a correlated series of insinuations
that God is a malicious double-crosser" (p. 153).

Marius Bewley attacks Thompson's position in *The Eccentric Design* (New
York, 1959); he points out that Thompson's quoted passage occurs in a context
that undercuts Thompson's interpretation. He shows that the vision of the
heavenly council is given by Ahab's only true prophet as a warning against
the false prophecies of four hundred others who told Ahab what he wanted
to hear. Hence the passage would appear to throw the responsibility for Ahab's

that part of Ahab's story that seemed to illustrate God's control of Satan, to support his claim that God's ordering of the creation through providence is indeed exhaustive. Wanting Ahab to set out on a suicidal military adventure, God appointed Satan to induce him to do so. "God sends Satan to Ahab, with his own Divine command that he should be 'a lying spirit in the mouth of all the kings prophets.' Thus the impostor spirit becomes the minister of the wrath of God, to blind the wicked."[2] For Calvin, of course, God used Satan against Ahab without incurring any culpability.

Melville inverts this element of Calvinist teaching as he indicates that Fedallah is an impostor spirit sent by an evil God to entrap Ahab. The heavily sardonic and insinuating passage that introduces the Parsee hints at this aspect of their relation: "Whence he came in a mannerly world like this, by what sort of unaccountable tie he soon evinced himself to be linked with Ahab's peculiar fortunes; nay, so far as to have some sort of a half-hinted influence; Heaven knows, but it might have been even authority over him; all this none knew" ("Ahab's Boat and Crew. Fedallah," p. 199). Later Melville drops a hint that is squarely in line with the Calvinist teaching: "Ahab seemed an independent lord; the Parsee but his slave. Still again both seemed yoked together, and an unseen tyrant driving them" ("The Hat," p. 439). Fedallah becomes the agent of an "unseen tyrant" rather than the minister of a holy God who does not share the evil of the errand on which he sends Satan. But Melville suggests also that Fedallah is a projection of Ahab's own self-determining purpose: he presents the pair "fixedly gazing upon each other; as if in the Parsee Ahab saw his forethrown shadow, in Ahab the Parsee his abandoned substance." This peculiar divorce of shadow and substance, and the suggestions of a divine overruling, characterize Ahab's own nature, as be-

---

fate entirely upon Ahab. Bewley declares that "it is a little difficult to see how Mr. Thompson's reading can be accepted as plausible at any level of interpretation" (p. 195).

It is abundantly clear that Melville's treatment of Ahab takes up many themes of Calvinistic theology, and specifically employs Calvin's own use of the Biblical Ahab, including Calvin's use of the passage in question to prove that God used Satan to deceive Ahab.

2. Calvin, *Calvin's Calvinism*, p. 240.

comes clear as the passage concludes: "For be this Parsee what he may, all rib and keel was solid Ahab" ("The Hat," p. 439).[3]

To analyze the inner workings of Ahab's inveteracy, Melville employs the orthodox characterization of sin as an alien tyrant ruling man's life. John Owen's *Indwelling Sin* proposes the sinner as the victim of an occupying presence: the power of sin "appears in the violence it offers to the nature of men, compelling them to sins, fully contrary to . . . the reasonable nature wherewith they are endued from God." Owen depicts the sinner's struggle in accordance with the psychological theory that Calvinists used to describe the process of spiritual "rebirth." He posits an original rational nature, God's image in man as created before the Fall, that survives in marred and diminished form under the subjugation of sin.[4] Correspondingly, Melville says that Ahab's "great natural intellect" had been the "living agent" in him before his injury, but then became the instrument of his madness. Ahab's madness is a usurping tyrant that "stormed his general sanity, and carried it, and turned all its concentred cannon upon its own mad mark" ("Moby Dick," p. 161). Thus in sleep Ahab's rational soul struggled to break free from the mad purpose that had forced it into servitude: "it spontaneously sought escape from the scorching contiguity of the frantic thing, of which, for the time, it was no longer an integral." Ahab's purpose had "by its own sheer inveteracy of will, forced itself against gods and devils into a kind of self-assumed, independent being of its own. Nay, could grimly live and burn, while the common vitality to which it was conjoined, fled horror-stricken from the unbidden and unfathered birth" ("The Chart," p. 175).

When Ahab bursts howling from his cabin in agonies of psychic disintegration, Melville tells us that he was for the time being "a vacated thing," so radical is the divorce sought by what remained of his rational self. Ahab's victimization is the torment of a Prometheus who has created his own vulture, Pro-

---

3. I have given a fuller discussion of Fedallah in "Calvinism and Cosmic Evil in *Moby-Dick*," *PMLA*, 84 (1969), 1613-1619.

4. John Owen, *The Nature, Power, Deceit and Prevalency of Indwelling Sin in Believers* (Philadelphia, n.d.), pp. 245-246. See also James Tanis, *Dutch Calvinistic Pietism in the Middle Colonies: A Study in the Life and Theology of Theodorus Jacobus Frelinghuysen* (The Hague, 1967), p. 104.

methean intellectual aspiration inseparably bound to Promethe-
an torment, and capable of existence only amid such torment.[5]
Just as the guilt of Jonah was only worsened by his strivings,
so the rage of Ahab is an inner furor in which effort and torture
are one. Owen declared that the mind of the sinner "is, as it
were, the upper region of hell; for it lies at the next door to
it for filth, horror, and confusion."[6] Melville shows his full appreciation of the moral theory inherent in this concept of hell as
he describes the horrors of Ahab's soul: "a chasm seemed opening in him, from which forked flames and lightnings shot up,
and accursed fiends beckoned him to leap down among them;
when this hell in himself yawned beneath him, a wild cry would
be heard through the ship" ("The Chart," p. 174).

The inner chaos that threatens Ahab does not finally overcome
him; on the contrary he succeeds in harmonizing his disunities
through ecstatic contact with the divine. In "The Candles" he
achieves a transfigured coherence in which his vision of God,
of nature, and of his own inner life is momentarily cleansed
of its ambiguities, annealed in the fires of a blasphemous conse-
cration.

Melville orders this spiritual drama by inverting the orthodox
scheme of "rebirth," in which the apparent contradiction between human freedom and God's deterministic decrees was resolved. According to Calvinist theory, those whom God elects
discover that their freedom is perfected in obedience. Spiritual
regeneration restores the primal nature of man, created by God
in his own image, freeing it from the tyranny of sin.[7] Thus the
reborn child of God can live out his truest nature; he is enabled
by grace to serve his creator with a whole heart. We may remember Father Mapple, who deploys the energies of "his own
inexorable self" in declaring his submission to the dispensations
of the Almighty.

Standing before the "trinity of flames" rising from the masts

---

5. Thomas Woodson, "Ahab's Greatness: Prometheus as Narcissus," *English Literary History*, 33 (1966), 351-369, gives a good analysis of the agony of Ahab's mind. He presents it, however, as essentially informed by the opposition of a humanistic self against the threat of thinghood.

6. Owen, p. 171.

7. Tanis, p. 104; Owen, p. 19.

of the *Pequod*, Ahab acknowledges the power of the spirit against which he has pitted himself. But he declares that it will not overwhelm him: "I own thy speechless, placeless power; but to the last gasp of my earthquake life will dispute its unconditional, unintegral mastery in me ... while I earthly live, the queenly personality lives in me, and feels her royal rights" ("The Candles," p. 417). Melville defines the royal status of the personality according to the liberal Christian theory that men have an inherent right to question the justice of whatever offers itself for worshipful submission. As William Ellery Channing had declared that human dignity rests on "a principle within us, which forbids us to prostrate ourselves before mere power,"[8] so Ahab addresses the spirit in the flame: "Come in thy lowest form of love, and I will kneel and kiss thee; but ... come as mere supernal power; and ... there's that in here that still remains indifferent" (p. 417).

Ahab cannot offer the worship of submission; he seizes another kind of worship, one that Channing did not envision. If God unjustly creates rebellious beings only to destroy them, those beings may offer him the worship suitable to their fate. "To neither love nor reverence wilt thou be kind; and e'en for hate thou canst but kill; and all are killed." Therefore Ahab achieves the truest and deepest expression of his own being by coming to the furious conviction that for him "right worship is defiance." In that worship he can join the hell-fire in himself with the confirming and answering hell-fire of rage that he finds arrayed against him, and so pursue objectives that are most truly his own and at once harmonious with the ultimate context in which his life is set. "Oh, thou clear spirit, of thy fire thou madest me, and like a true child of fire, I breathe it back to thee." Whereas the elect finds the freedom of his own truest life in submission to the divine decrees, the reprobate finds his deepest fulfillment in defiance. Thus Ahab celebrates his unification with the divine: "I leap with thee; I burn with thee; would fain be welded with thee; defyingly I worship thee!" ("The Candles," p. 417).

Just as the elect continues to be tempted to show defiance,

---

8. William Ellery Channing, *Works*, 6 vols. (Boston, 1849), I, 232.

so Ahab is tempted to repent, to relinquish the mad hatred by which his quest is driven. Pip's loyalty and affection have such an influence. "There is that in thee, poor lad," says Ahab, "which I feel too curing to my malady. Like cures like; and for this hunt, my malady becomes my most desired health" ("The Cabin," p. 436).

In "The Symphony," Ahab's struggle with his fated course receives poignant treatment. The beauty of the day touches him: "That glad, happy air, that winsome sky, did at last stroke and caress him; the step-mother world, so long cruel — forbidding — now threw affectionate arms round his stubborn neck, and did seem to joyously sob over him, as if over one, that however wilful and erring, she could yet find it in her heart to save and to bless. From beneath his slouched hat Ahab dropped a tear into the sea; nor did all the Pacific contain such wealth as that one wee drop" (p. 443).

This allusive comparison of Ahab's tear to the widow's mite (Mark 12:41-44) suggests that the tear represented all the repentance left in the scorched interior of Ahab's soul. The scene takes on appalling force when it is measured against the liberal theologians' charge that Calvinism envisages a God who holds out a false promise of salvation to the damned:

They [the reprobate] are called to return unto God — to repent . . . no one of which calls could they possibly obey; and yet, for not obeying, every time they refuse, their damnation is increased. Is not this awful — frightful! Could Satanic cruelty display greater malevolence than is here supposed? Every mercy, every call, every seeming good, is so arranged as necessarily to sink the poor, miserable victim deeper into the quenchless flames of eternal damnation. Thou glorious God of the universe, whose very nature is love, what a representation of thy character! — holding out to thy hapless, miserable creatures, an empty semblance of good, which it is *impossible*, in the nature of things, for them to attain. . . . Dreadful! dreadful! dreadful! Thou great Spirit of the heavens, art thou such a monster as this![9]

9. R. S. Foster, *Objections to Calvinism* (Cincinnati, 1849), p. 99.

Starbuck, inspired by the beautiful scene, pleads with Ahab to remember his wife and child and abandon the crazy hunt. Ahab for a moment relents, as his natural love for his own is aroused; the rational soul that his madness had subjugated suddenly asserts itself.[10] But that impulse is quashed as Ahab grimly declares that for him the glorious day, with all its suggestions of salvation, has been a ghastly deceit. "What is it, what nameless, inscrutable, unearthly thing is it; what cozening, hidden lord and master, and cruel, remorseless emperor commands me; that against all natural lovings and longings, I so keep pushing, and crowding, and jamming myself on all the time; recklessly making me ready to do what in my own proper, natural heart, I durst not so much as dare?" ("The Symphony," pp. 444-445).

Ahab's purpose is thus once again expressed as a victimization. He now states the quandary of his own self-assertion in terms that unmistakably link it with Calvinistic providence. "Is Ahab, Ahab? Is it I, God, or who, that lifts this arm? But if the great sun move not of himself; but is as an errand-boy in heaven; nor one single star can revolve, but by some invisible power; how then can this one small heart beat; this one small brain think thoughts; unless God does that beating; does that thinking, does that living, and not I" ("The Symphony," p. 445). Ahab then challenges Starbuck to reckon with the meaning of so drastic an indictment of God: "Where do murderers go, man! Who's to doom, when the judge himself is dragged to the bar?" (p. 445).

After the second day of the chase, Ahab shouts down Starbuck's pious expostulations by invoking the decrees of the power that has damned him. As in "The Candles" chapter, Ahab's cosmic fury overcomes the cleavage between the impulse of his rational nature and the madness of his quest. He reasserts his inner unity as the integrity of one whose damnation was sealed in the eternities prior to creation itself. "Ahab is for ever Ahab, man. This whole act's immutably decreed. 'Twas rehearsed by thee and me a billion years before this ocean rolled. Fool! I am the Fates' lieutenant; I act under oders" ("The Chase — Second Day," p. 459). Just as the orthodox claimed to achieve

10. Owen, pp. 247-249, discusses the affection for one's children as an impulse of man's created nature that is violated by the power of sin.

true manliness through obedience to the God of their salvation, so Ahab, vindicating his personal dignity, insists on his unavoidable and Satanic obedience to the God who has damned him.

Magnified in moments of contact with the Beyond, Ahab's demonic energy contributes to his awesome spiritual stature. But as his energy mounts in intensity he also becomes morally repellent. Ahab's battle with cosmic evil, for all its heroism, spawns evils of its own. As a result Ishmael withdraws his allegiance from Ahab, and continues his own quest with an increased burden of uncertainty. The contrast between Ahab's titanic force and the "incompetence of mere unaided virtue or right-mindedness in Starbuck" "Moby Dick," p. 162) displays Ahab's impressiveness and his evil. The degradation of Starbuck dramatizes the "fall of valour in the soul" that prompted Ishmael's early doubts about the possibility of believing in "the great democratic God."

* * *

In the tradition of Calvinist pietism, mere intellectual assent to correct doctrine was inadequate. One who had a rational understanding of the faith without having personally experienced its transforming power was called a "literal" man,[11] and efforts were made to encourage his entry into the spiritual experiences of which doctrine was considered an external expression. Intellect had only a secondary function; the true life of man was defined by an underlying spiritual disposition. Without the assistance of God's grace, it was taught, man's reason cannot even maintain a rational morality. Since man is challenged by Satanic evil, from within his nature and beyond, God's support was considered indispensable to his continued virtue. This scheme of conflicting spiritual vitalities is adapted by Melville to analyze Starbuck's moral collapse.

Starbuck perceived the blasphemous meaning of Ahab's purpose as soon as that purpose was declared, but this insight has not spurred him to effective resistance. Silenced by Ahab's early declamations, he broods over his unwonted submission: "My soul is more than matched; she's overmanned; and by a madman! Insufferable sting, that sanity should ground arms on such a

---

11. Tanis, pp. 108-110.

field! ... I think I see his impious end; but feel that I must
help him to it. Will I, nill I, the ineffable thing has tied me
to him; tows me with a cable I have no knife to cut" ("Dusk,"
p. 148). Ahab's frenzy touches the mate in the depths of his
being, and uncovers there a disposition to comply with the impious quest: "but he drilled deep down, and blasted all my reason
out of me." Aware that he is unequal to the task of stopping
Ahab, Starbuck founds his hope on the substantial possibility
that the issue will not be forced. Reminding himself that "the
hated whale has the round watery world to swim in," Starbuck
comes to the plausible conclusion that "God may wedge aside"
Ahab's "heaven-insulting purpose" (p. 148).

The impotence of Starbuck's rational virtue is emphasized
once again in a setting that shifts the issue from Ahab's "blasphemy" to the practical effects of his actions. Finding Ahab
asleep in the cabin, Starbuck ponders his own moral dilemma.
He asks himself the central question: "shall this crazed old man
be tamely suffered to drag a whole ship's company down to
doom with him? — Yes, it would make him the wilful murderer
of thirty men and more, if this ship come to any deadly harm;
and come to deadly harm, my soul swears this ship will, if Ahab
have his way." Starbuck perceives that his own reasonings will
never stop the mad captain, but he is so appalled by the spiritual
terrors of Ahab that he feels it would be impossible to imprison
him. "He would be more hideous than a caged tiger, then. I
could not endure the sight; could not possibly fly his howlings
... inestimable reason would leave me on the long intolerable
voyage." Starbuck pursues his reasonings until they bring him
to a delicately balanced indecision; it occurs to him that killing
Ahab would be analogous to a divine intervention. "Is heaven
a murderer when its lightning strikes a would-be murderer in
his bed? ... And would I be a murderer, then, if — ." Now
standing with a loaded musket aimed at the sleeping Ahab's
head, Starbuck wavers on the knife-edge of his uncertainty as
though waiting for the slightest heavenly confirmation of his
plan. "Great God, where art thou? Shall I? shall I? " ("The Musket," p. 422). But no divine impetus is given for the deed, and
he shrinks away.

After this crisis Starbuck's acquiescence becomes increasingly

pathetic. Since his courageous right-mindedness could not fulfill
its own imperatives, and received no divine reinforcement, he
becomes a hapless utensil in Ahab's hands. Eager to sight the
whale, Ahab has himself hoisted aloft in a basket and appoints
the mate to stand watch over the rope that secures him. "It
was strange," Melville observes, "that this was the very man
he [Ahab] should select for his watchman; freely giving his whole
life into such an otherwise distrusted person's hands" ("The
Hat," p. 440). Ahab finds a use for the reliable docility into
which Starbuck's spiritual courage has decayed.

Just as Ahab's madness touches parts of Starbuck's soul that
have the power to subvert his reason, so Ahab's vision of the
world centers on realities whose meaning Starbuck cannot face.
Starbuck is able to maintain the pious expectation that no final
catastrophe will overtake the *Pequod* because his piety finds confirmation in tranquil seascapes that encourage him to forget the
evidences of divine malice that the whale fishery presents. One
lovely day he gazes into the ocean depths, and is inspired to
murmur a frank confession of his wishful faith. "Tell me not
of thy teeth-tiered sharks, and thy kidnapping cannibal ways.
Let faith oust fact; let fancy oust memory; I look deep down
and do believe" ("The Gilder," p. 406). The final confrontation
with Moby Dick completes the devastation of Starbuck's manliness, forcing him to contend with the dread realities from which
his belief had shielded him. During the second day of battle
he fears that his devout hope may indeed have been vain, crying
"Great God! but for one single instant show thyself " ("The
Chase — Second Day," p. 459).

Starbuck's consternation reveals his incapacity to cope with
the dark meanings of Ahab's quest. He shouts a frantic protest
that summarizes the portents, but only succeeds in confirming
Ahab's cosmic rage. "In Jesus' name no more of this, that's worse
than devil's madness. Two days chased; twice stove to splinters;
thy very leg once more snatched from under thee; thy evil shadow gone — all good angels mobbing thee with warnings: —
what more wouldst thou have? — Shall we keep chasing this
murderous fish till he swamps the last man? Shall we be dragged
by him to the bottom of the sea? Shall we be towed by him
to the infernal world? Oh, oh, — Impiety and blasphemy to

hunt him more!" ("The Chase — Second Day," p. 459). Whereas
Ahab reads these signs as further indications of divine malice,
Starbuck reads them as merciful warnings; and he is confounded
by Ahab's invulnerable determination. Unable to grasp the implications of Ahab's purpose, Starbuck is paralyzed by confusion
and dread; he attains only a dim apprehension of the fact that
Ahab's action presupposes a God totally alien to his own. "God
keep us, but already my bones feel damp within me, and from
the inside wet my flesh. I misdoubt me that I disobey my God
in obeying him!" ("The Chase — Third Day," p. 461).

The final events of the chase vindicate Ahab's vision of divine
malevolence and vengefulness: as the exasperated whale bears
down upon the *Pequod*, Starbuck's desperation bespeaks a man
whose faith has been betrayed. Instead of wedging aside Ahab's
purpose, the manifestations of the divine appear now to have
brought on a catastrophe in which life is wantonly destroyed.
"Is this the end of all my bursting prayers? all my life-long fideli-
ties?" Instead of sustaining his rational courage, Starbuck's wishful faith is reduced to mere wishfulness. He can only pray abject-
ly that he may not meet death "in a woman's fainting fit" ("The
Chase — Third Day," p. 467). Melville does not portray the
destruction of Starbuck's valor with contempt, but with outrage
against a Beyond that could permit such a shameful spectacle.
He contrasts Ahab and Starbuck so as to suggest that the divine
offers no resource by which Ahab's supernatural energy might
be overmatched. But it is also made clear that the force that
blasted Starbuck's manliness was conveyed principally through
Ahab himself.

*　*　*

Melville's larger account of Ahab's debasement follows an
analogous pattern, revealing further his paradoxical complicity
in the cosmic evil he seeks to oppose. Ahab's role as a spokesman
for the legitimate grievances of mankind gives moral weight to
his outcries against divine injustice; but as Melville extends his
analysis of Ahab's relation to his fellow men he reveals Ahab's
incompetence as a source of moral truth or spiritual insight.

At the outset of the quest, Ahab's leadership establishes a
commonalty of damnation; he brings an appeal against the

heavens in behalf of reprobated mankind. His personal sense
of injury and his charges of injustice become Man's case against
God. Ahab and his crew are compared to the "representatives
of mankind" brought before the French Revolutionary Assembly
by Anacharsis Clootz; a "deputation from all the isles of the
sea, and all the ends of the earth, accompanying Old Ahab in
the Pequod to lay the world's grievances before that bar from
which not very many of them ever come back" ("Knights and
Squires," p. 108).[12]

As with Carlyle's "Heroes" and Emerson's "Representative
Men," Ahab's personal experience is presented as a point of
focus in which concerns of general human significance become
sharply visible. His life illuminates the life of Man under the
character of the Damned Soul. His injury becomes a figure for
all the unmerited injuries of men; his fuming exasperation, with
its intellectual and spiritual depth, summarizes all the "rage
and hate felt by his whole race from Adam down." This aspect
of Ahab's relation to Man is distinctly expressed as Melville
describes his collapse after the first day's combat with Moby

---

12. The Hayford and Parker text of *Moby-Dick* (New York, 1967) reads
"ever came back" at the line cited. Hayford and Parker acknowledge that
their reading lacks documentary authority, but give no specific explanation
of this alteration. (See pp. 492-493.)

The relevant immediate context is as follows: "Yet now, federated along
one keel, what a set these Isolatoes were! An Anacharsis Clootz deputation
from all the isles of the sea, and all the ends of the earth, accompanying
Old Ahab in the Pequod to lay the world's grievances before that bar from
which not very many of them ever come/came back. Black Little Pip —
he never did!" ("Knights and Squires," p. 108.)

Hayford and Parker assume the antecedent of "them" to be "Isolatoes,"
and that Melville means simply that "not very many of the *Pequod's* crew
ever came back." But the language that intervenes between "them" and "Isolatoes" broadens the issue in a way that justifies the verb "come." Just as Anacharsis Clootz assembled representatives of mankind, so the crew of the *Pequod*
represent mankind in Melville's trope, by bringing "the world's grievances."
Melville's language presupposes his notion that mankind has grievances to
lay before the divine bar. That enlarged meaning is carried forward by
"come," which is an abstract present referring to a permanent condition of
things.

If "come" is retained, "them" acquires an understood antecedent suitable
to the broadened meaning of the passage, something like "men with their
grievances." Pip, in the sentence following, becomes one of "them" as reasonably in this case as when the phrase is altered to refer only to the crew of
the *Pequod.*

Dick. "In an instant's compass, great hearts sometimes condense to one deep pang, the sum total of those shallow pains kindly diffused through feebler men's whole lives. And so, such hearts, though summary in each one suffering; still, if the gods decree it, in their life-time aggregate a whole age of woe, wholly made up of instantaneous intensities; for even in their pointless centres, those noble natures contain the entire circumferences of inferior souls" ("The Chase — First Day," p. 451).

By making Ahab a hero of the damned, Melville inverts the orthodox practice in which such figures were set forth to dash the boldness of the reprobate, and cheer the hearts of the elect. In terms that emphasize the reversal of pious teaching, Stubb warmly praises Ahab's determination to play out the cards that have been thrust into his hands. "And damn me, Ahab, but thou actest right; live in the game, and die in it!" ("The Quadrant," p. 413). But Melville develops aspects of Ahab's relation to his crew that undermine the moral validity of his heroism.

Since he knows he cannot rely entirely upon the heroic response of the crew, Ahab has schemed to maintain them in his purpose: "Granting that the White Whale fully incites the hearts of this my savage crew, and playing round their savageness even breeds a certain generous knight-errantism in them, still . . . they must also have food for their common, daily appetites." Reflecting that "the permanent constitutional condition of the manufactured man . . . is sordidness," Ahab keeps up the pretense of hunting whales for profit, beguiling his crew with the promise of an eventual payday. He also carefully preserves the usages belonging to a Captain's preeminence so as to discourage the recognition that he is "open to the unanswerable charge of usurpation." By committing the voyage to the pursuit of his personal revenge he has created a situation in which "with perfect impunity, both moral and legal, his crew if so disposed, and to that end competent, could refuse all further obedience to him." Hence Ahab gives a "heedful, closely calculating attention to every minute atmospheric influence which it was possible for his crew to be subjected to" ("Surmises," p. 184). He begins to act out what Channing meant when he asserted that the God of Calvinism, if made a model for human conduct, would turn men into monsters.[13]

13. Channing, *Works*, I, 238.

When Ahab discovers that defiance is the "right worship"of
the monster God, he immediately employs his unification with
the divine in order to cow the crew. The men are panic-stricken
as a tongue of flame flickers from the steel barb of his harpoon.
But Ahab stops them from setting sail for home by "snatching
the burning harpoon . . . [and] swearing to transfix with it the
first sailor that but cast loose a rope's end." Although he ex-
ultantly claims to "blow out the last fear" by extinguishing the
flame with a blast of his breath, it is quite clear that he means
to inspire superstitious dread. He wants the crew to obey him
with the same abject terror that they feel when God makes
known his wrath. "At those last words of Ahab's many of the
mariners did run from him in a terror of dismay" ("The Candles," p. 418).

Ahab finds an opportunity to consolidate his tyranny when
he learns that the men are terrified because the storm has reversed the compass. Although the reversed needles were perfectly
adequate to steer by, Ahab seizes the occasion to establish himself as a wizard. He creates new compass needles by a technique
unknown to his men, and with showmanship appropriate to the
intended effect he invites them to inspect the result. "Look ye,
for yourselves, if Ahab be not lord of the level loadstone!" Melville emphatically condemns Ahab's manipulation of the men
and the contempt for them it reveals. "In his fiery eyes of scorn
and triumph, you then saw Ahab in all his fatal pride" ("The
Needle," p. 425).

The chivalrous spirit Ahab had at first aroused in the crew
disappears altogether as the chase approaches its climax; Ahab's
purpose "domineered above them so, that all their bodings,
doubts, misgivings, fears, were fain to hide beneath their souls
. . . All humor, forced or natural, vanished" ("The Hat," pp.
437-438). Ahab's battle to maintain his personal integrity against
the "divine dominion" can only be waged, it seems, by denying
personal significance to other men. Under his intimate and unceasing despotism the sailors are scarcely persons at all. "Alike,
joy and sorrow, hope and fear, seemed ground to finest dust,
and powdered, for the time, in the clamped mortar of Ahab's
iron soul. Like machines, they dumbly moved about the deck,

ever conscious that the old man's despot eye was on them" (p. 438).

Melville completes his portrayal of Ahab's moral deterioration as he associates Ahab and his quarry with the most notorious of Biblical tyrants, King Herod. Only a few days before the encounter with Moby Dick, wild cries are heard in the night "like half-articulated wailings of the ghosts of all Herod's murdered Innocents" ("The Life-Buoy," p. 428). It is soon proposed that the cries were those of men from the whaler *Rachel* who were dragged over the horizon by Moby Dick. Captain Gardiner of the *Rachel* discloses that one of his sons was aboard the missing boat, and begs Ahab for help in the search to find it. "Do to me as you would have me do to you in the like case. For *you* too have a boy, Captain Ahab." But Ahab abruptly refuses: "I will not do it. Even now I lose time. Good bye, good bye, God bless ye man, and may I forgive myself, but I must go" ("The Pequod Meets the Rachel," p. 435). Melville concludes the chapter by reinforcing his allusion to the Biblical account of the slaughter of the innocents: "She was Rachel, weeping for her children, because they were not" (p. 436).[14]

This scene indicates that Ahab desires revenge because of personal resentment, not because of a compassionate awareness of injustices against mankind. Ahab's violation of human decency, framed by Melville as a breach of the Golden Rule, is linked with the blasphemous arrogance by which he proposes to forgive himself. Melville invites us to measure Ahab's callousness: Ahab refuses an opportunity to relieve suffering caused by the whale, so as to pursue his revenge for an injury that cannot be repaired.

Thus Ahab becomes an accomplice of the divine malice to which he offers the worship of defiance. Believing that he is victimized by the malevolence of the powers beyond, he sets out to gain satisfaction for his undeserved injury. But his quest ironically becomes an extension of the evil upon which he seeks

---

14. Wright, pp. 70-71, associates the *Rachel* with the "spiritual mother of all Israel" invoked in Jeremiah 31:15 as grieving over the Israelites when they went into exile. Melville's earlier reference to Herod indicates, however, that he had in mind the New Testament quotation of the Jeremiah passage, where the slaughter of the innocents was presented as a fulfillment of the prophet's words. See Matthew 2:17-18.

to revenge himself. He becomes an implement in the hands of the presiding forces, not only as he brings about his own destruction but as he exploits and finally destroys his crew. A medium through which a cosmic evil seems transmitted to the world is discovered in the one who pits himself against that evil in the quest for revenge. Whether the powers beyond are truly malevolent, or simply indifferent, the inner process of symbolic affront with its corresponding quest for symbolic revenge occurs as though by a dynamism of its own.

X

Ishmael Adrift

The unfolding relation of Ahab and Ishmael
works to convey Melville's awareness that there is no way to
achieve a unitary vision of divine Truth capable of sustaining
and guiding the moral self. Melville had hoped to find such
a basis for man's spiritual life by cultivating a prophetic consciousness whose characteristics are indicated in certain of Ishmael's meditations. Even as the meanings of Ahab's hunt grow
darker, Ishmael's own quest is brightened occasionally by
glimpses of divine beatitude. In fact, Ishmael's struggle with
religious doubt is affirmed to be a necessary condition of those
moments in which his positive yearnings appear to receive the
promise of fulfillment. "For, d'ye see, rainbows do not visit the
clear air; they only irradiate vapor. And so, through all the thick
mists of the dim doubts in my mind, divine intuitions now and
then shoot, enkindling my fog with a heavenly ray. And for
this I thank God; for all have doubts; many deny; but doubts
or denials, few along with them, have intuitions. Doubts of all
things earthly, and intuitions of some things heavenly; this com-
bination makes neither believer nor infidel, but makes a man
who regards them both with equal eye" ("The Fountain," p.
314). Both believer and infidel take their bearings from stated
canons of belief, from standards already formulated. But the
intuitions of religious genius illuminate the clouds of doubt and
confusion that precede formulation. They indicate an immedia-
cy of contact with the raw materials of man's spiritual constitution.

Melville intimates that Ishmael's struggle is a primordial spiritual agony that is suffered by a noble minority, by men who
contend radically for the Truth. The progressive cycles of toil

aboard the whaler reflect man's spiritual history; we see him
passing through stages, repeatedly testing an ancient heroism
and making slow additions to the stores of human understanding. "For hardly have we mortals by long toilings extracted from
this world's vast bulk its small but valuable sperm; and then,
with weary patience, cleansed ourselves from its defilements, and
learned to live here in clean tabernacles of the soul; hardly is
this done, when — *There she blows!* — the ghost is spouted up,
and away we sail to fight some other world, and go through
young life's old routine again" ("Stowing Down and Clearing
Up," p. 358).

Melville's vision of this prophetic consciousness receives its
most eloquent and confident expression through Ishmael's experience in "The Grand Armada." The *Pequod's* boats chase a large
number of whales that fan out into an immense circular pattern
of flight. Ishmael's boat is dragged into a calm that forms at
the center of the great commotion, and looking down, he sees
"the nursing mothers of the whales, and those that by their enor-
mous girth seemed shortly to become mothers." He observes
the suckling whales, and a new-born still attached to its mother
by the umbilical cord. "Some of the subtlest secrets of the seas
seemed divulged to us in this enchanted pond. We saw young
Leviathan amours in the deep" (pp. 325-326). This central calm,
in full view of the bloodshed and agony all around, and with
gigantic breeding and nurture in its depth, becomes the symbol
of a creative spirit that encompasses all joys and horrors, master-
ing an abundance so diverse as to disable lesser souls. "And
thus, though surrounded by circle upon circle of consternations
and affrights, did these inscrutable creatures at the centre freely
and fearlessly indulge in all peaceful concernments. . . . But even
so, amid the tornadoed Atlantic of my being, do I myself still
for ever centrally disport in mute calm; and while ponderous
planets of unwaning woe revolve round me, deep down and
deep inland there I still bathe me in eternal mildness of joy"
(p. 326).

This reverential spirituality is quite harmonious with the
mockery of religious custom elsewhere given as an aspect of Ishmael's temper. Ishmael's claim that "doubts of all things earthly" permit him to receive "intuitions of some things heavenly"

has its equally valid converse: an inspired spiritual voyager must condemn the authority vested in religious teaching that will not bear examination. Melville scoffs at those who are intimidated by empty traditions as he explains that the stripped carcasses of whales have been mistaken for shoals by mariners who know nothing of whaling. Hence "with trembling fingers is set down in the log — *shoals, rocks, and breakers hereabouts: beware!* And for years afterwards, perhaps, ships shun the place; leaping over it as silly sheep leap over a vacuum, because their leader originally leaped there when a stick was held. There's your law of precedents; there's your utility of traditions; there's the story of your obstinate survival of old beliefs never bottomed on the earth, and now not even hovering in the air! There's orthodoxy!" ("The Funeral," p. 262).

Melville's fearless questionings, however, bring him to issues on which the inquiry itself founders. Any who attempt to ground man's moral life in divine Truth must face questions about the moral structure of the divine realm itself. Such a demand for ethical validity is an essential component of Ishmael's quest. But Ahab and his hatred are the irreducible nub of the question whether man's striving toward the Good is supported by an ultimate ground. Ahab not only perceives the divine as malicious, but is confirmed in his vision by accessions of apparently supernatural energy. If the steadfastness of Father Mapple testifies to a holy and righteous God, then Ahab's "unsurrenderable wilfulness" equally bears witness to a divine monster. If ultimate reality is itself morally incoherent, in some Manichean cleavage, it will not afford a basis for the ordering of man's moral life.[1] Both Mapple and Ahab embody Melville's belief that the self must be disciplined to the contour of an ultimate Truth, a theocentric reality immanent to man's life, as well as transcending it. This implicit criterion of Melville's quest is evident in the way he shapes Mapple and Ahab as contrasting versions of the theocentric conception of moral integrity. But such integrity it-

---

1. A persuasive argument linking Melville's view with ancient cosmic dualism has been brought forward by Thomas Vargish, "Gnostic *Mythos* in *Moby-Dick*," PMLA, 81 (1966), 272-277. The gnostic theory in question supposes a hierarchy, as the origin of evil is explained through doctrines of an evil creator God, inferior to the supreme God. Melville's presentation of the issue, by contrast, establishes no such divine coherence.

self becomes impossible if the final Truth in which the individual soul participates is fractured into disparate and conflicting truths. The demolition of Starbuck's character suggests just such a cosmic discontinuity; his integrity is destroyed by realities he had been compelled to exclude from awareness as he sought to anchor that integrity in a scheme of divine goodness.

Ahab's undeniable wickedness violates the cosmic order if human moral judgments reflect the character of that order. But Melville does not invoke a transcendent sanction in his condemnation of Ahab; on the contrary, he uses Ahab to attack the notion that ethical insights may carry the authority of religious truth. To claim that the portrayal of Ahab's deterioration is meant to confirm a metaphysical standard of virtue is to miss the radicalism of Melville's explorations. As Matthiessen observed, Ahab's tragedy "admits no adequate moral recognition";[2] we are given no cathartic moment of restoration to moral reality. This omission ensues from the fact that *Moby-Dick* does not establish a transcendent moral economy sufficient to resolve the metaphysical issues of Ahab's quest.

***

Ishmael's disengagement from Ahab's quest does not signal the achievement of a broader scheme within which Ahab's questions are answered; it reflects a yet profounder skepticism in which the inquiry itself is doubted. On a night when the try-works are in operation, boiling blubber, Ishmael stares down from his post at the helm and guesses at the meaning of the strange sight: "the rushing Pequod, freighted with savages, and laden with fire, and burning a corpse, and plunging into that blackness of darkness, seemed the material counterpart of her monomaniac commander's soul." As such visions engage his spirit Ishmael insensibly goes to sleep, then awakens in dreamlike horror to find that the tiller had become reversed so that the *Pequod* is swinging up into the wind, in imminent danger of being capsized. Moralizing this near-disaster, Ishmael warns against fiery fixations: "Look not too long in the face of the fire, O man! . . . believe not the artificial fire, when its redness makes all things look ghastly. To-morrow, in the natural sun, the skies will be bright . . . the glorious, golden, glad sun, the

2. F. O. Matthiessen, *American Renaissance* (1941; reptd. New York, 1968), p. 456.

only true lamp — all others but liars!" ("The Try-Works," p. 354).

Clearly referring to his fascination with Ahab, Ishmael issues a warning: "Give not thyself up, then, to the fire, lest it invert thee, deaden thee; as for the time it did me." But this rejection of the fiery quest does not mean that the world revealed by the glorious sun is hospitable to the spiritual aspirations of man. "Nevertheless the sun hides not . . . all the millions of miles of deserts and of griefs beneath the moon. The sun hides not the ocean, which is the dark side of this earth, and which is two thirds of this earth. So, therefore, that mortal man who hath more of joy than sorrow in him, that mortal man cannot be true — not true, or undeveloped. With books the same. The truest of all men was the Man of Sorrows, and the truest of all books is Solomon's, and Ecclesiastes is the fine hammered steel of woe. 'All is vanity.' ALL" ("The Try-Works," pp. 354-355). Ishmael rejects Ahab and his perverse spiritual certainties because he has come to the realization that *all* such certainties are vain.

If the theocentric believers who ascribe benevolence to the Godhead are placed in a hopeless quandary by the "problem of evil," then old Ahab's belief in a malevolent God is disrupted by a corresponding "problem of good." Ishmael's skeptical rejection of Ahab results partly from Ishmael's abundant and candid responsiveness to natural beauty. This contrast between Ishmael's spirit and Ahab's becomes clear as Ishmael reveals that he cherishes moments of "land-like feeling towards the sea":

The long-drawn virgin vales; the mild blue hill-sides; as over these there steals the hush, the hum; you almost swear that play-wearied children lie sleeping in these solitudes, in some glad May-time, when the flowers of the woods are plucked. And all this mixes with your most mystic mood; so that fact and fancy, half-way meeting, interpenetrate, and form one seamless whole.

Nor did such soothing scenes, however temporary, fail of at least as temporary an effect on Ahab. But if these secret golden keys did seem to open in him his own secret golden treasuries, yet did his breath upon them prove but tarnishing ("The Gilder," pp. 405-406).

Thus Melville asserts his awareness that Ahab's monomaniacal passion mars a true loveliness. Despite his fascination with Ahab's dark ecstasies, which fuse his conception of the universe as a realm of evil, Melville was capable of moments of vision in which the whole of things is experienced as benign. In writing to Hawthorne during the final stages of his work on *Moby-Dick*, he commented on the limitations of ecstatic consciousness in terms that illuminate his way of handling this issue. Scoffing at Goethe's belief that the torments of mortal existence can be eliminated if one will *"Live in the all,"* he points out that the admonition to "bring to yourself the tinglings of life that are felt in the flowers and woods" would have little appeal for a man with a raging toothache. The inner meaning of this jest is explored in the character of Ahab, where Melville shows that acute and protracted suffering can yield its own vision of the "all," and that such a vision is as compelling in its moments of intensity as any transcendent joy. This awareness does not lead Melville to the conclusion that the "all feeling" yields no insight into the nature of reality, but persuades him that it yields only a partial insight. "What plays the mischief with the truth," he asserts, "is that men will insist upon the universal application of a temporary feeling or opinion" (*Letters*, pp. 130-131). Melville does not reject Goethe's maxim on the ground of mundane common sense; nor does he reject it because his own powers of ecstatic consciousness were weak. It was the prodigality with which he could evoke such moments of mystical insight that led him to reckon with the significance of their variety.

Ishmael's golden moment, in which fact and fancy appear unified, is taken not as an earnest of the theocentric vision he had sought, but as a transient experience whose truth is real but not final. "Would to God these blessed calms would last," he cries wearily. Instead of leading to a glorious culmination, this moment takes its place along the trail of a wandering that seems to have no end. "There is no steady unretracing progress in this life; we do not advance through fixed gradations, and at the last one pause: — through infancy's unconscious spell, boyhood's thoughtless faith, adolescence' doubt (the common doom), then scepticism, then disbelief, resting at last in manhood's pondering repose of If. But once gone through, we trace

the round again; and are infants, boys, and men, and Ifs eternally. Where lies the final harbor, whence we unmoor no more?
In what rapt ether sails the world, of which the weariest will
never weary?" ("The Gilder," p. 406).

If moral insight and ecstatic vision both lead to the conclusion
that reality is ultimately incoherent, then the arduous, isolated
search for a rejuvenated theocentric vision will have no end,
and appears a deluded enterprise in which the seeker is despoiled
of his energies. Instead of reaching a final harbor where his soul
may be sustained, the exhausted quester yields to an awareness
of his failure. Melville ironically celebrates this act of resignation
as a climax of mystical vision. In "A Squeeze of the Hand,"
Ishmael works the whale sperm in his hands and is overcome
by its lovely aroma: "I forgot all about our horrible oath; in
that inexpressible sperm, I washed my hands and my heart of
it . . . while bathing in that bath, I felt divinely free from all
ill-will, or petulance, or malice, of any sort whatsoever" (p. 348).

Ishmael forgets the oath in an access of fellow feeling that
revives the homosexual motif established in the initial scenes
with Queequeg:

> Squeeze! Squeeze! squeeze! all the morning long; I squeezed
> that sperm till I myself almost melted into it; I squeezed that
> sperm till a strange sort of insanity came over me; and I found
> myself unwittingly squeezing my co-laborers' hands in it, mis-
> taking their hands for the gentle globules. Such an abounding,
> affectionate, friendly, loving feeling did this avocation beget;
> that at last I was continually squeezing their hands, and look-
> ing up into their eyes sentimentally; as much as to say . . .
> Come; let us squeeze hands all round; nay, let us all squeeze
> ourselves into each other; let us squeeze ourselves universally
> into the very milk and sperm of kindness. ("A Squeeze of
> the Hand," pp. 348-349).

The homosexual suggestions here are not arranged, as in the
earlier instance, to indicate the defiance of convention required
by Ishmael's lonely effort to achieve Truth. They do not help
to define a setting-forth, in which outlandish experience is sought
despite orthodox claims that such "devilish" doings are the sign
and seal of man's spiritual blindness. On the contrary, Melville

reintroduces the homosexual motif in order to portray the acceptance of defeat, to acknowledge the futility of his spiritual investigations. This scene depicts a sentimental retreat from the harsh
frontier of the quest. "Would that I could keep squeezing that
sperm for ever!" Ishmael continues, "For now . . . by many prolonged, repeated experiences, I have perceived that in all cases
man must eventually lower, or at least shift, his conceit of attain-
able felicity; not placing it anywhere in the intellect or the fancy;
but in the wife, the heart, the bed, the table . . . the country"
("A Squeeze of the Hand," p. 349).[3]

Ishmael's skepticism leads him back to a sardonic acceptance
of conventional domestic comforts, as he relinquishes the hope
that "the intellect or the fancy" might provide spiritual fulfillment. At the outset of the quest, Melville had praised the
heroism of Bulkington, who fled "safety, comfort, hearthstone,
supper . . . [and] all that's kind to our mortalities" ("The Lee
Shore," p. 97) in order to maintain the fierce independence of
his spiritual struggle. But even in celebrating Bulkington's reso-
luteness Melville had intimated that it might prove futile: "Terrors of the terrible! is all this agony so vain?" (p. 98). Now in
the warmth and intimacy of communal sperm-squeezing an af-
firmative answer to that question is accepted, and the apotheosis
promised to the grim demigod is foresworn. Echoing the words
in which Eliphaz rebuked Job for inquiring into divine truth
(Job 4:13), Melville sarcastically concludes his admission that
such efforts are indeed quite vain: "In thoughts of the visions
of the night, I saw long rows of angels in paradise, each with
his hands in a jar of spermaceti" ("A Squeeze of the Hand,"
p. 349).[4]

---

3. I have discussed this passage more fully in "Homosexuality and Spiritual
Aspiration in *Moby-Dick*," *The Canadian Review of American Studies,* 6 (1975),
50-58.

4. The Hayford and Parker text of *Moby-Dick* (New York, 1967) reads "In
visions of the night" on page 349 at the line cited. Hayford and Parker explain
this emendation as follows: "we are assuming that Melville first wrote 'In
thoughts of ' and then changed it to 'In visions of ' without adequately marking
the first phrase for deletion" (p. 493). They are also assuming, quite rightly,
that the construction "In thoughts of the visions of the night" seems redun-
dant. But it clearly echoes the opening phrases of Eliphaz' vision (Job 4:13,
"In thoughts from the visions of the night"), whose general bearing is perfectly
apposite to Melville's thematic interests in the passage containing the allusion.

Sperm-squeezing fellowship is not sustained as a characteristic of Ishmael's final skepticism. He resumes his solitary aloofness, embracing the Solomonic austerity of the "wisdom that is woe," while disengaging himself from the "woe that is madness" that he sees in Ahab ("The Try-Works," p. 355). He asserts the loftiness of soul by which he has striven with mighty issues, even though his striving has yielded no final apotheosis in heavenly sunshine; "there is a Catskill eagle in some souls that can alike dive down into the blackest gorges, and soar out of them again and become invisible in the sunny spaces. And even if he for ever flies within the gorge, that gorge is in the mountains; so that even in his lowest swoop the mountain eagle is still higher than other birds upon the plain, even though they soar" (p. 355). The heroic isolation of the Truth-seeker remains heroic even when the search fails, leaving him alone in a black abyss that swallows all the religious conceptions from which ordinary men take their bearings.

In the end Ishmael is truly adrift and alone, the only survivor of the *Pequod*, clinging to the coffin turned into a life-buoy on which Queequeg had transcribed his mysterious tattoos. This tattooing, which had horrified Ishmael at their first meeting, is revealed at length as a hieroglyph: "a complete theory of the heavens and the earth, and a mystical treatise on the art of attaining truth" (Queequeg in his Coffin," p. 399). But it is a hieroglyph that no one can read, so that "these mysteries were . . . destined in the end to moulder away with the living parchment whereon they were inscribed, and so be unsolved to the last" (p. 399).

This complex figure is one of several in which Ishmael considers the possibility of weaving a coherent pattern from the disparate impressions and truths of his experience. Freedom, fate, and chance are interwoven in "The Mat-Maker"; life and death are interwoven in "A Bower in the Arsacides"; fact and fancy "form one seamless whole" in an instant of momentarily revived confidence that immediately yields to the grim conclusion that the secret of man's paternity is hidden in the grave: the interweaving of life's source with its end. This deep texture, the interweaving of life and death, preoccupies Ishmael from the opening sentences of the book: Queequeg's undecipherable tattoo, transferred from his living body to the coffin that then becomes a life-buoy, is complicated and recomplicated as a symbol for this profoundest secret of experience. But it conveys finally its own inscrutability; Melville complicates it intentionally so as to body forth the unreadable. The elaborate mute ikon is useful only to keep Ishmael afloat in the watery wilderness, the means of a survival whose ultimate significance is left in doubt.[5]

The thematic bearing of Ishmael's concluding speech is given by its epigraph: "AND I ONLY AM ESCAPED TO TELL

---

5. Ishmael's survival has stimulated diverse critical interpretations. Holman argues that "this unique salvation of Ishmael is essential to the theme of the novel," signaling the "lesson of acceptance" he has learned. "The mixed good and evil in all things, the prevalence of suffering in the world, the horror in which at times the universe seems formed — these he has come to take without fright and without affront." Ishmael may have come to accept these things, but hardly as the features of what Holman terms "the moral order of the universe in which Melville puts him." See C. Hugh Holman, "The Reconciliation of Ishmael," *South Atlantic Quarterly*, 57 (1958), 490.

William Rosenfeld, "Uncertain Faith: Queequeg's Coffin and Melville's Use of the Bible," *Texas Studies in Literature and Language*, 7 (1966), 317-327, aptly summarizes several studies of Ishmael's survival and seeks to harmonize them in his own sensitive and well-informed discussion. His argument becomes dubious, however, when he states that the concluding moment signifies Melville's reverence for human sympathy: "As Ishmael embraces the coffin-lifebuoy, the inner circle of 'sympathetic awe' which joins Queequeg, Bulkington, and Ishmael expands to spiritual dimension" (p. 323). Rosenfeld states that Queequeg's "physical death in the Pequod's sinking is beside the point" (p. 322); but it is very hard to see why Melville would have left Ishmael completely isolated had his fundamental intention been a celebration of the "heavenly impulse of love" (p. 325). Rosenfeld acknowledges that "the lack of exuberance in Ishmael's experience is an index to Melville's [religious] uncertainty and helps to expose the essential complexity of *Moby-Dick* and others of his writings" (p. 324). Melville's "uncertainty" is centrally at stake here, but for the nonce he succeeds in objectifying it as conscious art, to make a forthright statement. Rosenfeld appears to hold that it controlled Melville's mind at a level beneath awareness so that it "compelled him to set Ishmael on a troubled passage to faith" (p. 327). Yet Ishmael is not set on a passage; he is decisively set adrift.

The amoral unpredictable divine in *Moby-Dick* never ceases to bring in its surprises. It is true that Ishmael drifts in a calm, "on a soft and dirge-like main. The unharming sharks, they glided by as if with padlocks on their mouths; the savage sea-hawks sailed with sheathed beaks" ("Epilogue," p. 470). But the significance of this calm is given by the fact that in every previous instance such benign appearances precede overwhelming catastrophe, and that in this instance they precede a lucky chance.

THEE" ("Epilogue," p. 470). Instead of taking his keynote from the conclusion of Job, where the questionings are stilled, Melville uses the words of the messengers who brought Job news of disaster. Ishmael is not "saved" because he has discovered the ground of a triumphant Goodness which overcomes Ahab's triumphant Evil. He is rescued by chance, escaping alone to tell us of a catastrophe in which divine Truth is struck down as a moral standard.

Conclusion

T he conclusion of *Moby-Dick* brings Ishmael full circle to the stance in which we found him at the outset. The same skeptical, affectionate, whimsical, chastened, and profoundly wise Ishmael has recounted for us the whole crazy turbulence and glory of the quest. If both Ishmael and Melville have failed to discover the Truth that they sought, a large part of Melville's creative achievement lies precisely in the mastery with which he relates the spiritual catastrophe. When Melville's way of handling religious traditions is clarified, it becomes apparent that *Moby-Dick* evokes the most elusive and critical phase of all fundamentally creative endeavors. It conveys the crisis of uncertainty in which familiar conceptions lose their authority as representations of reality and are forced to reveal their provisional and limited character. Melville's presentation of the struggle is not controlled by any predetermined *telos;* the very openness of Melville's investigation gives it, in the end, its august grandeur and sadness. Instead of setting a confident new spiritual course, Melville leaves us with the great shroud of the sea rolling on as in immemorial ages. It is the image of an eternal mystery that finally limits the structures of meaning that men devise, thus assuring that the human spirit will never exhaust its materials, never lose its opportunity to deal directly with the unfathomable terror and abundance of life.

Just as Ishmael rejects Ahab's quest because it fails to do justice to authentic beauties and joys, so Melville's final skepticism is informed by his consciousness of the basic multiplicity of experience. When he remarked in "Hawthorne and His Mosses" that "it is not so much paucity, as superabundance of material that seems to incapacitate modern authors" ("Mosses," p. 544), he foresaw a major reason for the breakdown of his effort to achieve a unified vision of Truth. In "A Bower in the Arsacides," Melville presents such a confrontation with unknowable mystery.

He describes the rich and complicated verdure of a jungle, from the carpet of ground-vines to the interlacings of the highest tree-tops, as an image of the vast fabric of life. The "weaver-god" who generates this fabric is as inscrutable as any Calvinistic sovereign, but not because of the degeneracy of his creation. On the contrary, human inquiries are deafened by the humming of the great loom, the prodigious creative force that catches them up. In the midst of this ceaseless growing lies the skeleton of a whale, so bedecked by the living vines and tendrils as to suggest a reality more complex than the productions of the weaver-god alone. The skeleton and the vines make a more comprehensive fabric in which life and death are intermingled.

Having evoked this religious mystery, Melville defines its relation to the dead systems of dogma over which official guardians keep watch. He observes that the skeleton was maintained as a shrine by a band of priests who resent his effort to explore its interior. When he frankly asks them to give their views concerning its scale and significance, they fall into a disorderly quarrel among themselves and leave him to his own inquiries ("A Bower in the Arsacides," pp. 374-375). Melville's spiritual courage included an exceptional tolerance for ambiguity, a capacity to maintain opposing intimations and possibilities of truth without insisting that they compose themselves into a coherent pattern. This vitality of mind is attested by the disconcerting abundance of meanings that he uncovered as he probed the enigmas within the framework of religious belief generally accepted in his time, enigmas that prompted frantic controversies among official guardians of the structure.

In *The Conflict of Ages*, Edward Beecher traced the opposition of liberal and orthodox doctrine to a dilemma that he had perceived twenty-six years before, and had confided to his notebook in a tense and cryptic paradigm: "Evil exists. If it does prove malevolence in God we are lost, or else must love a partial being. We cannot analyse the thing."[1] Beecher kept his problem secret, even after he had devised a solution for it, revealing only to selected intimates the spiritual turmoil that plagued him. The reasons for his silence were complex, but among them seems

---

1. Robert Merideth, *The Politics of the Universe, Edward Beecher, Abolition, and Orthodoxy* (Nashville, 1968), p. 45.

to have been the recognition that if a Christian scholar acknowledged the existence of this fundamental quandary, the moral
authority of religious knowledge would be jeopardized. His
brother Charles knew the story from the inside, and later explained that Edward feared an open declaration might "tend
to unhinge and distract society," that the "wicked and impure
might scoff, and the holy feel hurt."[2]

In *Moby-Dick*, Melville thoroughly analyzed Beecher's enigma,
reaching conclusions that Beecher earnestly desired to evade.
Beecher did not want to settle for a "partial being"; he wanted
to vindicate the monotheistic authority under which Christian
teaching had sought to mobilize the religious impulses of man;
he wanted to proclaim a unified metaphysical system that could
form the basis of a coherent moral life. Melville's explorations,
by contrast, brought him to observe that "truth is ever incoherent" (*Letters*, p. 143); he celebrated the whale as an embodiment
of the divine, but not as the manifestation of a supreme unitary
Godhead. He declared that the whale's divine preeminence will
be recognized only when man's spiritual awareness is no longer
ordered by a single all-embracing principle, but is freed to develop a sophisticated polytheism:

> If hereafter any highly cultured, poetical nation shall lure
> back to their birth-right, the merry May-day gods of old; and
> livingly enthrone them again in the now egotistical sky; on
> the now unhaunted hill; then be sure, exalted to Jove's high
> seat, the great Sperm Whale shall lord it.
>
> "Champollion deciphered the wrinkled granite hiero-
> glyphics. But there is no Champollion to decipher the Egypt
> of every man's and every being's face. Physiognomy, like every
> other human science, is but a passing fable. If then, Sir Wil-
> liam Jones, who read in thirty languages, could not read the
> simplest peasant's face in its profounder and more subtle
> meanings, how may unlettered Ishmael hope to read the awful
> Chaldee of the Sperm Whale's brow? I but put that brow
> before you. Read it if you can." ("The Prairie," pp. 292-293).

Such forthright evocations of the divine mystery of the whale

---

2. *Ibid.*, p. 63.

occur frequently in *Moby-Dick,* and when they are compared
to the presentation of leviathan in the Book of Job, it becomes
clear that Melville has reversed the moral bearing of their Biblical counterpart. God finally demands and receives obedience
in the Biblical account, for Job accepts the divine authority;
the ineffable wonders of the creation propound a single ruling
creator to whom Job entirely submits.[3] Melville does not interpret the inscrutable whale as the figure of a morally authoritative
Godhead; to him the enigma on the plane of religious reality
implies a corresponding enigma in morals. He arranges his presentation of Ahab and Ishmael to convey the assertion that no
unitary divine power can properly require such obedience:
through them he assails the "egotistical sky."

We return finally to Melville's personal stake in this insurrection against the regnant spiritual ethos of his time. In "Hawthorne and His Mosses" Melville reveals that he had been
restrained from pursuing his explorations for reasons that resemble Beecher's. There he had spoken of "probings at the very
axis of reality" that produce dangerous revelations: "things,
which we feel to be so terrifically true, that it were all but madness
for any good man, in his own proper character, to utter, or even
hint of them" ("Mosses," pp. 541-542). Once he had dismantled
the theocentric system in *Moby-Dick,* Melville suffered something
more serious than physical or mental exhaustion; he suffered
the disorientation of returning from his heightened consciousness,
in which the madness of his visions made sense, to the everyday
world where conventional forms of thought still had currency,

---

3. Nathalia Wright, "Moby Dick: Jonah's or Job's Whale?" *American Literature,* 37 (1965), 190-195, argues that Ishmael sees the whale as "symbolic of
a universe which, for all its marvels, is not only amoral but inscrutable —
perhaps, indeed, a complete illusion. Excepting the last possibility, it is essentially the view of the universe expressed by the Hebrew Wisdom writers, most
notably the author of Job" (p. 192). Yet the Book of Proverbs is a major
repository of Wisdom writing, and it is filled with notations of the earthly
benefits God grants the virtuous and the punishments that befall the wicked.
See Robert H. Pfeiffer, *Introduction to the Old Testament* (New York, 1941), pp.
650-659. The Book of Job, though it attacks the pious smugness of Job's comforters, scarcely evokes an "amoral" universe. The speeches concerning leviathan, and the wonders of the created order generally, have an unmistakable
moral force. "I abhor myself," Job replies, "and repent in dust and ashes"
(Job 42: 6).

both in the public world and in his own personality. He found it difficult to resume "his own proper character" as a man who would shy away from terrific truths. Yet Melville's madness was sane; his religious doubts fixed on true questions, and his instinct was sound. Time would vindicate his intuition that traditional religious discourse was in a state of fundamental disarray. For the present, however, he needed reassurance against the fear that his madness was nothing more than personal aberration.

Melville's elaborate speculations on the metaphysical significance of madness should not blind us to the fact that he was really afraid that his own mental instabilities would get out of hand. When Charles Fenno Hoffman was committed to an insane asylum, Melville commented in terms that illuminate his misgivings: "This going mad of a friend or acquaintance comes straight home to every man who feels his soul in him, — which but few men do. For in all of us lodges the same fuel to light the same fire. And he who has never felt, momentarily, what madness is has but a mouthful of brains. What sort of sensation permanent madness is may be very well imagined — just as we imagine how we felt when we were infants, tho' we can not recall it. In both conditions we are irresponsible & riot like gods without fear of fate" (*Letters*, p. 83). The presumption that moral standards had to be grounded in divine principles was innate to Melville's thought; it was the central claim of that theocentric system of understanding by which he had grown to adulthood. Having evoked the breakdown of theocentric authority in *Moby-Dick*, Melville was left with the fear that no way of ordering consciousness remained.

Melville was tremendously elated therefore when he received from Hawthorne a letter about *Moby-Dick*, for it persuaded him that Hawthorne had understood the book. Melville attached a religious significance to Hawthorne's appreciation because it counteracted his deepest anxieties. But he found this significance hard to explain. His reply to Hawthorne traces the changes of consciousness that he experienced in trying to come to terms with this moment of deep reassurance. As he struggles for a way to articulate the religious import of his personal response his language finally becomes surreal, almost nightmarish in its recasting of familiar images.

He tells Hawthorne that he cannot in fact express his first
response to the letter because circumstances prevented him from
replying the moment he received it. "In me divine magnanimities are spontaneous and instantaneous — catch them while
you can. The world goes round, and the other side comes up.
So now I can't write what I felt. But I felt pantheistic then
— your heart beat in my ribs and mine in yours, and both
in God's" (*Letters,* p. 142). In this first expression of the solidarity
that he feels with Hawthorne, then, Melville directly invokes
theocentric conventions. Hawthorne's understanding of the book
manifests a shared spirituality (so Melville affirms) that is rooted
in the Godhead.

But that "pantheistic" moment has given way to a very different phase of consciousness, in which Melville affirms a polythe-
istic amoralism, like that celebrated in wine at the banquets
of pagan gods. Using language that recalls his meditation upon
the irresponsibility of madness, Melville informs Hawthorne that
"a sense of unspeakable security is in me this moment, on account of your having understood the book. I have written a
wicked book, and feel spotless as the lamb. Ineffable socialities
are in me. I would sit down and dine with you and all the
gods in old Rome's Pantheon. It is a strange feeling — no hope-
fulness is in it, no despair. Content — that is it; and irresponsibility. . . . I speak now of my profoundest sense of being, not
of an incidental feeling" (*Letters,* p. 142). Now there is no central
deity upon whom the divine fellow-feeling is grounded, no supreme Unit to give this commonalty an ultimate coherence.
Despite the quietude that Melville finds in this "strange feeling,"
it is clear that the major stress of this passage falls upon his
inner uncertainties. Affirming the "divine magnanimities" that
Hawthorne's letter aroused, Melville describes the drastic shifts
that are taking place in his sense of what it means. Earlier it
was mutual participation in the Godhead; now it is a feast of
separate divinities.

The banquet of the gods provides an image that accords well
with the multiplicity of religious consciousness that he had celebrated in *Moby-Dick,* but it still does not altogether satisfy Melville as a description of his present state of mind. He moves
on to yet a third image in which the divine reality, no longer

unified into One, still cannot truly be represented as individual divinities. Melville's final apprehension is not of plurality, a collectivity of autonomous gods among whom great artists like himself and Hawthorne deserve membership; his deepest consciousness is of fragmentation. "Whence come you Hawthorne? By what right do you drink from my flagon of life? And when I put it to my lips — lo, they are yours and not mine. I feel that the Godhead is broken up like the bread at the Supper, and that we are the pieces. Hence this infinite fraternity of feeling" (*Letters,* p. 142).

Here psychic and religious dislocation are expressed together. The bread at the Supper, in traditional terms, represents the opportunity of men to participate in the divine source and ground of their existence by partaking of the Body of Christ. In Melville's adaptation of the image, the partakers have disappeared, leaving human persons that are themselves pieces of God. As his spiritual investigation had broken up the Godhead on which all personhood was grounded, so Melville experienced himself as a fragmentary being. His image of the shared flagon, likewise, with its evocation of his lips surrealistically transformed into Hawthorne's lips, indicates the degree to which Melville found the contours of his own personality to be indefinite and liable to unnerving transformations.

As he permitted this internal plasticity to reveal itself to Hawthorne, Melville became uneasily aware that he was saying some very strange things. "My dear Hawthorne, the atmospheric skepticisms steal into me now, and make me doubtful of my sanity in writing you thus. But, believe me, I am not mad, most noble Festus! But truth is ever incoherent, and when the big hearts strike together the concussion is a little stunning" (*Letters,* pp. 142-143). Melville knew that his alterations of personality were associated with his spiritual inquiries; he insisted that the incoherencies he found in himself resulted from the incoherence of ultimate Truth that he had come to discern. His claim that the Godhead was broken up is in part a cry of triumph at what he had achieved. And yet the uncertainties now afflicting him were so grievous that he could not judge his own intellectual development securely. At one moment he insists upon having made a positive advance: "Lord," he exclaims, "when shall we

be done growing?" But in the next moment he confesses that
he hardly knows what to make of himself. He informs Hawthorne that a reply to his letter, addressed to "Herman Melville," will be missent. "For the very fingers that now guide
this pen are not precisely the same that just took it up and
put it on this paper. Lord, when shall we be done changing?"
(*Letters*, p. 143). Was he "growing" toward some suitable fulfillment? Or was he merely "changing," passing from one state of
consciousness to another with no standard by which to measure
the direction of change?

The "atmospheric skepticisms" that crept into Melville as he
wrote this letter to Hawthorne may have had an additional
source. He believed that Hawthorne understood him and his
book because he most passionately needed and wanted to believe
that. But he also may have had a canny awareness that Hawthorne did not necessarily share the "infinite fraternity of feeling" about which he was himself so excited. As his later remarks
indicate, Hawthorne at length found Melville's prodigious dis-
courses upon religious subjects to be quite tedious; he was simply
not the soul mate that Melville wanted him to be. Melville had
articulated in *Moby-Dick* an apprehension of reality that none
of his contemporaries shared. Certain reviewers and friends had
complimentary and admiring things to say about the book, but
it was not until well into the twentieth century that readers
began to glimpse the breathtaking magnitude of what he had
achieved. There was now really no one for him to talk to.

INDEX

Abraham, 105
Adam, 121, 124, 125, 154
Ahab (Biblical), 10 *n*, 118, 121, 142-144
Ahab, Captain, 66, 102
   the "all feeling," 164
   bigotry of, 90
   blasphemy, 119, 142, 146, 150-152, 157
   compared to the Biblical Ahab, 143
     n-144 *n*
   cosmic evil, 153, 158
   cosmic fury, 117-118, 149
   damnation, 117-119, 124-125, 139, 141,
     149-150, 153-154
   death of, justice in, 10 *n*-12 *n*
   defiance, 146-147, 156-157
   demonism, 124
   God, concept of, 147, 149, 156, 163
   hell concept, 146
   heretical aspect, 40
   as hero of the damned, 155
   heroism, 92, 116, 123, 150
   the inscrutable, 122-123
   Ishmael and, 127-128, 132, 133 *n*-134 *n*,
     139, 141, 150, 159, 162-163, 174
   Jonah and, 10 *n*, 118, 133 *n*, 146
   madness, 92, 123, 141-142, 145, 149, 152,
     167
   reprobate, 120-121
   monomania, 36, 141, 164
   predestination, 142, 147-149, 157-158
   rage, 119-121, 125, 146, 147, 152, 154
   rational soul, 149
   repentance, 118-119, 148
   as the reprobate, 117-126, 147
   revenge, 119-120, 126, 141-142, 157-158
   self-assertion, 142, 144, 149, 161
   sin, 118
   as a spiritual quester, 1, 46
   as spokesman for mankind, 153-155
   Starbuck and, 149-153
   transfiguration, 141-158
   Truth, 91-92, 123, 127, 161
   as a tyrant, 155-157
   vengeance, 142, 153
   wickedness, 10 *n*-12 *n*, 162
Aiken, Henry D., 83 *n*
Albany Academy, 62
Alma, 75, 76
American Christianity . . . (Smith, Handy,
   and Loetscher), 34 *n*

American Literature, 11 *n*, 133 *n*, 174 *n*
American Renaissance (Matthiessen), 70 *n*,
   162 *n*
Arminianism, 5, 38-40, 60
Arminius, Jacobus, 38
Arvin, Newton, 10 *n*-11 *n*, 53 *n*, 70 *n*
Augustine, Saint, 5

Baird, James, 6 *n*, 9 *n*-10 *n*
Barrett, William, 83 *n*
Battenfield, David, 111 *n*
Battles, F. L., 121 *n*, 143 *n*
Beaver, Harold, 1 *n*
Beecher, Charles, 173
Beecher, Edward, 7-8, 11, 16, 88-89, 124
   n, 172-174
Bentley, Richard, 69, 70
Bercovitch, Sacvan, 53 *n*
Berger, Peter L., 3 *n*
Bewley, Marius, 143 *n*-144 *n*
Bezanson, Walter, 9 *n*
Bible, the, 9 *n*, 10 *n*, 57, 97, 105, 109-113,
   117, 118, 121, 125, 133-135, 142-146, 154,
   166, 174
   allegory vs. fact, 135-136
   business practices and, 47 *n*
   on homosexuality, 99
   See also Melville, Herman; *Moby-Dick*
Bible and Men of Learning, The (Mathews),
   59-60, 91 *n*
Bickersteth, Edward, 34 *n*
Bildad, Captain, 101, 104, 105, 117
Billy Bud, Sailor and Other Stories (Melville),
   1 *n*
Bland, 80
Blasphemy, 119, 142, 146, 150-152, 157
Booth, Thornton Y., 134 *n*
Brodhead, Jacob, 33, 114
Brodhead, John Romeyn, 33-41
Brower, William Leverich, 35 *n*
Browne, Sir Thomas, 76 *n*
Buck, Charles, 34 *n*
Buckminster, Joseph Stevens, 31, 52 *n*, 53
Bulkington, 168 *n*
   heroism, 114-116, 166
Bunyan, John, 34, 35 *n*
Bushnell, Horace, 23, 27, 61
   on God, 25-26, 45, 46
   on reality, 25-26

Call Me Ishmael (Olson), 70 *n*, 78 *n*
Calvin, John, 11 *n*, 30 *n*, 38, 98, 109,
   112-113, 133 *n*
   concept of God, 121-125, 142-144
   on sin, 118, 121-122, 142
Calvinism
   Arminianism, 5, 38-40, 60
   baptism ceremony, 28
   business practices and, 47, 63-65
   Dutch Reformed Church, 28-42, 57-58,
      111
   deathbed stories, 59-60
   Second Great Awakening, 33-35
   fear, importance of, 111, 113, 120
   free will and, 131
   God, concept of, 5, 11 *n*-12 *n*, 30 *n*, 35,
      38-41, 148
      God/man relationship, 5-11
      inscrutable aspect, 57-58, 61, 121-122,
         134 *n*
      malevolent aspect, 11 *n*, 89, 124-125,
         148
      repentance, 119
      sovereignty, 84, 115, 121-124, 134 *n*,
         142-144
      vengeance, 120
      wrath of, 111-113, 124-125
   idolatry and homosexuality, 96-100
   imagination, mistrust of, 130-132
   innate depravity, 72, 75, 80, 82, 110-114
   pietism, 30, 33 *n*, 61, 110 *n*, 146, 150
   predestination, 38-40, 80, 82, 142, 146
   reason, 90, 109, 121-122, 150
   rebirth, 145
   repentance, 148
   reprobation, decree of, 38-39
   Sabbath School Union, 41-42, 59
   scientific knowledge and, 138-139
   sin, 35, 39, 79, 80, 111-113, 118-122, 142,
      145, 146
      original sin, 72-75, 80
   submission, virtue of, 113-114
   Synod of Dort (1618-1619), 38-39
   wickedness, 120-121
Calvin's Calvinism (Calvin), 38 *n*, 122 *n*, 143
   n, 144 *n*
Canadian Review of American Studies, The, 166
   n
Candid Examination (Taylor), 124 *n*
Carlyle, Thomas, 154
Caryl, Joseph, 112 *n*
Champollion, Jean Jacques, 173
Channing, William Ellery, 40-41, 75-77,
   80, 89-91, 111, 131 *n*, 147, 155
Christian Intelligencer, 59 *n*
Christian Nurture (Bushnell), 25-26, 27, 61
Clarel (Bezanson), 9 *n*

Clark, Harry Hayden, 9 *n*
Clootz, Anacharsis, 154
Coe, Edward B., 63 *n*
Cole, Henry, 122 *n*
*Collegiate Reformed Protestant Dutch Church
   . . .* (eds. Brower and Miller), 35 *n*
Commentaries on the Epistle of Paul . . . (Cal-
   vin), 98 *n*
Commentary on the Epistle to the Romans, A
   (Hodge), 98 *n*
Conflict of Ages, The . . . (Beecher), 7-8,
   88-89, 124 *n*, 172-173
Constitution of the Reformed Dutch Church, The,
   28 *n*, 58 *n*, 60*n*
Corwin, 33 *n*, 35 *n*, 36 *n*
Cosmic dualism, 161 *n*
Cosmic evil, 153, 158
Cosmic fury, 117-118, 149
Curti, Merle, 9 *n*

Damnation, 117-119, 124-125, 139, 141,
   149-150, 153-154
"Daniel Orme" (Melville), 1
Davis, 78 *n*
Dayton, Abram C., 33 *n*
"Dissertation on Divine Justice, A"
   (Owen), 120 *n*
Doddridge, Philip, 34-35, 58 *n*, 110, 137
   n
Dort, Synod of (1618-1619), 38-39
Dramatic Works, The (Shakespeare), 78 *n*
Driver, S. R., 143 *n*
*Dutch Calvinistic Pietism in the Middle Colonies
   . . .* (Tanis), 33 *n*, 110 *n*, 145 *n*, 146
Dutch Reformed Church, 28-42, 57-58, 111
   deathbed stories, 59-60
   Second Great Awakening, 33-35
Duyckinck, Evert, 11-12
Dwight, Timothy, 34

Early Settlers of Nantucket (Hinchman), 106
   n
Eccentric Design, The (Bewley), 143 *n*-144 *n*
Edwards, Jonathan, 39 *n*, 124 *n*
Eliphaz, 166
Emerson, Ralph Waldo, 154
Emerson Society Quarterly, 134 *n*
English Literary History (Woodson), 146 *n*
English Notebooks, The (Hawthorne), 12 *n*,
   18 *n*
Erikson, Erik H., 3 *n*, 15, 66 *n*
Erikson, Kai, 66 *n*
Everett, Edward, 31
*Exposition with Practical Observations upon the
   Book of Job, An* (Caryl), 112 *n*

Fedallah, 143 *n*, 144
Feidelson, Charles, Jr., 130 *n*
Fine Hammered Steel of Herman Melville, The
  (Stern), 10 *n*
Foster, R. S., 124 *n*, 148 *n*
Freud, Sigmund
  on God, 25, 45
  on reality, 23-26
  theory of neurosis, 13-14
Fromm, Erich, 15
Future of an Illusion, The (Freud), 24

Gabriel, 125
Gansevoort, Catherine, 29-30, 34, 43, 62
  n
Gansevoort, Peter, 29-30, 43, 62
  Melvill (Allan) and, 47-52
Gansevoort-Lansing Collection (GLC), 27
  n-32 *n*, 34 *n*, 47 *n*, 48 *n*, 49 *n*, 51 *n*, 62
  n
Gansevoorts of Albany . . . (Kenney), 29 *n*
Gardiner, Captain, 157
Geertz, Clifford, 3 *n*
Germany (Stael), 138 *n*
Gilman, William H., 28 *n*-33 *n*, 41 *n*, 45
  n, 49 *n*-53 *n*, 58 *n*, 62 *n*, 64 *n*, 66 *n*, 67
  n, 136 *n*, 138 *n*
God, concepts of
  Bushnell, 25-26, 45, 46
  Calvin, 121-125, 142-144
  Calvinism, 5, 11 *n*-12 *n*, 30 *n*, 35, 38-41,
    148
    God/man relationship, 5-11
    inscrutable aspect, 57-58, 61, 121-122,
      134 *n*
    malevolent aspect, 11 *n*, 89, 124-125,
      148
    repentance, 119
    sovereignty, 84, 115, 121-124, 134 *n*,
      142-144
    vengeance, 120
    wrath of God, 111-113, 124-125, 148
  Freud, 25, 45
  Hawthorne, 16-18
  Melvill (Allan), 47-54, 58
  Melvill (Maria), 58-61
  Melville, 10 *n*-12 *n*, 45-46, 54-55, 60, 61,
    74 *n*, 139
    Egyptian heritage, 87
    God/man relationship, 5-6, 9-11
    question of sovereignty, 84-85, 134 *n*
    Moby-Dick, 10 *n*-12 *n*, 102-105, 147, 149,
      156, 163
    judgment by God, 117-118
    malevolence, 124-125
    wrath of God, 111-113
  Paley, 136-139

Roman Catholic Church, 38
  Unitarianism, 5, 30, 40-41
Goethe, Johann Wolfgang von, 164
Golding, Arthur, 113 *n*
Goold, William H., 120 *n*
Gordis, Robert, 133 *n*
Great Christian Doctrine of Original Sin, The
  (Edwards), 124 *n*
Growth of American Thought, The (Curti), 9
  n

Hackensack Insurrection, 39 *n*
Hagar, 105
Hamlet, 18, 73
Handy, Robert T., 34 *n*
Harvey, John W., 111 *n*
Hawthorne, Nathaniel
  annihilation considerations, 16
  God, concept of, 16-18
  Melville and, 12, 16, 17, 19, 76
    correspondence, 83, 86, 139, 164, 175-
      178
    Melville's assessment of, 70-75
Hawthorne, Sophia, 78 *n*
"Hawthorne and His Mosses" (Melville),
  70-75, 86, 102, 171, 174
  innate depravity, 72, 75
  on the literary Christ (Shiloh), 71, 73,
    82
  literary nationalism in, 71-74
  madness, 73-74
  original sin, 72-75
  "power of blackness," 72-75
  sane madness of vital Truth, 2, 18, 70-75,
    78 *n*, 123
Hayford, 154 *n*, 166 *n*
Herman Melville, Cycle and Epicycle (Met-
  calf), 78 *n*
Herod, King, 157
"Heroes" (Carlyle), 154
Heroism
  Ahab, 92, 116, 123, 150
  Bulkington, 114-116, 166
  Father Mapple, 109-116
  Ishmael, 160, 167
  Queequeg, 101
Hinchman, Lydia S., 106 *n*
Hodge, Charles, 98 *n*
Hoeltje, Hubert H., 70 *n*
Hoffman, Charles Fenno, 175
Holder, Charles Frederick, 106 *n*
Holman, C. Hugh, 91 *n*, 133 *n*, 134 *n*, 168
  n
Homosexuality, 96-100, 165-166
  the Bible on, 99
Hopkins, Samuel, 39 *n*
Horney, Karen, 15

Horsford, Howard C., 87 *n*, 130 *n*
Howard, Leon, 9 *n*, 69 *n*
Hume, David, 103 *n*

Iago, 18, 73
Idea of the Holy, The (Otto), 111 *n*
Identity, Youth and Crisis (Erikson), 3 *n*, 15
    n, 66 *n*
Idòlatry, 96-100
Indwelling Sin (Owen), 43, 145
Institutes of the Christian Religion (ed. Mc-
    Neill), 121 *n*, 143 *n*
Interpretation of Cultures, The (Geertz), 3 *n*
*Introduction to the Literature of the Old Testa-
    ment, An* (Driver), 143 *n*
Introduction to the Old Testament (Pfeiffer),
    143 *n*, 174 *n*
Isabel, 13 *n*-14 *n*
Ishmael
    Ahab and, 127-128, 132, 133 *n*-134 *n*, 139,
        141, 150, 159, 162-163, 174
    evil, 127
    Father Mapple and, 96
    heroism, 160, 167
    homosexuality, 96, 99, 100, 165-166
    idolatry, 96-100
    imagination, problem of, 139-140
    intuition, 159-161
    natural theology, 136-140
    problems of orthodoxy, 96-100
    Queequeg and, 95-105
    rights of man, 126
    skepticism, 90, 92, 95, 128, 131, 136,
        166-167, 171
    as a spiritual quester, 1, 95-107, 164-165
    survival of, 167-169
    Truth, 91-92, 102, 106, 127-128, 131, 159,
        161, 165, 167, 169, 171
    universal religion, 101-102
    vanity, 163
    whiteness, symbolism of, 127-131
Ishmael (Baird), 6 *n*, 9 *n*-10 *n*
Ishmael (Biblical), 99, 105

Jackson, 79
James, Henry, Sr., 8 *n*
Jennings, D., 137 *n*
Jeremiah, 110 *n*
Jesus Christ, 114
Job, 47 *n*, 57, 113, 117, 133-135, 166, 174
    allegory vs. fact, 135
Jonah, 109-113
    Ahab and, 10 *n*, 118, 133 *n*, 146
    allegory vs. fact, 135
Jonathan Edwards (Miller), 124 *n*
Jones, Sir William, 173
Joshua, 106

Journal of the History of Ideas, 106 *n*
Journal of a Visit to Europe and the Levant
    (Melville), 87 *n*
Jung, Carl Gustav, theory of neurosis, 13-
    14, 15 *n*

Keach, Benjamin, 132 *n*
Kenney, Alice P., 29 *n*
Kierkegaard, Soren, 9
King Lear (Shakespeare), 78 *n*
Knox, John, 26-27
Kuhn, Thomas, 6 *n*-7 *n*

Landmarks of the Reformed Fathers (Van
    Eyck), 39 *n*
Langer, Susanne, K., 6 *n*
Langley, Harold D., 81 *n*
Larrabee, H. A., 65 *n*
*Last Days of Knickerbocker Life in Old New
    York* (Dayton), 33 *n*
Lear, 18, 73, 78
L'Estrange, Sir Roger, 76 *n*
Leviathan, 112, 113, 133-135, 160, 174
Leyda, Jay, 12 *n*, 28 *n*, 52 *n*, 53 *n*, 57 *n*,
    59 *n*, 64 *n*, 125 *n*
Life of Andrew Melvill (M'Crie), 27 *n*
*Life of the Mind in America from the Revolution
    to the Civil War, The* (Miller), 34 *n*
Loetscher, Lefferts, A., 34 *n*
Luckman, Thomas, 3 *n*

M'Crie, Thomas, 27 *n*
McCulloh, Gerald O., 38 *n*
McNeill, John T., 35 *n*, 121 *n*
Madness
    basic conceptual frameworks, 4-5
    Melvill (Allan), 46, 51-53
    Melville, 18, 78-80, 89-90, 175
    Moby-Dick, 92, 104, 123, 141-142, 145,
        149, 152, 167
    reprobate, 120-121
    reason and, 78 *n*, 90
    sane madness of vital Truth, 2, 18, 70-75,
        78 *n*, 123
    See also Neuroses
Magazine of the Reformed Dutch Church, 38
    n, 39 *n*, 59 *n*, 98 *n*, 113 *n*, 120 *n*
Main Currents in American Thought (Parring-
    ton), 41 *n*
*Man's Faith and Freedom, the Theological In-
    fluence of Jacobus Arminius* (ed. McCulloh),
    38 *n*
Mansfield, Luther, 78 *n*
Mapple, Father, 10 *n*-11 *n*, 36, 101, 105,
    118, 146, 161
    heroism, 109-116
    Ishmael and, 96

Marcel, Gabriel, 82-83
Mardi and a Voyage Thither (Melville), 60
  n, 69, 70, 75-79
  madness, 78-79
  reason, 75-79
  Revelation, 75
  sin, 77
  Truth, 75-78
Mathews, J. M., 28, 59-60, 91
Matthiessen, F. O., 70 *n*, 162
Mead, Sidney Earl, 39 *n*
Melvill, Andrew, 26
Melvill, Allan, 26-33, 62 *n*, 64-65, 67
  background of, 26-27, 30-31
  death of, 45, 46, 53-54, 57, 60
  disgrace of, 27, 45-53
  family pride, 43
  Gansevoort (Peter) and, 47-52
  influence on son (Herman), 45-46, 51-57,
    60-61
  madness, 46, 51-53
  question of personal honor, 48-50
  religion of, 26-33, 42-43
    business practices and, 47-53
    God, concept of, 47-54, 58
    hypocrisy in, 46
Melvill (Melville), Maria, 26-27, 31, 50, 53,
  62
  religion of, 29, 30, 57
    God, concept of, 58-61
    joins Dutch Reformed Church, 57-58
Melvill, Thomas, 27, 29 *n*, 31, 44
Melvill, Thomas, Jr., 52 *n*
Melvill family, 43-44
  change in spelling of the family name,
    27, 62
  conflict of religious views, 27-44
  family pride, 32, 43, 62, 67-78
Melville (Miller), 17 *n*, 53 *n*, 70 *n*
Melville, Allan, 59
Melville, Augusta, 59
Melville, Gansevoort, 33 *n*, 62, 64, 65
Melville, Helen, 59
Melville, Herman
  the anima experience, 13 *n*-14 *n*
  annihilation threats, 12, 17 *n*
  antiflogging movement, 81
  attack on missionaries, 68
  autobiographical aspect of writings, 14
    n-15 *n*
  background of, 26-29
  baptism of, 27, 28, 32
  the Bible, use of, 10 *n*, 42, 97, 110 *n*,
    121, 133 *n*, 135, 143 *n*
  childhood, 2, 5-6, 45-56
  on the condemned, 60 *n*
  delusions, 46

demonic consciousness, 67
early success as a writer, 69
economic hardships, 62-68
education, 42, 62
family pride, 32, 67-68
father's influence, 45-46, 51-57, 60-61
financial ruin, fear of, 86-87
God, concept of, 10 *n*-12 *n*, 45-46, 54-55,
  60, 61, 74 *n*, 139
  Egyptian heritage, 87
  God/man relationship, 5-6, 9-11
  question of sovereignty, 84-85, 134 *n*
Hawthorne and, 12, 16, 17, 19, 76
  correspondence, 83, 86, 139, 164, 175-
    178
  Melville's assessment of, 70-75
house-religion, 61-62
intellectual idiom of, 9
madness, 18, 78-80, 89-90, 175
  sane madness of vital Truth, 2, 18,
    70-75, 78 *n*, 123
manliness concept, 27, 46, 60
on Messianic role of America, 80-82
neurosis, 12-19
  Erikson on, 15
  Freudian theory, 13-14
  Jungian theory, 13-14, 15 *n*
  obsessiveness of, 11-12, 16
  Oedipus Complex, 13 *n*-14 *n*
as prophet of spiritual revolution, 9
psychic distress, 83, 86-88
on the reading public, 85-87
reality, 86, 176-178
  guilty secret in, 46
  models of, 3-4
  ultimate structure of, 6, 37
scientific knowledge and, 138-139
selfsovereignty, 83-85, 86
Shakespeare and, 70, 78 *n*
  Melville's assessment of, 70-73
skepticism, 130 *n*, 171, 177-178
theocentric system, 6, 9-11, 15, 18, 45,
  175, 176
  breakdown of, 87-90
  business cycle and, 62-65
  negative dimension in, 66-67
  suppressed revolt against, 65-66
Truth, 3, 82, 86, 159, 171-173, 177
undeserved suffering, 79, 80, 82
universality of writings, 15 *n*
See also names of works (especially
  "Hawthorne and His Mosses;" *Moby-
  Dick*)
Melville's Quarrel with God (Thompson), 11
  n-12 *n*, 74 *n*, 99 *n*, 110 *n*, 143 *n*-144 *n*
Melville's Use of the Bible (Wright), 10 *n*,
  110 *n*, 143 *n*

Meredith, Robert, 8 n, 172 n
Metcalf, Eleanor Melville, 78 n
Miller, Edwin Haviland, 17 n, 53 n, 70 n
Miller, Henry P., 35 n
Miller, Perry, 34 n, 124 n
Moby-Dick (Melville), 65, 68, 82-83, 88 n,
  95-178
  aesthetic structures of, 9, 37, 91
  the "all feeling," 164
  allegory vs. fact, 135-136
  annihilation, 129
  assessment of, ix-x, 2-3, 18-19, 178
  the Bible and, 42, 92 n, 105, 106, 109-114,
    117-118, 121, 124, 133-234, 135 n, 143
    n-144, n, 157, 163, 166, 174
  blasphemy, 119, 132, 142, 146, 150-152,
    157
  cosmic fury, 117-118, 149
  cosmic resentment, 127-140
  creative synthesis in, 91-92
  damnation, 117-119, 124-125, 139, 141,
    149-150, 153-154
  demonism, 124, 129
  depravity of man, 110-113
  "devilish" concepts, 104-105
  evil, 109, 127, 153, 158
  God, concept of, 10 n-12 n, 102-105, 147,
    149, 156, 163
    judgment by God, 117-118
    malevolence, 124-125
    wrath of God, 111-113
  hell concept, 146
  heroism, 92, 101, 109-116, 123, 150, 160,
    167
  homosexuality, 96, 99, 100, 165-166
  human dignity, 102, 106, 109-116, 126
  idolatry, 96-100
  imagination, problem of, 128-131, 139-
    140
  impersonal natural law, 139
  the inscrutable, 122-123
  intuition, 159-161
  madness, 92, 104, 123, 141-142, 145, 149,
    152, 167
    reprobate, 120-121
  manliness, 114-115
  predestination, 125-126, 142, 147-149,
    157-158
  prophetic consciousness, 159-160
  punishment, 117
  rage, 119-121, 125, 146, 147, 152, 154
  rebirth theme, 110, 113, 114, 146
  repentance, 118-119, 148
  reprobation, 117-126, 147
  Revelation, 132-133
  revenge, 119-120, 126, 141-142, 157-158
  rights of man, 126
  self-assertion, 142, 144, 149, 161
  sharkishness of man, 134
  sin, 110-113, 115, 118
    original sin concept, 104, 109
  skepticism, 90, 92, 95, 128, 131, 136,
    166-167, 171
  submission, virtue of, 113-114
  theocentric system, 90, 127, 132, 141,
    161-162, 174
  transfiguration, 141-158
  Truth, 83, 88, 91-92, 102, 105, 106, 123,•
    127-128, 130, 131, 137, 159, 161, 165,
    167, 169, 171
  use of tradition in, 91-92
  vengeance, 142, 153
  whaling technology, 134-135
  whiteness, symbolism of, 127-131
  wickedness, 10 n-12 n, 162
  See also names of major characters
Modern Christian Movements (McNeill), 35 n
Modern Fiction Studies, 130 n
"Moral Argument against Calvinism"
  (Channing), 40
Mosses from an Old Manse (Hawthorne), 70
Mullahy, Patrick, 15 n
Murray, Dr. Henry, 12-15, 17 n

Nathaniel Hawthorne, a Biography (Stewart),
  16 n
*Nathaniel William Taylor, 1786-1858, a Con-
  necticut Liberal* (Mead), 39 n
Natural theology, 136-140
Natural Theology . . . (Paley), 136-139
*Nature, Power, Deceit and Prevalency of In-
  dwelling Sin in Believers, The* (Owen),
  121 n, 145 n, 146
Nature of Evil . . . (James), 8 n
Neuroses, 12-19
  basic conceptual frameworks, 4-5
  Erikson on, 15
  Freudian theory, 13-14
  Jungian theory, 13-14, 15 n
  See also Madness
*New England Primer, The: Containing the As-
  sembly's Catechism*, 100 n
New York Male High School, 42
Nicodemus, 114
Nietzsche, Friedrich Wilhelm, 9
Nineteenth-Century Fiction, 133 n, 134 n

Objections to Calvinism (Foster), 124 n, 148
  n
Olson, Charles, 70 n, 78 n
Omoo (Melville), 68
"On the Ontological Mystery" (Marcel),
  83 n
Orme, Daniel, 1

Oro, 77, 78, 79
Otto, Rudolf, 111 n
Owen, John, 34, 35 n, 43, 98 n, 120 n, 121
     n, 145, 146, 149 n

Paley, William, 136-139
Panic of 1837, 62-65
Parker, 154 n, 166 n
Parrington, Vernon Louise, 41 n
Parsee, 144-145
Parsons, Talcott, 47 n
Paul, Saint, 97, 99
Pearce, Roy Harvey, 106 n
Pelagius, 5
Peleg, Captain, 101, 117
Pequod, 10 n-12 n, 95, 101, 103, 117-120,
     126, 133 n, 147, 152, 153, 154 n, 157, 160,
     162, 167
Pequods (Pequots), the, 106
Pfeiffer, Robert H., 143 n, 174 n
Philosophy in a New Key . . . (Langer), 6 n
Philosophy in the Twentieth Century (eds. Bar-
     rett and Aiken), 83 n
Pierre or, The Ambiguities (Melville), 1, 12-15,
     46, 55-56
     the Isabel relationship, 13 n-14 n
Pietism, 30, 33 n, 61, 110 n, 146, 150
Pip, 148, 154 n
Politics of the Universe . . . (Meredith), 8 n,
     172 n
Predestination, 38-40, 80, 82
     Calvinism, 38-40, 80, 82, 142, 146
     Moby-Dick, 125-126, 142, 147-149, 157-
     158
Presbyterians, 39 n, 99-100, 104
Process and Reality (Whitehead), 17 n
Protestant Ethic and the Spirit of Capitalism,
     The (Weber), 47 n
Psychoanalysis: Evolution and Development . . .
     (Thompson and Mullahy), 15 n
Puritanism, 106, 130

Quakers, 105-106
Quakers in Great Britain and America, The
     (Holder), 106 n
Queequeg
     coffin of, 167-168
     heroism, 101
     homosexuality, 96, 99, 100, 165
     idolatry, 96-100
     Ishmael and, 95-105
     undeserved agony, 138

Rachel, attack on, 157
Ramadan, the, 103
Reality
     Bushnell, 25-26

Freud, 23-26
Melville, 86, 176-178
     guilty secret in, 46
     models of, 3-4
     ultimate structure of, 6, 37
religious conceptions of, 4, 6, 23
Reason, 75-79
     Calvinism, 90, 109, 121-122, 150
     madness and, 78 n, 90
Redburn, His First Voyage (Melville), 45, 54,
     60 n, 69, 79-81
Redeemer Nation: The Idea of America Millen-
     nial Role (Tuveson), 82 n
Religio Medici (Browne), 76 n
Religion and the Rise of Capitalism (Tawney),
     47 n
"Representative Men" (Emerson), 154
Revelation, 75, 90, 132-133
Reynolds, Edward, 113 n, 119 n
Rise and Progress of Religion in the Soul (Dod-
     dridge), 34-35, 58 n, 110
Robinson, Thomas, 118
Robson-Scott, W. D., 24 n
Roman Catholic Church, 91, 101
     God, concept of, 38
Rosenfeld, William, 110 n, 168 n
"Ruin and Recovery of Mankind, The"
     (Watts), 137 n

Sabbath School Union, 41-42, 59
Samuel Enderby, 137
Sarah, 105
Satan, 121, 124, 144
Scripture Characters (Robinson), 118
Scripture Doctrine of Original Sin (Taylor),
     123-124
Sealts, Merton M., Jr., 78 n, 97 n, 100 n,
     114 n, 121 n, 124 n, 134 n
Seneca, Marcus, 76 n
Seneca's Morals by Way of Abstract . . . (L'Es-
     trange), 76 n
Serenia, Island of, 75-79, 80, 83
Sermons by the late Rev. J. S. Buckminster, 52
     n
Sermons . . . upon the Book of Job (Calvin),
     113 n
Shakers, the, 125
Shakespeare, William, 18, 116
     Melville and, 70, 78 n
     Melville's assessment of, 70-73
Sin, 77, 125, 149 n
     Calvin on, 118, 121-122, 142
     Calvinism on, 35, 39, 79, 80, 111-113,
     118-122, 142, 145, 146
     original sin, 72-75, 80
     Moby-Dick, 110-113, 115, 118
     original sin, 104, 109

Skepticism
  Hume, 130 n
  Melville, 130 n, 171, 177-178
  Moby-Dick, 90, 92, 93, 128, 131, 136,
    166-167, 171
Smith, H. Shelton, 34 n
Social Construction of Reality, The (Berger and
  Luckman), 3 n
Social Reform in the United States Navy (Lang-
  ley), 81 n
Solomon, 19
South Atlantic Quarterly, 92 n, 133 n, 168 n
Stael, Madame de, 138 n
Starbuck, 102, 119, 123, 142
  Ahab and, 149-153
  degradation of, 150-153, 162
  impotent aspect, 151-153
  rational virtue of, 151
  spiritual disintegration, 150-153
Stern, Milton R., 10 n
Stewart, Randall, 16 n, 18 n
Stout, Janis, 133 n
Stovall, Floyd, 9 n
Structure of Scientific Revolutions, The (Kuhn),
  6 n-7 n
Stubb, 134, 155
Studies in the Novel (Werge), 88 n
Sullivan, Harry Stack, 15
Symbolism and American Literature (Feidel-
  son), 130 n

Taji, 1, 46
Tanis, James, 33 n, 110 n, 145 n, 146, 150
  n
Tawney, R. H., 47 n
Taylor, John, 123-124
Taylor, Nathaniel William, 39 n
Texas Studies in Literature and Language, 110
  n, 168 n
Thompson, Clara, 15 n
Thompson, Lawrance, 11 n-12 n, 74 n, 99
  n, 110 n, 143 n-144 n
Timon, 18, 73
Tommo, 1
Transcendentalism, 10 n, 130 n
Transitions in American Literary History (ed.
  Clark), 9 n
Tropologia, a Key to Open Scripture Metaphor
  (Keach), 132 n

Truth
  Mardi and a Voyage Thither, 75-78
  Melville, 3, 82, 86, 159, 171-173, 177
  Moby-Dick, 83, 88, 91-92, 102, 105, 106,
    123, 127-128, 130, 131, 137, 159, 161,
    165, 167, 169, 171
  sane madness of vital Truth, 2, 18, 70-75,
    78 n, 123
Trying Out of Moby-Dick, The (Vincent), 10
  n
Tuveson, Ernest Lee, 82 n
Typee (Melville), 68

Unitarianism, 31, 32, 91, 124 n
  God, concept of, 5, 30, 40-41

Van Eyck, William O., 39 n
Van Loon, Charles, 66-67
Vargish, Thomas, 161 n
Vermilye, Thomas, 47 n, 63-65
Vincent, Howard P., 10 n, 78 n

Washington, George, 31
Watts, Isaac, 137
Wayward Puritans: A Study in the Sociology of
  Deviance (Erikson), 66 n
Weber, Max, 47 n
Weigle, Luther A., 25 n, 61 n
Werge, Thomas, 88 n
Whitehead, Alfred North, 17
White-Jacket or The World in a Man-of-War
  (Melville), 69, 78 n, 79-81
  antiflogging movement, 81
  madness, 80
Winny, James, 76 n
Woodruff, Stuart C., 134 n
Woodson, Thomas, 146 n
Works (Channing), 40 n, 41 n, 75 n, 76,
  90-91, 131 n, 147 n, 155 n
Works (ed. Goold), 120 n
Works (eds. Jennings and Doddridge), 137
  n
Works (Reynolds), 113 n, 119 n
Wright, Nathalia, 10 n, 110 n, 133 n, 134
  n, 143 n, 157 n, 174 n

Yojo, 100, 103
Young Martin Luther (Erikson), 15 n
Young Men's Association for Mutual Im-
  provement, 63-65